THE SOFT ADDICTION SOLUTION

Also by Judith Wright

THE ONE DECISION

THE
SOFT ADDICTION
SOLUTION

Break Free of the Seemingly
Harmless Habits That Keep You
from the Life You Want

A Revised and Expanded Edition of Judith Wright's Classic
There Must Be More Than This

JUDITH WRIGHT

JEREMY P. TARCHER / PENGUIN
A MEMBER OF PENGUIN GROUP (USA) INC.
NEW YORK

JEREMY P. TARCHER/PENGUIN
Published by the Penguin Group
Penguin Group (USA) Inc., 375 Hudson Street, New York, New York 10014, USA · Penguin Group
(Canada), 90 Eglinton Avenue East, Suite 700, Toronto, Ontario M4P 2Y3, Canada (a division of Pearson
Penguin Canada Inc.) · Penguin Books Ltd, 80 Strand, London WC2R 0RL, England · Penguin Ireland,
25 St Stephen's Green, Dublin 2, Ireland (a division of Penguin Books Ltd) · Penguin Group (Australia),
250 Camberwell Road, Camberwell, Victoria 3124, Australia (a division of Pearson Australia Group
Pty Ltd) · Penguin Books India Pvt Ltd, 11 Community Centre, Panchsheel Park, New Delhi–110 017, India ·
Penguin Group (NZ), Cnr Airborne and Rosedale Roads, Albany, Auckland 1310, New Zealand (a division
of Pearson New Zealand Ltd) · Penguin Books (South Africa) (Pty) Ltd, 24 Sturdee Avenue, Rosebank,
Johannesburg 2196, South Africa

Penguin Books Ltd, Registered Offices: 80 Strand, London WC2R 0RL, England

This is a revised and expanded version of *There Must Be More Than This:
Finding More Life, Love, and Meaning by Overcoming Your Soft Addictions* (Broadway, 2003) and
Soft Addiction Solutions: Companion Workbook to There Must Be More Than This (Lakeview Press, 2005).

One Decision™ and Soft Addictions™, with their related trainings and materials,
are trademarks of Judith Wright and the Wright Institute, Inc.

Most Tarcher/Penguin books are available at special quantity discounts for bulk purchase for sales promotions,
premiums, fund-raising, and educational needs. Special books or book excerpts also can be created to fit
specific needs. For details, write Penguin Group (USA) Inc. Special Markets, 375 Hudson Street, New York,
NY 10014.

Library of Congress Cataloging-in-Publication Data

Wright, Judith, date.
The soft addiction solution: break free of the seemingly harmless habits that keep you
from the life you want / Judith Wright.—Rev. and expanded ed.
p.   cm.
Rev. ed. of: There must be more than this.
ISBN-13: 978-1-58542-532-7
ISBN-10: 1-58542-532-X
1. Self-actualization (Psychology)   2. Spiritual life.   3. Quality of life.
I. Wright, Judith, date. There must be more than this.   II. Title.
BF637.S4W75   2006   2006023063
158.1—dc22

Printed in the United States of America
1 3 5 7 9 10 8 6 4 2

Book design by Jennifer Ann Daddio

While the author has made every effort to provide accurate telephone numbers and Internet addresses at the time
of publication, neither the publisher nor the author assumes any responsibility for errors, or for changes that
occur after publication. Further, the publisher does not have any control over and does not assume any responsibility for author or third-party websites or their content.

CONTENTS

INTRODUCTION

What an amazing journey it has been these past few years since the first version of this book began helping people gain more time, money, intimacy, and satisfaction by breaking free of their "soft addictions."™

From working with thousands of people at my trainings, I knew the importance of helping people overcome soft addictions, but I had no idea that the concept would catch the attention of America the way it has. Nor did I imagine that soft addictions would speak to people so universally—across cultural, ethnic, and national divides. Labeling this phenomenon—putting a name to something that was operating under the radar of our consciousness—triggered a collective "A-ha! That's it!"

Most people only needed to hear the term, and they immediately had an automatic, almost intuitive, understanding of soft addictions and how ubiquitous they were. Their response was, and continues to be, nothing short of amazing. Even more amazing is the time, money, love, and fulfillment they reclaim when they deal with their soft addictions. At my seminars, people calculate the actual costs of their soft addictions. To my surprise, the lowest actual cost that a person has calculated for soft addictions—from coffee to Internet shopping—was just shy of $3,000 a year. And the average in most seminars has been somewhere between $15,000 and $18,000! If this is what you can reclaim in real dollars, just imagine the lost intimacy and satisfaction you can regain.

Facing soft addictions and their costs can make you vulnerable. I felt I was given a precious window into the lives of countless people as I traveled across the country talking to them about their dreams. In bookstores, on planes, in hotel lobbies, on college campuses, in churches, or corporations, everyone seemed to understand that soft addictions were blocking them from the life they want. There wasn't one place I visited that people didn't want to get more of what really matters out of life—what I call MORE.

People resonated with the call to greater personal freedom, fulfillment, and satisfaction—everyone from taxi drivers in some faraway city to the CEOs I consult with, from security personnel at airports as I got ready to leave for another appearance to the students I coach. These personal and precious contacts gave me a lens into the hearts and minds of thousands of people, who allowed me to peek beneath the surface, to see what matters most to them and what is keeping them from living the lives they want.

National and local media alike caught the importance—more than 50 TV programs like the *Today* show and *Good Morning America,* more than 350 radio programs, and more than 35 newspapers and magazines, including *The San Francisco Chronicle, Fitness,* and *Marie Claire.*

Whether I was being interviewed on a country music station or National Public Radio, a sports or late-night jazz program, a talk show or a fast-paced early-morning drive time, the same truths were shared: everybody has soft addictions; there are huge costs to the quality of their lives and to society as a whole; and everybody wants MORE out of life. I have been deeply touched by how people have shared so openly and honestly about the trap of their soft addictions; their feelings of being stuck, settling, giving up, or being frustrated at not getting everything out of life that they deeply desire, or about their universal desire for MORE in their lives.

I encountered results-oriented executives who saw how their nonproductive patterns were limiting their accomplishments and satisfaction, and couples whose relationships had lost the thrill as they spent their evenings zoned out instead of blissed out on life. Parents shared how their family members were in different rooms of the house at night, glued to a different screen, watching TV, playing video games, participating in a computer chat room, or surfing the Internet. Singles admitted to isolating or posting not-so-accurate depictions of themselves for online dating rather than risking going out and being seen for who they really are. Women discussed comforting themselves with Ben and Jerry's rather than going out and meeting a real Ben or Jerry. Children talked about TV, computers, video games, and oversnacking instead of playing outside or being with other kids. Men admitted to being hooked on sports, gadgets, and pornography, while women confessed to overshopping, overglamorizing, overcleaning, overworking out, and gossiping.

Soft addictions are universal, yet while some are very common, others are more personal in nature:

"I'm buried in clutter."

"I'm wasting hours surfing the Internet."

"I'm sleeping my life away and hiding from my life."

"I'm losing days of my life just watching TV I don't care about."

"I'm staying at work later and later so I can avoid going home. I feel competent at work, but not in my personal life."

"I'm spending every weekend at garage sales, trying to find things for my collection."

Once addressed, executives' careers are renewed, families discover new ways to be close, children get better grades, and even marriages are saved. You will be amazed at the resources and satisfaction you have available as you replace your soft addictions with MORE of what you really want. In order to do this, you must overcome "Yeah, but . . ."

YEAH, I HAVE SOFT ADDICTIONS, BUT . . .

As much as people acknowledged the problem, they weren't always all that keen to do something about it. They were still in denial about the costs of their soft addictions, and still too attached to the pseudo-comfort they thought they derived from them to consider living another way. They saw the problem but weren't always willing to release their soft addictions even if the rewards of overcoming them was unprecedented. But over time, this seems to be changing.

If you are like the thousands of people I have met who now identify with the term *soft addictions*, you are waking up and doing what it takes to free yourself for MORE. Where the job of the first book seemed to be to bring the problem of soft addictions to your attention, this new expanded version seems to be emerging at a time for you who are willing to solve the problem, through the Soft Addiction Solution.

I know from my own experience that the Soft Addiction Solution really works. I discovered the eight key skills within this book and, by applying them, changed my life. Now thousands of other people have done the same. The Soft Addiction Solution did far more than just help me change a bad habit or two; it transformed my life and the lives of those who have heeded its call.

Your soft addictions have important information for you, if you allow yourself to listen. They provide windows into your deepest dreams and desires. Once over your denial, you experience the paradoxical mix of laughing loud and long at your foibles while reaching sublime spiritual spaces that put you in touch with your deepest hungers and the sacred emptiness within you. You experience the healing power of admitting the ridiculous stuff you do—the wild rituals, the excuses and rationalization riddled with stinking thinking, and the lengths you go to hide your habits—with compassion and humor. Out of all the trainings we do at the Wright Institute, the Soft Addiction Solution training has always been one of my favorites, and I think it's for this reason: it is so deeply personal, so tenderly human, so divinely revealing—and so powerfully effective.

RESULTS: INSIDE AND OUT

The Soft Addiction Solution isn't just about the external results of more money, time, energy, intimacy, and productivity—although they are considerable—but it is also about the internal shifts for those who apply these skills. As you embark on this journey, you gain more self-acceptance, self-esteem, self-respect, satisfaction, fulfillment, self-love, and compassion. You understand that you aren't crazy or weak-willed or hopeless. You, like all of us, are simply misguided in your attempts to take care of yourself and need to learn new skills to meet your deeper needs.

Through this book, you will come to understand that you have deep and sacred hungers that deserve to be met, and that no soft addiction (no matter how many you try!) will ever touch that place within you. The core of the Soft Addiction Solution is the One Decision—choosing to live a life of MORE. This is much more important and difficult than it sounds, which is why I wrote an entire book on the wonders of the One Decision. When you make your One Decision, your life becomes unified by a guiding philosophy. You have direction and are able to envision a beautiful life for yourself. Strengthened by your One Decision, you are more easily able to resist the habits that had previously prevented your dreams from coming true. You regain and tap the power of your feelings, instead of numbing them. Laughing, crying, brimming with energy and passion, admitting your fears, and getting the comfort and encouragement you need, you move forward into your life beyond anything you have experienced before. Each step you take creates MORE in your life. Not only do you break free of your soft addictions, but you also create a magnificent lifestyle that is nourishing, satisfying, inspiring, healthy, fun, creative, beautiful, and life-enhancing rather than life-deadening.

It hasn't always been this way for me. Let me tell you my story—how I discovered the problem of soft addictions and what you can do about them.

My Story

Growing up in Flint, Michigan, a factory town, I was hungry—hungry for more than all the snacks and junk food I was stuffing into my mouth. No matter what I ate or what I did, it wasn't enough. The hunger persisted. I kept feeling that there must be more to life. I didn't know then that it was my spiritual hunger that needed feeding.

As a child, I felt like something was missing, something wasn't right, but I couldn't describe it. Something was off, not just in me, but also in the world around me. People didn't seem really happy or alive. They were in the house, but not home; they were busy, but not engaged. While they may have been doing something that *should be* fun, they weren't *having* fun. They talked, but did not make contact. Life was lonely in this world, full of activity without deep engagement—activities without aliveness, full of zoned-out spaces and zoned-out faces. It felt foggy, as if everyone were wrapped in cotton. I worried sometimes that I was the weird one and the world was fine. But deep inside I knew something was missing in the way people lived. I couldn't articulate *then* how it should be, so I continued my soft addictions—overeating, watching TV, biting my nails, and burying myself in my studies.

Few Role Models

I didn't have many models of people living the life they wanted. Most people seemed to live the life they settled for, or they complained about their lives but did little to change them. They had let go of their dreams and settled instead for a decent wage and benefits. I remember thinking that if this was what it meant to grow up, then I wasn't too interested! All I knew was that I wanted more, but I didn't have a clue what that was, how to get it, or if it even existed.

In some ways, I lived in two worlds. In one, I did what I could to try to have more in my life—becoming a good student, stretching myself, and always being first in my class. I filled my after-school time with studying, dance or music lessons, camp, volunteering, and Girl Scouts. I read a lot, rode my bike, and played with a diverse group of neighborhood kids. We wrote plays, acted them out, made costumes, sold tickets, and served refreshments. We held carnivals and played restaurant, shoe store, and grocery market. I set up lemonade stands, founded a revolving neighborhood library, and wrote a neighborhood newspaper as well as stories that my sister illustrated. In high school, I became class valedictorian and a student leader. I was editor of our yearbook, a class officer, and an award-winning drum majorette (yes, I even twirled a fire baton and wore those little white boots).

Yet in my blue-collar town doing well in anything other than sports meant little, and mediocrity was valued over excellence. My achievements were either ignored, unacknowledged, or scorned. Despite the lack of recognition, I felt more alive when engaged in these activities; I didn't feel quite so hungry.

Still, with all this activity and achievement, I was a fat, unhappy kid. I would still come home from school, plop my chubby self down in the recliner, flip on the television, and mindlessly eat bags of chocolate chip cookies with cartons of milk or chew my nails and lazily leaf through stacks of magazines during commercials. Zoned out, I drifted through the afternoons until I rallied myself to do homework or was called by friends to play.

When I wasn't busy distracting myself, I felt empty and hungry. My heart hurt, although I didn't know how to say it then in those terms. I often felt hollow or as if I were some kind of wispy ghost, barely existing. I knew something wasn't right but not what was wrong. I felt that life was supposed to be somehow different. Yet, this was the only formula I knew—working hard and achieving and then zoning out with the TV and stuffing my face.

Looking for Love in All the Wrong Places

I followed the same formula as a young adult. I was a great student in college and a high achiever as a young woman, so much so that I had reached national prominence in two different careers by the time I was twenty-eight years old. But despite my achievements, I still felt empty, unhappy, and dissatisfied. Searching for an answer to my upset, I decided that the *real* reason I was still unhappy was because I was fat. So I dieted and lost weight. And then, I was successful, thin—and unhappy.

I must be unhappy because I am not in a relationship, I reasoned. So I got into a relationship with my college sweetheart, a Sylvester Stallone look-alike with a genius IQ. Now I was sure that I had it all: success, the body I wanted, and a genius stud. But I didn't. I was still unhappy, empty, and feeling desperate.

Everything looked good from the outside, but on the inside I was miserable. I didn't know what else to do. I thought I had the formula, but it wasn't working. So I started to escalate, doing more of everything—working harder, partying more, buying more, finding more and more diversions. I shopped, watched TV, hung out, went out, and was wrung out. I felt worse and worse about myself and my life, increasingly empty, sad, lost, and frantic.

I was doing everything I knew to do and succeeding—and it still was not enough. I was twenty-some years old, thinking how horrible the rest of my life would be if all I had was more of the same. I had no idea what else I could be doing. At best, I felt like I was sleepwalking through my life. At worst, I felt desperate, lost, devoid of meaning and of hope.

The Dawning of Awareness

The desperation extended through my first two big jobs. Gradually, it dawned on me, through the haze, that there were other messages coming my way through the work I was doing. I had developed and run a model program for students with disabilities to successfully attend college. It was a demonstration project, one of the first such college programs in the country that helped establish the parameters for barrier-free education. Students with severe challenges—from deafness and quadriplegia to those recovering from strokes or with cerebral palsy, mental illnesses, and other chronic conditions—braved the challenges before them to win college degrees. I designed and ran the initiative, and also counseled students in this program.

Some of the students who came into my office were a total joy. They often displayed a remarkable sense of humor and perspective as they grappled with hard problems, demonstrating dignity, grace, or just plain guts. Those who delighted and inspired me the most were always learning and growing.

On the other hand, there were students who were like storm clouds, and it was painful to be around them. They felt victimized by their situations, were downcast, and seemed to drain the energy from a room. Often, these were the students with the least severe problems. This experience nagged at me like a loose tooth throughout the coming years.

My next assignment was as a director of clinical programs with a joint appointment at a state university and the state department of mental health to design and run model demonstration programs for children with developmental disabilities and their families. I developed and led a team that developed state-of-the-art services. We taught parents to love, accept, and help their children, many of whom were severely disabled and profoundly limited, sometimes even taking years to be able to just lift up their heads. But the most difficult part of the work was to help the parents release the picture of the child they had imagined and come to accept and love the child that they were given.

Remarkably, there were some families who actually became more fulfilled and happier after this so-called tragedy as they shifted their lives to focus on a deeper sense of love—celebrating their child's small developmental victories, expanding their perspective, becoming closer to each other and to spirit, and orienting to something higher together.

I began putting these two formative professional experiences together, and to my surprise, I realized that these students that lit up my days and these parents who inspired and touched me so deeply had a higher quality of life than I did, despite my many successes. Their success in life had nothing to do with having the perfect mind or the perfect body, the perfect spouse, or the perfect circumstances. It had nothing to do with perfection at all, or with the formula I had been following.

It dawned on me that I was being shown something much more important. The answer that I was looking for was right in front of me all along, and these students and families were showing it to me. They chose to live a life of MORE—independent of external or physical circumstances. They could not choose to orient to external accomplishments, because no matter what they did they weren't likely to win at that game. They could not compete in the rat race, eschewed the victimhood, and exercised the divine gift of choice in a way I had completely overlooked. Despite all the reasons in the world to live lives of victimhood and suffering, they had chosen satisfaction, fulfillment, and love. They were able to overlook or work around serious limitations to live days filled with spirit, joy, and love. They didn't wait until things were "perfect" because things were never going to be that way.

These students that lifted my spirit and the parents who transformed their lives in powerful ways had something in common. They had made what I now call a One Decision: they had chosen to live a good, fulfilling life, no matter what their circumstances. They were making the most of their lives. They had decided to embody an attitude of possibilities and gratitude.

My One Decision

It was at this time of my deepest upset, and my deepest insight, that the lessons of these blessed beings came home to me and I made my own One Decision—a decision so profound that it changed my life forever after. It was a clear turning point in my life when I declared to myself that I would no longer sleepwalk through life. I decided absolutely that I would *feel* my life, be conscious, awake, and alive, and do whatever it took to live this way and help others do the same. I would live a life of gratitude and be a vessel for Spirit—not some pasty, superficial Pollyannaish promise, but really turn myself inside out, like the beacons I had been blessed to observe.

It was out of this decision that I actively pursued MORE in my life, looking for what made me feel more conscious, present, and alive. And it was then that I was struck with a realization—all those things that I had been doing to try to feel better were actually making me not feel at all. My overeating, overshopping, overstudying, partying, gossiping, magazine-reading, and TV-watching addictions had numbed me. Even though I felt compelled to do them, they were simply diversions, distractions keeping me from the greater satisfaction I yearned for. I was chasing away the greater MORE I sought with what I came to know as, and call, soft addictions.

At last, I finally had a compelling reason to change my behavior. By filling my life with MORE—choosing activities and ways of being that refreshed, soothed, inspired, and helped me feel and be alive—my soft addictions lost their appeal and began to melt away. As I released my soft addictions, I experienced the greater MORE.

I realized that my relationship with my college sweetheart and first husband looked good on the outside but wasn't good on the inside. It was not an honest, truthful relationship. I was as addicted to it as I had been to all the other activities that weren't good for me. I was using my soft addictions to hide my awareness of his hard addictions. When he didn't make his One Decision, refused help, and then continued on unfazed, I realized that we couldn't resolve our issues and I left the relationship. Single again, I started to date more consciously men whose lives were guided by higher values. I then met my current husband (and partner in all ways), Bob, a deeply committed and passionate man who had made his own One Decision and lived it as fully as anyone I had met or have yet to meet. I was finally discovering the possibilities of real relating with deep, ever-growing intimacy, genuine contact, and a life of shared passion and meaning.

I realized that most soft addictions are misguided attempts to run away from emotions. By cutting down on my soft addictions, I learned to honor my feelings. I went toward my emotions rather than away. I cut down on sweets as I lived life more lovingly. I began to add more nourishing foods, activities, and satisfying ways of being to my life. A dip in the hot tub felt more relaxing than drinking wine and it didn't negatively alter my consciousness or leave any unwanted aftereffects. Belly laughing with abandon, praying, and experiencing moments of joy felt better than feeling buzzed or high. Reading great literature felt better than sitting dazed in front of the television. Spontaneous laughing, yelling, and even crying my guts out in deep sobs brought me peace as no amount of unconscious, numbing behavior ever could. Learning to tell my deeper truths, avoiding secrets, and revealing myself felt scary—yet freeing.

I even stayed thin without dieting, I was free! Free from revolving my life around food, free from this horrible merry-go-round of overworking and diversions. I had more energy, was more present, more satisfied, and more fulfilled. I was living the life I had always yearned for.

I discovered the eight key skills that I am sharing with you in this book that led me to break free of my soft addictions to live the life I want—a life of MORE.

The One Decision at Work

Once I made my One Decision, I changed my work. I started sharing with able-bodied people the gifts I had learned from those with disabilities. I developed a personal and spiritual growth business, which allowed me to keep my commitment of helping others "awaken," too. I was yet to coin the term *soft addictions*, but I was on the way.

At the same time, my husband Bob had a training business that helped people develop skills in areas of life, such as leadership, relationships, and careers. We used to refer to his business as masculine and mine as feminine, but the differences were deeper. The people he served were terrific. Working with Bob and his talented staff, they would accomplish many goals and develop skills in intimacy, assertiveness, and relationships—but they wanted more. They flocked to my business for workshops I led to get this extra something—a sense of spirit, compassion, humor, deeper meaning, and a relationship with God, a higher power, or the universe.

In both of our businesses, we observed the difference between people who kept growing and those who did not. There was more than skill needed to really learn and grow throughout life. Those who stalled in their personal development often had counterproductive soft addictions that stood in the way of their growth and the life they said they wanted. They worked hard in our personal growth seminars and coaching to uncover feelings. They let their emotions out, but then they frequently would return after a stimulating training weekend and no change occurred in their daily life or, if it did, the change was short-lived. They would indulge in soft addiction routines to numb what they had just unearthed. They would lose their momentum and the possibility of deepening their journey.

Many of them had skills beyond mine, but their lives were not better. I looked at my own life and saw how I had shifted my behaviors away from numbing habits and what a difference it had made to the quality of my life. I saw that the net of routine was trapping them, just as it had once trapped me. At that point, we coined the term *soft addictions,* because while they shared certain characteristics in common with hard addictions— compulsiveness, numbing effects, substituting for a lifestyle—the substances themselves would not kill you as they would with hard addictions.

We offered the first training in overcoming them in 1991. The response and the phenomenal results continued to grow until by popular demand and the urge to share our discoveries, the first edition of this book was written.

WHAT IS MORE?

The MORE I have discovered by overcoming my own soft addictions is the MORE that awaits you in your life. The MORE varies from person to person, but what you'll find in this book are the proven lessons, ideas, and tools that help you define it for yourself. Keep this in mind, though. When I speak about MORE in life, I mean the "big" MORE of life. This is the pursuit of MORE of everything that really matters—more love, satisfaction, meaning, and those aspects of life that bring us an abiding sense of fulfillment, joy, and love.

By actively pursuing MORE in life, you meet your deeper needs directly, release your soft addictions, and experience greater fulfillment. By not spending so much time and money on insidious soft addiction routines, you have more time, energy, and resources to pursue more meaningful activities. You feel more awake, alive, and conscious. You spend more time discovering and developing your gifts and talents, making more of a difference in the world. You are living the life you want.

Orienting to MORE positively impacts everyone in all areas of his or her life. Fathers discover greater contact with their children, spouses rediscover each other, careers take off, and some even develop the confidence to follow their dreams for the first time in their lives. Sales

professionals make more money, executives receive awards and promotions, mothers discover greater fulfillment as they grow with their children, tasting all the joys of life side by side with the children rather than waiting for the kids to grow up.

WHAT TO EXPECT FROM YOUR JOURNEY

Breaking free from soft addictions and embracing MORE in life has not been my experience alone. Thousands of people who read the first edition of this book and hundreds of people who have experienced the Soft Addiction Solution training and coaching at the Wright Institute have made a similar journey, and you'll find their stories as well as mine in this book. Together we've been able to overcome our habitual behaviors and have learned to live increasingly exceptional lives. We support each other in our quest for conscious living—choosing less television, caffeine, shopping, excessive exercising, daydreaming, isolation, and the 101 other things that reduce consciousness. We celebrate deep relating, risk taking, truth telling, rest, full engagement, and other infinitely available nourishing acts of consciousness.

Over the years, the students in my workshops have helped me refine the process of overcoming soft addictions and finding more meaning. By taking this journey, they have created new ways to live lives of ever-increasing MORE. These discoveries come together in eight key life skills:

1. Make your One Decision.
2. Identify your soft addictions.
3. Mind your mind and clean up your stinking thinking.
4. Discover the "why" beneath your soft addictions.
5. Fulfill your spiritual hungers.
6. Develop a vision.
7. Learn the Math of MORE.
8. Get support and be accountable.

These eight skills are the components of a proven process that takes you to the next level of living the life you want and beyond what most people have dreamed possible.

SPIRIT AND MORE

Throughout this book I talk about spirit, spiritual hunger, and God. I use these terms to reflect a broad concept of spirituality and God; they are not meant to represent any particular religion or spiritual tradition. At the Wright Institute we serve people on all paths, be it religious traditions (Catholic, Protestant, Jewish, Muslim, Buddhist, or other) or a purely secular alignment with higher purpose. We even have students and clients who are priests, ministers, and rabbis in Anglican, Franciscan, Dominican, Methodist, Adventist, and Reform orders. They are drawn to the Institute because we believe in supporting people to live their own beliefs as fully as possible, as long as those beliefs include truth and love.

Many of our atheist and agnostic students choose to hear these spiritual terms as synonymous with life, love, or whatever abstractions they find most powerful. Please use these spiritual references throughout the book as an opportunity to reflect on what fulfills your deeper hunger and makes your heart sing—whether it's a general spiritual sense, a particular religious tradition, a connection with God, Jesus, Buddha, Goddess, Universe, Creator, your higher self, other aspects of a creative spirit, or higher principles such as love and truth.

The fact that you've picked up this book means that you are interested in living the richest life you can, the life you want—a life of MORE. While we all have soft addictions, not all of us are willing to admit that they are a barrier to the life we want and deserve. By reading this book, you make a positive statement and join many others who have made conscious living a reality through their One Decision. As you'll discover, your soft addictions contain enormous amounts of information about your deeper needs. Once you obtain this information and act on it, you are in a much better position not only to manage your soft addictions but also to live the life of your dreams.

Although breaking free of soft addictions is a concrete benefit of this book, it is not the only one. Each step of the process brings with it tremendous self-knowledge. The information in each chapter is designed to prepare you for a lifelong journey, a continual awakening of your spirit as you overcome the numbness of your addictions.

The first chapter shows you how we become locked into our soft addiction routines and habits and lose sight of the more meaningful things

life has to offer. We will explore how pursuit of MORE provides a spiritually satisfying alternative to our myriad routines. The following eight chapters delineate the eight key skills, showing you a path you can follow toward the life you desire. It provides a process for releasing soft addictions as well as discovering and satisfying deeper hungers. It introduces you to the One Decision, teaches you to identify your particular web of soft addictions, and guides you in developing a vision for your life. These chapters lead you toward an increasingly conscious, authentic lifestyle. The final chapters provide a vision for the support and inspiration we all need to succeed on our journey.

The last section, at the end of the book, is a workbook with tools, exercises, and ideas for you to apply the skills you are learning. You can complete the exercises in the workbook as you read, along with the chapters, or complete it after you have finished reading the main body of the book. It's your personal tool kit to help you apply the concepts you'll be learning throughout the book.

You will notice a variety of sidebars and elements scattered throughout the chapters:

- MORE-sels are nuggets (morsels) of inspiration to encourage you on your journey.
- MORE to Think About invites you to reflect on the theme of the chapter.
- MORE to Do gives you a task to apply what you are learning about achieving MORE.
- MORE Alert is a caution that alerts you to possible blocks or barriers to living MORE.
- Individual testimonials or stories keep you inspired by sharing others' real-world successes.

Each of these tools will help you build your vision of MORE. They add to the wealth of approaches that will fit into the Soft Addiction Solution.

Remember, the path of MORE is not about deprivation. People who embark on this journey need not fear that they will have to quit all their addictions cold turkey. The journey, however, will lead you to abundance and fulfillment. Rest assured that quitting everything and feeling deprived is not the goal, nor is it even desirable. Instead, you learn to add soul-satisfying activities to your life with the by-product being a natural reduction of soul-numbing activities. Consciousness is the key. If you want more out of life, then you need to practice being more aware of yourself in the moment. As you attune to the choices you face every day, you will naturally and easily grow in consciousness and satisfaction.

Just reading this book will serve you by raising your consciousness, but you won't create a life of MORE unless you take action. Although you can do this by yourself, many have found they are more likely to stick to it with support. Share the process with friends. Support makes for better follow-through, and developing support is one of the ways to have MORE in every aspect of life. Chapter 9 is filled with ideas for creating support for yourself, but you don't need to wait. You can find like-minded and like-spirited buddies, start a group of your own, be part of an online community, register to start a group in your area, attend a training, or even become a trainer yourself by logging on to my Web site at www.judithwright.com. You'll find bulletin boards, quizzes, soft addiction computer games, and more to encourage and support you on your path. You can join our MORE groups and ask questions or share thoughts with people who have been on the journey for a long time—people whose stories appear in these pages—and others who are just starting on their own personal journeys. You can also receive a special limited-time offer just for reading this book. Go to www.judithwright.com, click on "Soft Addictions Solution Special Offer," and enter the code 4M6R3. Your offer will appear.

Support and inspiration are powerful ingredients of a life of MORE. You deserve to have all of the support in the world to create a life of MORE. As the saying goes, what do you have to lose?—mind-numbing, consciousness-deadening habits, behaviors, and moods that rob you of energy, time, and resources, and keep you from having the life you truly want. And what then do you stand to gain? MORE!—more life, more money, more love, more time, more emotional fulfillment, more challenge, more of everything that is the fabric of life.

May you experience more of everything that matters to you and have the life you want!

Judith Wright

GETTING MORE OUT OF LIFE

"Can't you see, I want my life to be more than just long."

PIPPIN

The book you're holding in your hands is a ticket to living your dreams, a passport to the life you've always wanted, a permission slip for unleashing your power and living the life you were born to live. Sound like a tall order? Not to worry, thousands of people have already paved the way for you—from CEOs to stay-at-home moms, salespeople to health-care professionals, artists to artisans, students to doctors. Countless people are living their dreams in a way they never imagined possible because they were willing to tell the truth about their lives, to have the courage to recognize that their same old routines weren't bringing them the satisfaction and fulfillment they craved or deserved, and to admit that they wanted something more.

Each of us yearns to get more—more of what really matters—out of our lives. We hunger to feel more fulfilled, to have more meaning, to make a difference, to be part of something greater, or to live a life of love and peace. Oftentimes, we're not even aware of this yearning, because we are conflicted about our own wanting. *Do I want too much or not enough? I have more than I thought possible. Why aren't I happy? Is it okay to want more?* Consider this quote from Chris Evert (all-time-great women's tennis champion at the peak of her career while married to John Lloyd): "We get into a rut. We play tennis, we go to a movie, we watch TV, but I keep saying, 'John, there has to be more.'" If wealth and world fame weren't enough for tennis champion Chris Evert, then we are in good company in asking ourselves these simple yet profound questions about having MORE.

Whether we are high achievers, world champions, underachievers, or somewhere in between, we all desire MORE. Ironically, at the same time that we hunger to get MORE out of life, we are not doing what we need to do to actually *get* it. Statistics show that almost every one of us, overachievers and underachievers alike, is engaged in activities and habits that not only interfere with the MORE we seek, but actually rob us of its pleasures even when we get it. Our lives pass us by while we waste our precious resources—our time, energy, consciousness, and life force—watching too much TV, overshopping, surfing the Internet, overeating, gossiping, or engaging in the numerous ruts and routines that I call soft addictions.

Without even realizing it, the years pass, and we have built our entire lifestyle around these habits to the point that we have left behind our dreams and replaced them with a collection of automatic routines. But it does not need to be this way. The skills you will learn in this book will show you how to get more of what really matters—more than you ever dreamed possible.

FROM LESS TO MORE

How can breaking through bad habits and routines lead you to your dreams? In essence, soft addictions are distractions from our destiny. They put us in a fog, keep us from thinking clearly or being really present, distract us from our higher values and true purpose, prevent us from connecting to others, and distance us from our loved ones. Soft addictions decrease our productivity and numb us from our true feelings. They keep us from getting MORE out of life, lead us to less, and sabotage our dreams.

The Soft Addiction Solution will help you break free of the seemingly harmless habits, patterns, and behaviors that in actuality keep you from living the life you truly want. Freeing yourself from what numbs your body, mind, emotions, and spirit, you reclaim precious time, money, energy, satisfaction, and intimacy. Make no mistake, this is not simply about overcoming your bad habits and then feeling deprived as a result. The Soft Addiction Solution is *the* key to living a fulfilling life with more of everything you want—more time, money, intimacy, love, satisfaction, energy, and meaning.

As you lessen the hold that your soft addictions have on you, you will experience the greater MORE of life. You reach beneath the surface of your habits to discover your deeper hungers and longings, opening windows to new worlds. You apply the skills to one habit and suddenly you experience the magic of MORE—your life begins to transform in every area. You have more feelings and are more conscious and present. Your life is more satisfying, you make more of a difference, you feel more connected to yourself, others, spirit, and the world around you. You experience more intimacy, more passion, more truth, and more genuineness—and become more you.

This is not a path of deprivation, but one of abundance. It is a journey of learning how to satisfy your deepest desires, adding elements of inspiration and nourishment to your life, understanding yourself at a deep level, developing more support, and crafting a bigger vision for your life. It is a journey of learning to love yourself and your life even more. It is *the* path to getting MORE out of life.

MY SOFT ADDICTIONS: BEFORE THE MORE

A Cycle of Achievement and Zoning Out

Biting my nails, snarfing chocolate chip cookies by the handful, mindlessly thumbing through magazines, watching too much TV, zoning out over my textbooks, or wandering aimlessly through the mall—these were the previous building blocks of my lifestyle. An overachiever, I excelled in academics and in my work. I rose to national prominence in two different careers by the time I was in my late twenties. Yet even with this success, and after losing the weight that had plagued me my entire life, I was still reading recipes like they were the secret to life, obsessing over what I was going to eat, when I was going to eat, how much I was going to eat.

I worked very hard and was successful, yet when I wasn't leading an event or receiving an award for a program I developed, I would be endlessly shopping or browsing through things I couldn't possibly afford to buy, gossiping about mutual friends or celebrities' lives, disappearing into catalogs, or imagining myself in the latest fashions. The harder and longer I worked, the more I achieved. The more acclaim I received, the more I felt justified to buy even more, or zone out more. (*I work hard so I deserve this.*) Despite the high-quality results I produced, I was always rushing around, being late to just about everything, with clutter building up everywhere, dirty dishes in the sink, yesterday's clothes strewn all over the bedroom. I would ruminate on everything I did wrong, beat myself up inside, and minimize any compliment I received.

MORE in My Life

Now my life is very different. I still shop and I have very nice "stuff," but it is an accent to my life, a reflection of the woman of substance I have become. I am more apt to search for meaning or a deeper connection with myself than to launch a desperate quest for the latest bargains. I have a lot more fun—spontaneous belly laughing, good times, bubbling feelings of joy—instead of the artificial and short-lived high of a shopping binge. Rather than looking forward to a trip to the mall, I now look forward to dinner with my husband, or to dancing to great music, or to strapping on my cross-country skis and immersing myself into the quiet beauty of the snowy woods. No longer watching too much TV, I'm reading great books (or even writing them!). The list of activities that fulfill me is long and always growing.

Instead of stuffing my emotions and numbing them with cookies, I feel my feelings and am nourished by them and use them to help me solve problems. Rather than fantasizing about what I'd look like in some designer dress I saw, I am more likely spending time envisioning my future—a future of possibilities for me, my husband, our business, and the planet.

My work is even more satisfying; I actually feel better and have more energy at the end of the day than I did at the beginning. Instead of all the habits I indulged in to be "cool," I've learned to become "warm"—more real, more in touch with my heart. I'm now likely to share a deep truth or my dreams with my husband than to regale him with a juicy piece of gossip. I have a greater intimacy and closeness than I ever knew was possible—and it keeps growing. I have more love, satisfaction, energy, and even more time. I am making a bigger difference and being more myself. I

love my life! It's not that my life is more exciting, but that I am more excited about and engaged in my life. To be sure, I still have pain and
anger; in fact, I am more likely to feel hurt because I am no longer
numbing my feelings. But it's all part of experiencing the MORE of life.

WHAT ARE SOFT ADDICTIONS?

To experience MORE, we must be willing to take an honest look at our
soft addictions. But what are soft addictions and how do we know if we
have them? Soft addictions are those seemingly harmless habits—like
overshopping, overeating, watching too much TV, surfing the Internet,
gossiping, procrastinating—that actually keep us from the life we want.
Whether we realize it or not, our soft addictions cost us money, rob us of
time, numb us from our feelings, mute our consciousness, and drain
our energy. And we all have them.

A Harris Poll revealed that 91 percent of Americans admit to having
soft addictions. From my personal experience, I think that the other 9
percent are still in denial, because I have never met anyone who does not
have a soft addiction. In speaking with people of the United States and
the countless countries I've visited around the world—people of every
race, religion, age, and background—the question is not, *Do I have a soft
addiction?* but rather *Which soft addictions do I have* and *What are the costs?*

Soft addictions are not a sin. They are simply a misguided attempt to
take care of ourselves—a way to try to relax after a draining day, to distract
or amuse ourselves, or to cope with strong feelings. The problem is that
soft addictions don't add to our life; they actually drain us of the precious
resources that could be used toward fueling our dreams. They don't take
care of us, refresh us, or give us the comfort that we really deserve. They
take from us without giving us much back. We all need breaks from our
stressed-out lives. We need entertainment, refreshment, recreation, and
more. But we deserve great breaks—not just sneaking in a zoned-out
chipsfest while gazing at the computer screen or mindlessly flipping channels as we flop in front of the TV. We need satisfying and exciting ways to
nurture, restore, and entertain ourselves, which give us MORE, not less.

Breaking free of your soft addictions doesn't mean that you avoid TV
for the rest of your life, or that you forsake grande mocha forever, or that
you are forbidden to shop or surf the Internet. What it does mean is that

you design a fulfilling, satisfying life that feeds your body, mind, and your spirit. It means learning eight key skills that not only help you overcome your dependence on these life-robbing habits but that also then become the building blocks of a truly great life—a life of MORE.

People often ask me the difference between soft and hard addictions. With hard addictions, like drugs or alcohol, the substances themselves are dangerous and life-threatening. With soft addictions, the substances or behaviors are not in themselves dangerous. What makes them a problem is how we use them and overuse them. You don't have to have drugs and alcohol to live, but you do need to shop, eat, and use media. Consequently, you can't overcome the grip of soft addictions just by getting rid of the substance. Instead, you have to change your very relationship to the activity and learn new skills. Unlike hard addictions, soft addictions are socially accepted. They are popular activities that everyone does and that people often share together. They are constantly glamorized in media, ads, and magazines. Soft addictions are insidious and often operate beneath our radar, while stealing our life force and precious resources. They become so ingrained that our lifestyle simply becomes a web of our soft addictions. See if you can recognize any aspects of yourself in the scenario below.

> ### MORE-SEL
>
> *"You don't die from soft addictions. But you don't live, either."*
>
> —JUDITH WRIGHT

You wake up after multiple hits on the snooze button and jump into a series of mad dashes—getting the kids to school, catching the train or driving through rush hour, getting to work on time, making a project deadline, arriving on time for a meeting, and then picking the kids up from school. Conversations with friends or fellow workers revolve around office politics, local news, sports, celebrities, television shows, or investments. The conversations tend to be brief and fragmented, bouncing from one subject to the next and rarely address feelings, especially deeply held or troubling ones.

Your free time—what little you have—is devoted to meeting unfulfilling, acquired needs. You *need* to get a grande mocha from the local coffeehouse, to watch soap operas, to listen to a particular radio station, to read the sports pages, to check your e-mail, to work out. You have a

TOP TEN SOFT ADDICTIONS
(HARRIS POLL RESULTS)

The Harris Poll revealed these as the top ten soft addictions:

1. Procrastination
2. Watching too much television
3. Overworking
4. Acting moody, such as being grumpy, cranky, or overly happy
5. Overeating
6. Drinking too much coffee
7. Shopping impulsively
8. Daydreaming excessively
9. Complaining excessively
10. Surfing the Internet excessively

fleeting thought that you are overdoing it but are unable to think of something more productive to do.

Work alternates between anxiety-producing moments and the accomplishment of moderately satisfying tasks. You finish a project and your boss or client likes it, and you feel like you've accomplished something. This feeling, however, doesn't last, and it's not something you're particularly proud of or think about with great satisfaction.

At times, you watch the clock. You can't wait until lunchtime or until the end of the workday, even though lunch is nothing special and you don't have anything particularly exciting to do after work. You procrastinate and make excuses about why your project is late, yet you play computer games with your door closed. You yearn for vacations, new work, or retirement, thinking that *then* you will be happy.

At home, you hop to the needs of the family or you zone out. Perhaps you have a glass of wine or two to take the edge off the day. You channel-surf at night but don't remember later what you watched. You spend hours flipping through catalogs, coveting new outfits or nifty gadgets. You fantasize about various men and women, whether you're married or in a serious relationship or not.

Did you recognize yourself or anyone you know in this scenario? Yes, this may be an exaggeration of a typical day in anyone's life. But it's not so far from our reality as we might like to believe. If you're like most people, you recognize aspects of yourself in the examples depicted—activities and behaviors that we refer to as soft addictions. Though they're seemingly harmless, and somewhat pleasurable, they are ultimately empty routines. In the back of your mind you might even suspect that these routines prevent you from experiencing a more meaningful, fulfilling life.

Why, then, doesn't everyone immediately shift their activities and break their routines to gain a more satisfying existence? Unfortunately, it's easier said than done. These routines are soft addictions. They exert a powerful hold on us, and we see them everywhere we turn.

PARADOX OF OUR TIMES

Soft addictions reflect the age in which we live, an age of paradox. The world we live in facilitates both soft addictions and spiritual enlightenment. The opportunities for fulfillment and meaning are equaled by the opportunities for creatively wasting time. Our time is fraught with particular challenges from the sheer volume of what is available to buy, consume, utilize—and tempt us. Each new object, toy, or gadget—from PDAs, cell phones, and TiVo, to the coolest technological tools—becomes something that we think we need or want, even though we didn't even know it existed or even have the desire for it before.

Many forces come to bear in our era that make us particularly vulnerable to the allure of soft addictions. The cumulative effect of each of the following aspects of our society makes soft addictions more difficult to address—and at the same time more urgent:

- our increased dependence on technology
- our spotlight on wealth, redefining the "good life" materially rather than by our own goodness
- the increase in disposable income
- our need-for-the-new faddish society
- the proliferation of institutionalized gossip

- the emphasis on quick fixes rather than engaging in thoughtful solutions to complex problems

We move faster and farther, feeling like we are going nowhere. We earn more, buy more, do more, and feel like we are living less. Time-saving devices are taken for granted as we move at an ever-quickening pace, complaining that we have no time. Bigger isn't necessarily better, and more sometimes creates less— this is the paradox of our time. When we become trapped in this paradox and are content to do less with more, we fall prey to our soft addictions.

We possess greater opportunities to fulfill our spiritual hungers but are confronted with more distractions—a dazzling array of seemingly important pursuits. Because of all the books, workshops, and other vehicles devoted to the subject of spirituality, many of us have raised our consciousness. Yet because of the proliferation of video games, cultural fixation on celebrity gossip, and reality-based television shows, our consciousness has been similarly lowered.

> ## MORE-SEL
>
> *"The paradox of our time . . . We have more conveniences but less time. . . . We drink too much, smoke too much, spend too recklessly . . . read too little, watch TV too much, and pray too seldom. We have multiplied our possessions, but reduced our values. . . . We've learned how to make a living but not a life."*
>
> —ANONYMOUS

Consider the tremendous power and potential of the Internet—the ability to democratize information, the possibilities of connectivity, the opportunity to discover values and appreciate diversity and demolish boundaries. The notion of global consciousness is utopian, but the Internet is a medium that can bring that dream closer to reality. Given all of this, it is staggering that one of the most frequent uses of the Internet is for visiting pornography sites.

Our challenge is to reconcile the paradox of more leading to less. This requires learning to distinguish between soft addictions and meaningful activities, between escapist entertainment and forums for self-discovery. We live in a time where the lines blur. We're vulnerable to style over substance, the appearance of energy rather than the reality. The sophistication of soft addictions and their marketing create the illusion that they're meaningful, enriching endeavors. We celebrate our "connectedness" as we spend hours buying and selling trivial objects on eBay. Just as significantly, the rising level of stress most of us are under makes soft addictions seem necessary. We feel we "need" to get away and watch television to escape the stress. Some outlets are inherently positive while others are limiting, but all can easily become vehicles of avoidance. To avoid being trapped, we must be aware of the paradoxical nature of our society and the challenges it presents.

The immense creativity and phenomenal technology that creates more addictive substances and temptations are the very same resources that can be used for unlimited good. R. Buckminster Fuller, the futurist and visionary, said that we are poised on a precipice of creating utopia or oblivion. The choice is ours—to resolve the paradox of our times and choose MORE, not less.

The Promise of MORE: Choosing Utopia over Oblivion

Soft addictions are so numbing and so pervasive that we have often overridden the still, small voice within that reminds us of the possibilities of MORE. It is difficult to hear the call of our hearts when we are in the buzz of a caffeine or adrenaline high, or numbed from our fast-food frenzy, or in a zone from staring at our computer or plasma screen for hours. We too often discard our dreams, settle for less, and decide "this is all there is"—forsaking our destiny or life's quest.

But we all have a divine itch that needs to be scratched, and that itch is more powerful than the numbing of our soft addictions. The problem is that for most of us, this higher yearning does break through, but often only in moments of crisis, trauma, loss, or even death. Without these crises, we're easily confused about what's important in life. We think that if we only had more stuff, or made more money, or lost more weight, or had more designer clothes or gadgets, then we'd be happy. We fool ourselves into believing that numbness is good, yet deep inside, though we may be able to ignore it in the short-term, eventually we are called by the promise of MORE. And if you are reading this book, you have already begun to respond to the call.

From Not Wanting Enough to Wanting MORE

You've probably made at least one of the following statements out loud or to yourself or heard others say them:

"Is this all there is?"

"Sometimes I feel like I'm wasting my life."

"I'm just going through the motions."

"I want to make a difference."

"I don't want to continue leading a superficial life."

"I just want to feel deeply connected to another person."

"I wish I could discover my purpose for being on this planet and fulfill it."

"I want to bring God into my life."

"I long to be part of the universe, to be in harmony with something larger than myself."

"I feel empty inside."

"There must be more."

As these statements suggest, the hunger for MORE manifests in a variety of ways. We each express our MORE uniquely because of our different issues, lessons, purposes, and even different soft addictions in our lives. We start out in a personal place, struggling to emerge from our sleep of limited consciousness maintained by soft addictions. We may begin by searching for more meaningful ways to live our lives, or we may begin by seeking deeper relationships. But ultimately, MORE translates into a spiritual journey or a path of higher purpose for all of us.

But students don't always come to the Wright Institute seeking more in life. Rather, they usually come to achieve a specific goal or to solve a particular problem. They may want to have a better relationship, become a better leader, or get a promotion. They may have problems they want to solve, such as earning more or wanting to get out of a bad job situation or relationship. Perhaps they feel lonely and want to find a life partner. Often they think that their unhappiness is because they want too much in life and should settle for less. But once they step onto the path to MORE and let go of some of the soft addictions that had been keeping them numb, they can suddenly see the possibilities available to them. They begin to understand that they did not want enough, and they start to dream bigger. They achieve their goal or take care of the problem they had, but invariably, they understand that it was their limiting, unconscious beliefs and feelings that kept them from desiring MORE. They may have felt they didn't deserve MORE or may not have believed in an abundant universe. For whatever reason, they don't initially see the unlimited possibilities of living the life they want. But once they do, the sky is the limit.

Katie came to the Institute because her marriage was on the rocks. The best she could see was to end the relationship amicably and move on. A nurse by profession, her life did not reflect any type of health care. She was overweight, underexercised, and chronically sullen and moody. After making her One Decision (a personal life commitment you'll learn about in the next chapter) to make her mark on the world through nourishing herself and others, everything turned around. Of course, her relationship with her husband became more satisfying, but so did all of her relationships. She began to care for her body as a gift to herself and lost weight. She also began exercising more because she enjoyed her body so much more. As she took these steps, she kept discovering how much more she wanted. Rather than just escape from an unhappy relationship, she started to vision a life that was far more exciting—one where she and her husband supported and encouraged each other, where she was healthy and vital, where she would open herself up to reawakening her spiritual life.

Now Katie has a life that others envy. Not only did she and her husband not divorce, they deepened their relationship tremendously and even had a daughter. She moved from getting by in her career to switching organizations and being put in charge of implementing some major health-care change initiatives at her new hospital. She and her husband travel to sacred sites every year and share their deep faith and exploration with their daughter. Katie is the poster child for not wanting enough. All she wanted was to resolve her relationship problem. But by learning to want MORE, she discovered health, vitality, intimacy, career success, and a loving, supportive family.

THE DEEPER MORE v. THE SURFACE MORE: ACCEPT NO SUBSTITUTES

Like Katie, you may not readily know what you are missing or how your soft addictions keep you from it. Even if you see clearly the greater MORE you want, it helps to start naming and describing it in words, to differentiate the deeper MORE from the surface more.

Notice in the lists below the things we often mistake for the greater MORE. There is nothing wrong with wanting more clothing or a nicer car or house. It's just that having those things alone won't lead you to the bigger MORE of life. Seeing the two lists side by side can put into perspective how unlikely material things are to help you achieve your longing for a more meaningful life.

MORE TO THINK ABOUT

If someone were to ask you what's missing from your life, how might you respond? What do you want MORE of?

Deeper MOREs	Mistaken/Superficial Mores
More love	More gossip
More life	More house
More creativity	More caffeine
More adventure	More power
More knowledge	More media
More meaning	More avoidance
More peace	More oversleeping
More abundance	More "stuff"
More feelings	More possessions
More consciousness	More diversions

More energy	More fame
More connection	More vacations
More direction	More car
More truth and genuineness	More image
More life	More status
More of a difference	More escapes
More God/spirituality	More clothing

MORE ALERT

Be aware of these blocks to creating MORE:
- Not wanting enough
- Confusing more "stuff" with MORE
- Being stuck in the sticky web of soft addictions
- Fear of MORE
- Fear of risk and changes

PEOPLE WHO ARE GETTING MORE OUT OF LIFE

The Soft Addiction Solution skills evoke a certain magic. By pursuing MORE you naturally release your soft addictions, and by releasing your soft addictions you get MORE out of life. And as you apply the skills to get one of the greater MOREs of life, the rest naturally follow. You may choose to pursue more intimacy, but you find that because of your increased ability for connecting to people you end up making more money. Or you may create a life with meaning and find that a healthy lifestyle begins to develop without your even having planned it. Everyone who has followed these key skills to overcome their soft addictions has experienced exponential results. The results look different for each person, but in every case, the quest for MORE leads to finding more life, more love, and more meaning. Here are a few of their stories to inspire you.

Corey—MORE Connection, Time, and Money

"Eleven cups a day . . ." admitted Corey, telling the truth of his daily coffee habit. A stockbroker whose life had become nothing more than a web of soft addictions, Corey was a late-night TV junkie who channel-surfed until he dropped off to sleep in his chair. He launched his morning with multiple hits to the snooze alarm and mug after mug of coffee, just to get going. No wonder his maximum yearly income had never surpassed $80,000, which is low for his profession.

Not only was Corey trudging through his job, his marriage was on the fritz because he was so out of touch with himself and his wife. After attending Soft Addiction Solution training, Corey was sobered by what he saw in his lifestyle: he was out of control, unfulfilled, and spinning his wheels. He made a One Decision, a powerful life-changing commitment and the first step in overcoming soft addictions; at that point, everything changed. He uncovered a long-buried hunger for connection and committed to having quality relationships in every area of his life. After inventorying all the places where he was not creating quality connections with others, he started by making contact deeper with himself. Late at night he'd call a friend rather than mindlessly turning to the TV for comfort. He went to bed earlier and got up earlier in the morning to have quality time with himself before setting out on his day. He really cared about and tended to his clients in a way he hadn't before.

The results were dramatic. His salary kept increasing as he was better prepared for calls and served his clients more effectively. He went from making a maximum of $80,000 a year to $150,000 and then to $200,000 in a year the stock market was in the tank. At last check, his salary was $320,000, four times his original maximum. With his new-found ability to connect with people he dramatically transformed his relationship with his wife, awakening a long-hidden urge to have another child and opening up the possibility for adoption.

In his own words, Corey said, "When you are not watching as much television or doing other things that really don't add to the quality of your life, you have so much more time. I caught the first train to work at 5:51 a.m. instead of trying to stagger into work at 8:00 or 8:30. Those two extra hours really gave me an extra eight hours a day because the time was so beautiful and uninterrupted. I got to discover more prospective clients, talk to more people, and get into deeper relationships with the people I already knew. My work habits drastically changed. When I cleared away the rubble, made a commitment out of the vision of how I wanted my life, and did the work that was necessary, the universe just delivered like I couldn't believe. I learned a whole different way of talking to people. Instead of getting them to buy something, I was discovering what they needed. If I could provide it, I provided it. If not, I let it go. I now present myself to my customers as a real person, and look what a difference it has made. I have more time and more energy, and I have quadrupled my salary."

Jori—MORE Health and Satisfaction

"Single, slim, successful, smoke free, and loving my life," is how Jori described her lifestyle after working on breaking through many of her soft addictions. A regular smoker and consistently overweight, she was desperately looking everywhere for Mr. Right to ride in on his white horse and save her from her single life. Her day-to-day routine was one of work and recovery, work and checking out, work and escaping from the world.

A fortunate turn of events landed her in a Soft Addiction Solution training weekend, where she made her One Decision. She committed to love herself fully. Without even intending it on that training, she walked away from her cigarettes forever without looking back—a surprise to her since she had tried to quit many times before. Her commitment to love herself was the triumph that made a big difference everywhere she turned. After all, why would she poison the lungs of someone she loved?

After this first powerful step, she started looking more deeply at her web of soft addictions. She started eating foods that felt more right for her, eventually going on a diet and losing weight. She gained more confidence and decided she wasn't going to wait around for Mr. Right; instead, she was going to truly enjoy her single life. She set out to meet lots of great guys, to learn more about herself through the dating process, and to discover what mattered to her, what she cared about.

"I'm not even the same person anymore. Actually maybe I'm more of myself than I ever have been," she explained. "I feel great in my body. I exercise regularly, eat well, have a terrific group of friends and a very active social life. In a strange way, my soft addictions have been a gift to me. Since I started looking more deeply at them, I've completely changed my life. I completed a masters program with straight As and am now a successful counselor making a difference in the lives of many, many people. But most importantly, I love my life. How many people can say that?"

Tiffany and Ron—MORE Intimacy and Connection

Ron and Tiffany seemed to have it all. So good-looking that their friends called them Barbie and Ken, they had financial success, two beautiful children, the perfect home, and a wonderful lifestyle—except that Tiffany was spending hours upon hours away from her husband, children, and home because she was out shopping. Plus, she was consumed with decorating and redecorating their already lovely home, to the tune of $10,000 of custom carpet in one hallway, $8,000 curtains for two windows, and several other big-ticket items. And Ron had his own issues. He zoned out in front of the TV, was hooked on sugar, and obsessed about looking cool, always having the latest gadgets on hand before anyone else did. His successful sales job kept him on the road, and when he was home he distracted himself with his home projects. Tiffany, on the other hand, filled her time with shopping and redecorating.

After some heart-to-heart discussions they reached out for additional coaching and support. With a family history of alcoholism, Ron realized that even though he had stopped drinking himself, he hadn't learned how to deal with his feelings. He found a deep longing to relate to people but had invested so many years in looking cool, he didn't really know how to be genuine and connect with others. Tiffany realized that for years her self-worth had been based on how she looked, and she learned to apply the same formula to decorating her home or dressing her daughters. Underneath it all, she was hungry to learn who she was within and to be valued for it. Ron and Tiffany made a One Decision—Tiffany committed to living a life of substance and depth, and Ron committed to connecting deeply with others. Their mutual discovery had a ripple effect throughout every area of their lives. They both decided that the cycle of family addictions and unconsciousness would stop with them. They would commit to learning and growing and to transforming their lives so that they would leave a legacy for their daughters to build on.

Now their lives are dramatically different. As Ron learned to be more genuine with others, his already successful career skyrocketed. He was promoted and subsequently started his own company, bringing in $1 million in revenue in its first year. Tiffany went back to work in a fulfilling career of coaching and training, and recently completed her

master's degree. Together they developed a closeness and intimacy beyond anything they had ever imagined. As a family, they have a substance
and connection that is truly an inspiration for others—a far cry from
their Barbie and Ken history.

BREAKING FREE OF SOFT ADDICTIONS AND PURSUING MORE

You may have wondered why the first chapter of a book entitled *The Soft
Addiction Solution* is filled with information about getting MORE out of
life. That's because the secret to a great life is wanting and learning to expect a great life. If you allow yourself to want, the skills you will learn
for breaking free of soft addictions truly will give you that life, a life of
MORE. And by pursuing MORE directly, you will naturally break free of
your soft addictions. It's a divine formula that has had a tremendous impact on my life and the lives of thousands of others. In the next chapters,
you will discover the eight key skills that have the potential to bring you
the life you always dreamed of, beginning with the One Decision.

2

MAKE YOUR
ONE DECISION

*"We must make choices that enable us to fulfill
the deepest capacities of our real selves."*

—THOMAS MERTON

A great life requires a great decision—the One Decision. Your One Decision is a personal, life-defining commitment to the quality of your life—a commitment to living a life of MORE. When you make this choice, and learn to live accordingly, it positively impacts every aspect of your life. It serves as a powerful guide leading you to true satisfaction and steering you away from the false promise of soft addictions.

This is not just *a* decision. It is *the* One Decision that determines the quality and direction of your life. This powerful decision informs all your other life choices, guiding you to fulfillment and satisfaction in your career, self-esteem, relationships, service, spirituality, and even more.

Making the One Decision may be the most important decision you make in your life. Yet if you're like most people, you probably don't realize that the decision is yours to make. We often go through life thinking, *This is just the way it is.* It seems the best we can do is get by. We numb ourselves to the pain with soft addictions and just cope with the grind. Without the One Decision, we flounder. At times, we may realize that something isn't right and try to do something about it, but the nagging feeling lingers: *There must be more than this.* We haven't yet discovered the power of making the One Decision that leads to a life of MORE.

We all face the decision between living deep, conscious lives, or shallow, unconscious ones. If we don't consciously commit to what matters most to us, we commit to an unguided, unconscious life by default. When you commit to your One Decision, you have a reason to apply the skills to break free of your soft addictions. By using your One Decision as a guide, you design a fulfilling life, choice by choice, in which you are less dependent on your soft addictions. Making the One Decision ultimately becomes a commitment to a life of MORE and to the steps that you'll take to get the life you want.

> MORE-SEL
>
> *"You don't get to choose how you're going to die. Or when. You can only decide how you're going to live. Now."*
>
> —JOAN BAEZ

You have yet to formally identify your soft addictions, develop a vision of what this life looks like, and learn the skills of the process, but even now you stand at the edge of the great excitement and fulfillment that comes with making your One Decision. In making this decision and learning to live it, many of you will be learning about the very nature of commitment. You may be excited or afraid. But if you hunger for MORE—if you're fed up with your routines, sick of not being satisfied, or are determined to live a meaningful existence—then you possess the drive and the desire to make this commitment, one that will guide you through the steps of this book as well as your life.

GOOD-BYE WILLPOWER, HELLO FREEDOM

The way to release the bonds of soft addictions is to decide you are going to have a powerful, rich, and meaningful life. Breaking free of your soft addictions isn't about willpower; it is about aligning your thoughts and actions with this bigger commitment. With this beacon in front of you, soft addictions become less attractive. People I have worked with have tried a myriad of ways to overcome their soft addictions, but it is when they make their One Decision that they experience its transformative powers. Rather than trying *not* to indulge their soft addiction, they focus on living their One Decision.

"No more. I refuse to diet ever again!" Sandra exclaimed in frustration. "Over the last twenty years I've lost enough pounds to equal my total body weight, and probably yours too! And I've watched each pound creep right back on bringing more with them." Sandra tried every diet under the sun—no sugar, no fat, no salt, no wheat, the blood-type and body-type diets, high-fiber diets, liquid diets and special foods diets. She made New Age healthful attempts as well, including fasts, cleansings, acupuncture, and vegetarianism. She also tried any number of single-food-group diets like the cabbage broth diet, egg diet, celery diet, tuna diet, cottage cheese diet, grapefruit diet, etc. In her own words, "If I had mixed enough of them together, maybe I could have had a meal!"

Sandra finally refused to gain or lose another pound. She decided she wasn't going to waste any more energy on the weight-loss game, which clearly never worked for her. Quite by accident, or maybe by design, she signed up for a One Decision training. At that weekend she made her One Decision. *I love myself beyond measure as a unique gift of God's love.* As she began to guide her life according to her One Decision, she found herself asking questions that even impacted her meal times. *What would you feed someone you love right now? Is this the best thing for someone you love?* She thought, *I probably wouldn't tell them to stand in front of the refrigerator and eat out of the leftover containers!* Little by little, she began to take better and better care of herself. Without choosing to lose weight, she dropped twenty-two pounds. She also began to expect to be treated with more respect and she treated others with more caring. She became an even better manager, with a salary increase to show for it. Her work became more meaningful, her relationships deepened, and her house began to reflect the beauty she hungered for. Sandra knows she won't be thin overnight, but that isn't her focus. Her One Decision taught her to create the life she dreamed of—which just happened to include a more vital and healthy body, better relationships, and a higher quality of life.

THE UNDECISION V. THE ONE DECISION

As you read in the introduction, I made a lot of what I call "undecisions" in my own life before discovering and committing to my One Decision. Undecisions are the decisions you make that you think are going to make you happy or satisfied, but in fact, they often don't result in either.

As a teenager and young adult, I was overweight, overwrought, and underliving. I thought, *I'm unhappy because I am fat. That's my problem.* So I decided to lose weight, went on a food plan, and shed the pounds. But then I was thin—and unhappy. My life was still heavily involved with the soft addiction of food—what I would eat, what I wasn't going to eat, when I was going to eat, how much I was going to eat. I had decided to lose weight and succeeded at what I decided, but I hadn't decided to be satisfied, only thin. Disappointed, I searched for another solution. Then I thought, *I need a relationship, then I'll be happy.* So I hooked up with my college sweetheart. But, I was still unhappy, unsatisfied, and empty.

Once again, I had made an undecision. You can tell it was an undecision because of my *so that* thinking. I had decided to lose weight *so that* I'd be happy. I decided to get in a relationship *so that* I'd be fulfilled. But the problem was that although I had decided to lose weight and get in a relationship—I hadn't decided to live a great life.

Once I made my One Decision, everything changed. Suddenly, I kept my weight off with ease without dieting. I also found the right relationship to be in, the right life, and even what feels like the right "me." My days became satisfying; I was no longer waiting for some magical result to make me happy. Rather than making undecisions—losing weight, getting in a relationship—*so that* I would have a great life, I made my One Decision and went directly to the great life.

LIFE LITE OR LIFE DEEP

In the broadest sense of the term, the One Decision is a choice between opposites: a deeply felt life or a barely felt one; meaningful activities or escapist activities; spirituality or superficiality. It means choosing between living in a pleasant, anesthetized haze or experiencing life in all its authentic pain and pleasure; between a vague self-awareness or an acute

consciousness of our deepest feelings. It is choosing quality over
quantity, spirit over matter. Making the One Decision is choosing
to live a considered, conscious life,
rather than just drifting in a fog.
To be or not to be is the real decision, and whether or not we know
it, it's a decision we make every day
of our lives.

> MORE-SEL
>
> *"To be, or not to be:*
> *that is the question."*
> —WILLIAM SHAKESPEARE

MORE TO DO

Rent the movie *The Matrix* for a graphic illustration of a One Decision. The hero is given a choice of which pill to take—the one that
shows him the full reality or the one that numbs him into a con
trived, protected, unfeeling, consensual fantasy.

THE RIGHT STUFF WITH THE WRONG DECISION

Many of us think we have chosen a deep or high-quality life, but actually
we haven't. We may do some deep things or add some quality experiences, but we have not made an underlying decision that changes the fabric of our lives. I thought I was making an important decision when I
decided to lose weight, but it wasn't the One Decision that would change
my life. It was when I decided to live a conscious, deeply felt life that my
life changed. I realized that living this commitment is different from just
adding conscious activities to your life.

For example, I have met many people on a spiritual path who consider themselves very evolved, who meditate for hours each day, but who
then continually complain and indulge in mood and other soft addictions. They still live frustrating, semi-satisfying lives, out of touch with
their deeper wants. Adding a yoga class or in-depth courses in spiritual
development isn't enough without the One Decision. However, with the
One Decision, all the good things we do contribute to the larger whole
and take us where we ultimately want to go.

Maya wanted to be perfect. To her, perfect meant being a particular weight, having a toned body, and making sure her hair looked just right. She began her regimen. She worked out, dieted, and consulted with her hairstylist on the perfect hairdo. She learned styling techniques and makeup application. One day while on vacation at Club Med, she awakened in the morning and thought, *This is it. This is the day. I am perfect. My weight is exactly right, my body is toned and tan, I'm having a great hair day.* But then she realized, *I have no one to tell. What do I do with this? Go down to the beach and say, "Hey, I'm perfect today"? What's the point?*

A few years later, Maya is still in great shape, but she defines it differently. She's made a different decision. It's her mind, body, and spirit that matter to her. She meditates, does Pilates, has a great relationship with a wonderful guy, and uses her business acumen and contacts to help others live great lives. She still experiences twinges of envy when she sees her friend who is a fashion model, but Maya knows it is her whole life that matters, not just being a perfect size 8. Her body is in shape, but now it is *her* shape, which is fit and healthy but no longer "perfect."

THE POWER OF YOUR ONE DECISION

Your One Decision shines as a beacon. It beckons you and orients you through times of confusion. The One Decision guides your life in ideal situations, but it also influences decisions in difficult times. It gives you a sense of direction and control in times when you don't feel like you have much control. You discover that you can always align to a higher principle or value. You can always choose how you want to experience something and how to respond.

When you make your One Decision, you choose to pursue the greater MORE of life. Your One Decision then sustains you throughout the rest of the process. You'll be ready to identify and release your soft addictions because they hinder your path to a conscious life—the life you want.

How might your life change were you to decide to live more deeply and consciously every day, recognizing your spiritual hungers and aligning your thoughts and activities to fulfill them? What if all you do fits into a more meaningful whole? Imagine never thinking, *There must be more than this,* because you had found the life you want. Picture yourself at the end of a typical day feeling energized and sensitized to every aspect of your world—a day well-lived.

To be this way requires a decision. Of course, choosing our soft addictions constitutes a de facto decision. We usually aren't conscious of this decision and its implications; we don't understand that we've opted for a numb existence instead

> ## MORE-SEL
>
> *"I would rather be ashes than dust! I would rather that my spark should burn out in a brilliant flame than it should be stifled by dry rot. I would rather be a superb meteor, every atom of me in magnificent glow, than a sleepy and permanent planet. The proper function of man is to live, not to exist. I shall not waste my days in trying to prolong them. I shall use my time."*
>
> —JACK LONDON

of a fully alive one. At times the numbness wears off and we glimpse the terrible possibility that we are wasting our lives. But in our glazed, softly addicted state, we aren't sufficiently awake to consider the path of our life.

Our soft addictions steal our aliveness and short-circuit our soul's longing. As a result, we infrequently reach the point where we ask ourselves, *What do I want to say about myself at the end of my life?* Who would want to answer that they spent a gazillion hours online, daydreaming, and trying to make more money than they did the year before? Blinded by our soft addictions, we don't see that we can choose to ask if we have lived deep and meaningful lives, defined by our desires to be closer to ourselves, to others, to nature, and to God.

Sometimes a tragedy, illness, or loss jars people into awareness of what is most important to them. With this awareness, many make a commitment to change their lives. Most, however, shift for a while, but eventually return to their older patterns. They had a sudden awareness but didn't make the underlying life-altering decision. If you treat the One Decision like a New Year's resolution, you'll soon slip back into your soft addiction routines. I'd like to help you make a decision that you'll stick with and that you'll embrace with every fiber of your being, the One Decision that will endure and guide you for the rest of your life.

....

"Every year I make a New Year's resolution to follow a more rigorous exercise plan, and I never do. Instead, this year I made my One Decision to be a vessel for spirit. Without planning it, my workouts became more regular and more fulfilling. Because of my One Decision, I even meditated and prayed as I exercised. Now my exercise feels like sacred time rather than a punishment to keep my body to a certain size. And I was still able to lose my post-pregnancy weight in the process."

—Clare

....

COMMON CHOICES

Making the One Decision translates into many personal choices. If you decide to live a soulful life, it follows that you will change the way you spend your time and energy. For one person, this might mean spending less time mindlessly shopping and more time talking mindfully to close friends. For another, it might mean quitting a boring, unfulfilling job and pursuing one's life's work. Obviously, the One Decision has implications that vary from individual to individual.

But not every decision is on that scale. Each day, we make hundreds, if not thousands, of decisions. From what to wear to what to think about in our idle moments to what we're going to do for lunch, we are steeped in choices. All day long we make decisions without a real guiding philosophy. We are often confused by all our options or we fall into automatic routines that make our choices. Our One Decision can provide guidance, a yardstick with which we can measure all things.

Consciously making the One Decision saves us from thousands of ill-considered decisions and endless internal debate, bargaining, and mind chatter. We more easily see which activity or mood leads to a deeper rela-

> ### MORE-SEL
> ....
> *"Living is a constant process of deciding what we are going to do."*
> —JOSÉ ORTEGA Y GASSETT

tionship with ourselves, to higher consciousness, or even to God. People who are constantly agonizing about what to do or who let their routines decide for them have not made their One Decision.

The following are common decisions. Note which option out of each pair you would be more likely to choose. Try not to pick your idealistic answer, but rather a realistic one.

A. Flipping through the channels just trying to chill out and distract yourself until it's time for bed.

or

B. Searching the television guide for a program that addresses a topic or issue that you care about or that's related to a significant problem or event taking place in your life.

A. Sleeping a little late and then rushing off to work

or

B. Getting up a little early to journal and prepare for the day.

A. Talking with a friend about who's going out with whom.

or

B. Talking with a friend about what's going on inside of you.

A. Spending a weekend day continuously shopping, cleaning the house, and doing other chores straight through from morning to night.

or

B. Taking a break from weekend chores and spending time just by yourself in nature, listening to music or a thoughtful radio program, or meditating.

A. Consistently working six or seven days a week and complaining bitterly about "the stupid job."

or

B. Recognizing that your attitude is grinding down your soul and beginning a search for a more rewarding career.

A. Choosing to spend unnecessary time at work rather than participate in family activities.

or

B. Doing what you need to do at work so you have time to be with your family.

A. Gobbling fast food from plastic containers while watching hours of mediocre situation comedies.

or

B. Setting the table, playing great music, lighting a candle, and inviting yourself to dinner.

A. Fantasizing in idle hours at work or at home about material things or relationships with people you barely know.

or

B. Engaging more fully at work or taking a risk to go out and connect with a friend or meet someone new.

All of us, with or without a One Decision, sometimes make less conscious choices over more meaningful ones. The point of living the One Decision is not choosing perfection. However, for each of us, there is an enormous cost to making numbing choices versus choices that make us feel alive, vibrant, and engaged in our lives. We sacrifice our dreams, decision by decision, and if we forget to look, if we forget to remember what we're about, then our entire life can pass by without our realizing it. Breaking free of your soft addictions is a process you will learn more about in the following chapters. The first step is to make your One Decision.

While you may not be ready to make this life commitment now or even while you are reading this book, you may gain the benefits of it by trying one on for size. Choose MORE of what really matters in life and it can stand in for the more personal One Decision you will make when you're ready. Once you've starting aligning around this bigger decision, you'll find yourself gravitating toward choices that bring you more of what you really hunger for.

The One Decision is even
more powerful and has had more
impact than I thought when I first
discovered it. I initially used the
concept in my Soft Addiction Solution trainings, but as people began to make and live their One
Decision, the results went beyond

> ### MORE-SEL
>
> *"Purity of heart is to will one thing."*
>
> —SØREN KIERKEGAARD

just letting go of habits and behaviors. It had far-reaching effects, and
since then has become a critical foundation for all of our training and
coaching. In fact, it became the topic of my book entitled *The One Decision*,
which you may want to consult for in-depth support.

WHAT DOES A ONE DECISION LOOK LIKE?

The expression of the One Decision is personal and unique. Here are
some examples that people have made:

I am a person of integrity—I am truthful, genuine, and honest.
I love myself unconditionally.
I am a vessel for spirit.
I live my life as an adventure.
I am awake, engaged, and present.

These are all very different expressions of the same decision: to lead
a life of MORE. What unites the expressions is the recognition of our
yearnings for something greater than ourselves, for love, acceptance, or
truth. They lead to the recognition of being worthy and magnificent, deserving of an exceptional life. Tremendously powerful touchstones, their
"authors" can always come back to their decisions when in doubt or distress. No matter what type of problem or opportunity, they can always
refer to their One Decision. If they're feeling down, it can inspire; when
they're unsure, it points toward a course of action. It provides momentum and guidance as they climb the steps necessary to rise above their soft
addictions.

Making the One Decision, however, doesn't mean that you will never
indulge in your soft addictions again. That isn't the point. But the next

time you find yourself mindlessly channel surfing or engaging in hours of gossip, you will have a way of managing your soft addictions. Your consciousness of your actions will intrude: You'll recall the One Decision that you made, and it will help you limit the time and energy that you devote to these empty pursuits.

The One Decision helps you be with yourself in a new way. It allows you to ask yourself more interesting questions when you're engaged in a soft addiction. For instance, you'll ask yourself, *Why am I spending all this time in front of the television? Is it helping me get in touch with my deeper yearnings? Does watching this program add more meaning and resonance to my life than being with friends?* Instead of chastising yourself for watching so much television, making an excuse to justify your habit (*I've had a tough day; I deserve this*), or just zoning out and not thinking at all, you can refer to your One Decision and address your soft addiction differently. The One Decision to live a considered life helps you discover the Why underneath your soft addiction routines. Whether you have that One Decision in your mind or on a piece of paper, you can refer to it, view your activities or moods in a new light, and gain the strength and motivation to move toward more meaningful endeavors.

To illustrate the impact of the One Decision, let's take the example of two people, Laura and Jeff, who were preparing for a big meeting at work. Jeff woke up a nervous wreck. Everything seemed to go wrong. Filled with anxiety about the meeting, he tossed and turned all night rather than resting. Exhausted, he kept pushing his snooze alarm only to pop out of bed at the last possible minute and rush to the office. Barely mumbling to his wife and children as he flew around the house getting ready, Jeff gulped several cups of coffee to stay alert. He drove, frenzied, to the office, zigzagging and speeding through traffic while constantly pushing the radio buttons to distract himself.

Laura also woke up anxious about the meeting after a short night's sleep. But her One Decision, to be in touch with her feelings and to value herself, allowed her to make a series of choices that immediately calmed her. She began her morning by orienting to her One Decision, accepting the fact that she is going to feel anxious and scared. She spent a short time meditating, offering up a prayer for her day, sitting in a special place in her house where she knew she would be undisturbed. Refreshed from her meditation, Laura woke her husband and gave him a big hug, and relished feeling cared for and valued by his return embrace. Though her husband was responsible for waking their children and getting them ready for school this week, she stopped by each of their rooms, kissed them, and said good-bye. She left herself time to review her presentation. On the way to work, she listened to a CD she loved and even though she was scared, she was prepared with a positive outlook for the day.

The One Decision put all of Laura's other decisions into perspective. Jeff lacked a life-orienting perspective and so he alternately fled from his feelings and anxiety rather than addressing it head-on.

"I returned a call to a possible business prospect today. I have a soft addiction to being cool and fake, so normally I would say or do anything—even lie or agree with things that don't make sense to me—just to have the person like me or to get the business. Instead, I used my One Decision: I am a woman of integrity. I took risks and disagreed with the client on several comments he had made. To my surprise, rather than getting off the phone quickly like we might normally do, we had a much deeper conversation. I got not only new business but also an additional referral, just because I lived my One Decision."

—Beth

DECIDING TO GO ON A JOURNEY

I don't want to give the false impression that the moment you make your One Decision everything automatically changes. Deciding is simply the start of the journey, and along the way missteps occur, but your One Decision helps you assess your behavior, understand it, and reorient what matters most to you.

Glancing down at the ledger sheet, Kendra was shocked to see a total of $2,500 for coffee. Kendra was doing a cost inventory of her soft addictions and was taken aback when she saw that her gourmet coffee habit of several thousand dollars could have paid for a vacation she couldn't afford to take, a hefty annual sacrifice for something that made her feel anxious and jittery every day. She liked the buzz she got from drinking it, the ritual of stopping at her favorite coffeehouse, the familiar baristas and the cool way she placed her tongue-twisting order. The entire ritual made her feel important and special, and it was reassuring to be able to rely on the same behaviors daily and give herself a break.

But after attending my Soft Addictions Solution training, Kendra made her One Decision to fully embrace and experience her life. The more she chose to really feel alive, not just accept the caffeine buzz she substituted for aliveness, her coffee ritual wasn't appealing anymore. She started to add activities that would help her feel more alive and vital naturally. As a result, she began learning to dance, finding that grace and movement conferred a sense of freedom. She took risks in talking to friends and clients and found a natural energy and excitement that came from her relationships. She unleashed her creativity by writing short stories, designing and making quilts, and adding decorative touches to her home.

Kendra's journey has not been perfectly smooth. She talks about the stupid things she still does when she wants to impress a guy or how she clings to her procrastination soft addiction. She even indulges in a three-dollar cup of coffee now and then. Kendra, though, is intensely alert to these addictions as well as the activities that bring her authenticity and meaning. The One Decision woke her up. She consciously notices things in her life rather than sleepwalking through it. For Kendra, existing is much more intense and feeling focused. She feels she's going somewhere now that her life has a destination.

People ask me what it's like after you resolve to live a highly conscious life; how it feels to have made the One Decision. Rather than describing it, I share with you the actual words people have shared with me about the effect of The One Decision:

> *I'm making more money than I ever dreamed possible. . . . I've expanded my network of friends. . . . I take huge risks, and I'm very excited about what's next. . . . I am more satisfied. . . . I enjoy my work and my life so much more and just am having a heck of a time. . . . My life with my family, friends, and my wife has been three thousand percent better. . . . I've grown exponentially in terms of the power that I feel in my daily life. . . . I became the leader that I wanted to be. . . . I have*

self-respect now. . . . I'm a better parent. . . . I have a relationship with my kids
that I think other people envy.

Most of all, people talk about starting on a journey, opening a new
door onto a fresh path. While you may have miles to go before you become spiritually fulfilled or find the meaning in life you're seeking, you
experience a strong feeling of moving in a new direction. The journey
becomes fulfilling in itself. The excitement and energy of the path facilitate taking the next steps.

....

"I finally feel awake, literally. I had no clue how much I had been sleepwalking
through my life. I even used to fall asleep in meetings. Since I made my One Deci-
sion to be alive, awake, and engaged, I'm the one raising my hand or leading the
group on a new initiative or new idea. I used to hate looking at photos of myself be-
cause I was so zoned out, I looked really unattractive. Now people comment on how
photogenic I am. I finally feel alive."

—Lilliana

....

WHY YOU DON'T NEED TO BECOME
MOTHER TERESA OR GANDHI

Perhaps the One Decision sounds ominous, as if you're making a reverse
Faustian pact, an agreement with an angel rather than the devil. While it
is a momentous decision, it's not a black-and-white one. Making it
doesn't mean that you must live a purely spiritual life or that you can no
longer indulge in any soft addictions. It is nothing more—and nothing
less—than a shift in perspective, in how you see the world, in the quality
of your life. Don't expect to be transformed into a saint or a monk (unless that happens to be your path), but still expect major changes to occur. Here are the ones that most people experience.

Asking the Big Questions. You will stop obsessing over the small questions
and start asking the big ones. Rather than endlessly deliberating over:
What should I wear? What gadget should I buy? What dessert do I want?, you'll use your

One Decision to make those choices. You'll begin to see how we expend tremendous amounts of time and energy repeatedly asking ourselves the little questions, most of which relate to surface issues. While it's fine to look for a nice dress, it's not OK to agonize for weeks over what outfit to buy for a party and waste hours going from one store to another.

After making the One Decision, people will still ask these questions and they will still pick out a dress to wear or a gadget to buy. But the decision is more integrated, and the dress is more likely to reflect who they really are, and the gadget is more likely to have a higher purpose than to just have the latest and coolest thing. The small questions will transform into inquiries like, *Which choice helps me move toward my vision?* More important, they will start asking the Big Questions and spend time contemplating the answers. Big Questions include: *What is my purpose and what helps me fulfill it? Why am I here and how do I make my life count?* and *What gives my life meaning?*

Experiencing more intense feelings. You will experience more intense feelings. The numbness recedes once you make the One Decision. The joyfulness, energy, and even euphoria are part of an emotional rush that comes after deciding. At the same time, asking the Big Questions also makes you feel fear and sadness. Exploring your purpose can be a struggle, and you may have to confront years of wastefulness in which you acted without purpose. Be prepared to laugh with great joy and cry with great sorrow; you cannot experience one without the other.

Feeling more conscious and engaged. Your One Decision wakes you up to life. Becoming more aware and engaged, you notice the world around you and within you. As a result, life becomes more exciting. Rather than trying to escape from life's changes, you embrace them with the spirit of an adventurer.

Getting a new perspective on addictive behaviors. You will get a new perspective on your soft addictions. You'll start viewing every mood and activity through your One Decision. You won't eat, smoke, gossip, or daydream without thinking, *What am I feeling now? What is going on with me that I want to do this now? How will this lead me to knowledge about myself, to more awareness and more sustenance?* As a result, you'll reframe television watching as a window to worlds you wouldn't ordinarily experience. Instead of surfing the Internet in a mindless daze, you'll use it to focus on a specific inquiry designed to satisfy a deeper need. Instead of reading to escape, you'll read for knowledge, inspiration, and wisdom.

You'll begin to examine your motivations for doing what you do and feeling what you feel. This examination allows you to be less dependent on your soft addictions. Or more accurately, you change soft addictions into meaningful behaviors.

For example, as I was writing the previous paragraph, I started to feel anxious and noticed a clutch in my gut concerning an engagement tonight. All of a sudden, I wanted to check out: to take a nap, to grab a cup of coffee, to make some chorelike phone calls, and so on. But because of my One Decision, I noticed what was going on. My decision to be conscious and in touch with my feelings helped me realize that I was anxious and was looking for any way possible to avoid my anxiety. I knew to look beneath the urges for my soft addictions to discover what I'm feeling. Rather than checking out, I took a meaningful break. I listened to a favorite song, made a cup of great tea, and allowed any feelings I had to bubble to the surface. I closed my eyes for a moment, reviewing and adjusting my plans for the evening until I felt satisfied. I felt the tension release. Doing so relaxed me and allowed me to return to this writing, refreshed and aware that this was something important to me. There's a big difference between consciously choosing breaks and checking out.

CLAIMING A ONE DECISION

You have moved toward your One Decision by picking up this book and reading to this point. As I mentioned earlier, a One Decision isn't about being perfect, so at this point in your journey you don't need to worry about coming up with the perfect One Decision. In fact it's not really important *what* greater MORE of life you commit to. But it is very important *that* you commit. For now you may choose to orient simply to the greater MORE of live, however you define it. Or you can test-drive a One Decision and see what feels right for you. You may choose to stand for truth, to feel your feelings, to live life as an adventure, to live as if every moment counts. Again, it doesn't matter at this point which one you choose, but rather that you start to orient to something bigger. There are exercises in the workbook at the back of this book that can better help you explore your commitment.

Enjoy playing with possibilities. Think of your decision in the affirmative, not as a wish or by saying, "I want to." You are creating a living statement that can grow with you and become clearer as your One Decision comes into greater focus throughout your life. Remember, the decision is final, but the wording and understanding may vary over time. You are deciding to live the life you want, a life of MORE.

Your One Decision guides you and provides a foundation to support you as you learn to live the life of MORE you have chosen. It is a decision that leads you to recognize that you are a worthy, magnificent person who deserves a great life. With your One Decision in mind, you're now ready to move forward and identify the soft addictions that lead you to less, not MORE.

3

IDENTIFY YOUR
SOFT ADDICTIONS

"I generally avoid temptation unless I can't resist it."
—MAE WEST

Without fail, in the fifteen years since I coined the term *soft addictions,* people respond with an *aha!* when they first hear the term. They immediately identify a common soft addiction or even mention an addiction of their own: "Oh, yeah, like watching too much television," or "I spend a lot of time on the Internet." After they learn more, they generally discover even more soft addictions, such as gossiping, nail biting, or collecting things. Then there are always those who are more eloquent about the soft addictions of others: "My husband is a sports fanatic," or "My wife is into shoes."

Most of us can identify at least one activity that hooks us. It's the rare person who doesn't admit to being addicted to television, sports, shopping, work, or any of the typical leisure-time endeavors. What is more difficult is admitting the cost of these activities and the harm they do—how they keep us from the life we want. Most people dismiss the habit as a harmless pastime, or an outlet for stress, or a bothersome little habit, but have not come to grips with the costs of money, time, energy, productivity, intimacy, motivation, opportunities—the loss of a life of MORE.

Without realizing the cost, we aren't sufficiently motivated to survey our lives fully and identify the less apparent soft addiction routines that have us in their grip. They're not always as obvious as television, and they're often far more insidious. We're not used to thinking about moods as something that we might be addicted to, unaware of how we can use familiar moods as a refuge. Similarly, many people are addicted to avoidance patterns, such as procrastination or steering clear of social interactions.

In addition, we enmesh ourselves in scores of smaller routines, ones that may seem innocuous on the surface but whose cumulative impact is significant. We spend enormous amounts of unproductive time on these little things—from compulsive e-mail checking to nail picking to overgrooming (combing hair, putting on makeup) to getting weather updates ten times a day. As harmless as they may appear, these activities deprive us of time and energy that could be devoted to more meaningful pursuits. We may not realize that our drive to constantly check the status of our investments qualifies as a soft addiction, but it's one of many little habits that keep us trapped.

MORE TO THINK ABOUT

The average man clicks on the remote control every 28 seconds.*
Think about how many times that adds up to in just one hour.

Denial and defensiveness compound the difficulty of identifying our addictions. We'll focus on this problem in greater detail in the next chapter. For now you should be aware that you most likely deny, rationalize, or make excuses for at least some of your soft addiction routines. The odds are that you've developed credible explanations to yourself about why these routines are not a problem. It's also possible that you admit these soft addictions are a problem but not one of sufficient magnitude to worry about. Instead, you ascribe your addictive behaviors to being human and suggest that everyone has a weakness. Thus, you have trouble identifying your soft addictions because you view them as minor flaws rather than as obstacles to living the life you want.

*Francine Hardaway, "Under the Radar: Television 2.0," *BizAz* #5 (2002): 80.

THERE'S MORE THAN MEETS THE EYE

"I know. I know. I know," was Jason's typical response when people teased him about his addiction to Internet surfing. Jason was well aware that he wasted enormous amounts of time on the Internet, both at work and at home. He freely admitted to the endless hours he spent online gaming or surfing sports or sex-related Web sites. His wife's complaints and a couple of work reprimands about his personal Internet surfing motivated Jason to start tackling what he knew was a soft addiction for him. He made his One Decision to live life as an adventure and things started to change dramatically. Rather than waiting to get online, he began to have more good times with his wife and children—going to the zoo, playing games, planning creative meals together, talking about their dreams. He engaged in his work more deeply by challenging some long-standing policies that were outdated for his industry and started to enjoy the excitement of it in a way he hadn't thought possible.

What Jason didn't recognize as he first embarked on his journey was that this big soft addiction of Internet surfing was actually masking scores of smaller ones. "I don't know how I got here but my entire lifestyle is filled with soft addictions," he finally admitted to himself. For instance, every day Jason mindlessly snacked on candy bars and then every night he went to the gym and played basketball with the guys because he felt guilty about eating so much candy. To him, the snacking and exercising canceled each other out and they were simply activities that were a part of his lifestyle, rather than an unconscious routine he was stuck in.

As Jason's awareness increased he realized that when he wasn't online, he often got a buzz from fantasies or daydreams. Some of them were sexual; others revolved around fantasies of escape and vengeance. He felt that his bosses picked on him, and he imagined scenarios in which he exacted retribution for their unfair treatment of him. He hadn't realized how many hours he wasted in this fantasy world.

As he started to get closer to his wife and children, he realized that he had been addicted to acting aloof. His demeanor at home and at work was that of a stoic, never letting anyone see him upset (or joyous, for that matter). What Jason began to realize was how much his routines were really controlling him, and not the other way around. He had been stuck in a superficial existence. It was only by making his One Decision, and having the compassion to see his behaviors and moods for what they really were, that he started to experience the real adventure and closeness he had always craved.

Identifying soft addictions takes a bit of practice, but once you start doing it, you become perceptive about the linkages between various moods and behaviors. You realize that soft addictions may exist in all shapes and sizes, but they all serve the same purpose: they numb you to your feelings and your deeper, spiritual self.

It's often easier to identify the soft addictions in others. For example, think of someone you know well. You could probably list off the top of your head the more common soft addictions they have (television, gossip, shopping). Now imagine the smaller or idiosyncratic ones you've seen them do (coupon clipping, collecting salt and pepper shakers, hair twirling). Do they also have addictions related to moods, things, and avoidances? While it's more difficult to identify another's mood addictions, you may be able to venture a good guess based on themes in conversations with that person. For instance, someone who tells you that he or she spends hours dreaming about a television actor or who complains about always feeling blah is telling you what activities and moods he or she gravitates toward.

WHAT ARE SOFT ADDICTIONS?

To identify soft addictions, it's helpful to look more closely at what defines them, and what common characteristics they share. Soft addictions can be habits, compulsive behaviors, or recurring moods, ways of being, or thought patterns. Their essential defining quality is that they satisfy a surface want but ignore or block the satisfaction of a deeper need. They numb us to feelings and spiritual awareness by substituting a superficial high or a sense of activity for genuine feeling or accomplishment.

Many soft addictions involve necessary behaviors like eating, reading, and sleeping. They become soft addictions when we overdo them and when they are used for more than their intended purpose. Soft addictions, unlike hard ones such as drugs and alcohol, are seductive in their softness. E-mailing, shopping, and talking on the phone seem like perfectly harmless, pleasurable activities while we're engaged in them. When we realize how much time and energy we devote to them, however, we can see how they compromise the quality of our lives.

MORE TO DO

Rent the movie *About a Boy* for an eloquent example of a softly addicted life. The main character, played by Hugh Grant, lives a life centered around soft addiction routines until he discovers MORE through his unlikely relationship with a lovable and nerdy preteen boy.

Though you'll find a list of common soft addictions in this chapter, you should understand that an almost infinite variety exists. A soft addiction can be as idiosyncratic as any individual personality. While a universal soft addiction might be television watching, a more personal form might be collecting anything from comic books to movie memorabilia, or doodling geometric figures.

Some people have difficulty differentiating an occasional behavior or fleeting mood from a soft addiction. If you watch television one hour a day, is it only a harmless habit, but if you watch three to four hours per day (the national average*) is it a soft addiction?

We'll get into more detail about this later in the chapter, but keep the following in mind: the motivation and the function of your behavior determine whether or not it's a soft addiction. For instance, television can be a window into new worlds, stimulating viewers with new ideas and leading them into meaningful pursuits—or it can be a means of escape. I know a woman who enjoys television, because she uses it as "destination TV," picking something in advance to watch that is inspiring, educational, or helps her think about issues in a different way. She loves foreign cultures, nature, and the arts, so if she finds a program that aligns

*David G. Myers, *The American Paradox* (New Haven and London: Yale University Press, 2000), 200.

with her interests, she plans ahead and tunes in. On the other hand, another woman I know is simply a channel surfer. She leads a tough, hectic work life so she comes home stressed and looking for renewal, but instead ends up zoning out in front of the television for hours at a time, letting the programs wash over her, rarely caring or remembering what she saw. The biggest problem is that she never really feels renewed and inspired. In the end, she only feels more drained.

As you compare the two television watchers, the differences in motivation and function are clear. The first woman's motivation revolves around very specific goals to develop herself and learn more; the second's motivation is to numb herself. The first woman uses television to enhance her life; the second, to escape from her life.

Sometimes, however, the line between soft addictions and productive activities is less clear. Here are a few clues to help you define this line and recognize that your behavior is a soft addiction.

Zoning out. One way of identifying a soft addiction is to ask if you zone out while you're doing it. When we are zoned out, we are not fully engaged. We may be checked out or have a "nobody's home" look on our face. Zoning out suggests that the goal of our activity is numbness. Although we're physically engaged in an activity, our mind is elsewhere. After the activity, we often don't remember what we've done, seen, or read. While this often happens when watching television, it can also occur while shopping, working, having superficial conversations, or doing other activities.

Perusing catalogs was a soft addiction for me. On the surface, you might ask, what's the big deal? I didn't spend hours on it every day. But the problem was that the instant I opened the catalog, I started traveling in that imaginary world of new clothing, furniture, or travel and I was gone . . . I was checked out, in a semi-trance. If my husband asked me something, I would barely hear him. It was a chore to get myself back on track with my day after that. I was definitely zoned out and I really didn't like the feeling of trying to wake myself up again. Fortunately, using the skills I've shared in this book, I was able to shift. Sure, I still flip through catalogs when I need something, but it's no longer an Olympic sport for me.

MORE TO THINK ABOUT

Zoning out while surfing the Internet has become such a phenomenon that it has earned its own name. *Surfer's voice* no longer describes the dulcet tones of a tan, athletic Californian with a surfboard slung over his shoulder. Instead, the term has become a widespread description for the voice people use when they are surfing the Internet, are zoned out, and aren't really paying attention to someone who's "offline" and asking a question. It's a monotone, muttered, barely audible way of responding, typically with short meaningless phrases, like yeah, uh-huh, and sure.

Avoiding feelings. Does a given activity or mood grant you a reprieve from your emotions, especially intense emotions? We avoid feelings by being numb, enhancing the feelings we like to the exclusion of others, or even wallowing in one unpleasant feeling to avoid another. Many of us are uncomfortable with our deepest feelings, whether positive or negative. We don't know how to deal productively with our sadness or anger (or, in some instances, with our joy), so we find an activity or a mood that facilitates an emotion-muting state, leaving us with subdued sadness, low-level anger, or other unsettled feelings.

"Talk about avoiding feelings! I was in a car accident and all shaken up. Rather than calling my husband to tell him what happened and how I was feeling, I suddenly found myself at the counter of a shoe department handing over a credit card to purchase a pair of Jimmy Choos (shoes way out of my budget, for you non–shoe addicts). I clued in when I saw my hand shaking as I passed over my credit card."
—Elaine

Compulsiveness. Does an irresistible urge drive you to indulge a particular behavior or mood? Do you feel compelled to do, have, or buy something, even though you know you don't need it? This may be accompanied by a helpless, powerless feeling. You may be unable to stop or reduce the amount of time spent on a given activity. Though you may find some transient pleasure, you often don't feel good about yourself after engaging in it. You persist in following the routine, telling yourself you'll never do this again. Though you try to stop, you can't.

Denial/Rationalization. If you're defensive or making excuses for your behavior, chances are it's a soft addiction. Denial is a refusal to acknowledge, and rationalization is an excuse or explanation used to justify a compulsive behavior. Both blunt our self-awareness and lower our expectations of ourselves. To make our actions acceptable, we ignore, conceal, or gloss over the real motive or cost. Either we maintain that a habit isn't a problem or we rationalize why it's an acceptable or necessary way to spend our time. Saying you need designer clothes for work and questioning what's so bad about a few cups of coffee are typical rationalizations. We may deny that the hours spent surfing the Net are a waste of time and energy. The impulse to deny or rationalize a routine suggests a soft addiction.

Consider the following list of excuses and rationalizations we fall back on when confronted with our soft addictions:

"After working hard, I need to escape."
"It's just harmless fun."
"This is just my hobby."
"Everyone does this."
"I wouldn't know what to do if I couldn't do this."
"This is part of who I am."
"All my friends do the same things, so what would we do if we
    didn't do this?"

....

(MORE TO THINK ABOUT)

How might you defend your routines to a friend or loved one? How might you explain or justify your addictive behaviors? Would you act resentful at being accused of having an addiction?

....

It's natural to react defensively when someone points out your soft addiction; you feel guilty to be wasting so much time on a particular behavior. In a larger sense, however, there is nothing to feel guilty about: we all have our soft addictions. In their most benign form, soft addictions are harmless hobbies and necessary escapes from stress. To eliminate them entirely is difficult if not impossible. But what is important is increasing our awareness of these behaviors, especially when they prevent us from having the life we want.

Stinking thinking. Related to denial and rationalization, stinking thinking is distorted thinking based on mistaken beliefs. Overgeneralizing, magnifying, minimizing, justifying, blaming, and emotional reasoning are some examples. Stinking thinking creates the funny rules and logic of soft addictions, such as, "There are no calories if I eat standing up," or "I can't possibly work out if I've already showered." Woven throughout soft addiction routines, this type of thinking is addictive in itself. The distorted thoughts prompt indulging in a soft addiction in the first place and later let us justify the indulgence.

Hiding the behavior. Beware of habits that become guilty pleasures you seek to hide. Covering up the amount of time you spend on an activity and/or lying to others about how you frequently spend your time or your money are signs of soft addictions. In other words, you feel ashamed of what you're doing and that's why you want to hide it from others.

....

"I stash my shopping bags in the trunk of my car so my husband doesn't know what I bought. Then when he's not home, I pull off all the tags and hang them in my closet so he has no idea they're new."

—Susan

"I told my wife I would cut down on my ice cream habit, so one night when I ate half of a gallon I ran to the store and got the exact same kind to replace the carton in the freezer so she wouldn't know."

—Bill

....

....

"My whole family knows I've got an Internet thing. But I've become an expert at hiding it. I pull up our budget and expense spreadsheet on my computer, and then I log onto the Internet. If I hear anyone coming near the office, I just close the Internet window so that I look very busy."

—Joan

....

Avoiding feelings or zoning out are perhaps the most telling of these signs. Part of the allure of soft addictions is that they provide an escape from the pace and pressure of life. If we've had a tough day, we want to relieve the pressure. The same impulse that pushes people to have a drink rather than talk out tensions at the end of a hard day leads them to soft addictions.

Doing this is perfectly natural. We all need to zone out at times. Zoning out allows our unconscious mind to sort things out, giving us the downtime we need to regroup. It would be unusual to find anyone who didn't need to escape from his or her feelings at certain moments. The problem, of course, is when this becomes a way of life and soft addictions become deeply ingrained. We become like football players who have an injury but anesthetize themselves so they can get back in the game. As a short-term strategy, this may work. We convince ourselves that if we didn't have our soft addictions, we couldn't keep going to work, taking care of the kids, and generally keeping our life together. The danger to the football player, however, is that the underlying injury never gets treated and can even worsen. Similarly, we become accustomed to numbing ourselves and never consciously feeling any pain (or any intense emotion, for that matter). In this way, we become out of touch with our deeper self. We fail to meet deeper needs and move farther from our full potential.

CHANGING OUR PERCEPTIONS OF SOFT ADDICTIONS

Identifying our soft addictions is impossible if we resist categorizing them as addictions. Admittedly, *addiction* is a problematic word. For many people, the word denotes skid-row bums, needles, drunken binges, and the like. Even though most experts recognize that hard addictions represent a disease, there still remains the too widely held view that they are the result of a weak will or a moral flaw.

As a result, people don't like to admit that they're addicted to anything, be it soft or hard. What we need to come to terms with is the ubiquitous nature of addictions and how the addictive process runs through everyone's life. We all give ourselves over to things. In fact, the word *addiction* comes to us from Roman law, meaning "to give over."

....

"I came back from my vacation and everyone was asking me what I did. I hardly wanted to admit to them that I just spent the majority of my vacation organizing my DVD and CD collection. First of all, it's pretty sobering to think that I have so many DVDs and CDs that it takes me days to organize them. And that I spent my precious vacation time organizing it all. I finally had to admit it. I am addicted!"

—Martin

....

SEARCHING FOR RED FLAGS

Identifying addictions isn't a science. Some of your activities may fall on the cusp; others occupy a gray area where it's initially difficult to know with any certainty if they're soft addictions. For example, you may daydream at times (who doesn't?), but it's difficult to discern if your daydreaming is excessive or if it interferes with your ability to achieve your real dreams.

It's also possible that you have a lot of time wasters but your time commitment to each is relatively small—you don't do any of them to excess, making it difficult to detect their cumulative effect on the soft-addictions radar.

> MORE-SEL
> ....
>
> *"Lead me not into temptation. I can find the way myself."*
> —RITA MAE BROWN

At this point your goal shouldn't be to create a definitive list of every activity, mood, and avoidance in order of time consumed or energy zapped. Rather, identify and attach red flags to parts of your life that clearly lead you in the wrong direction. Let them generate self-awareness about the moods and activities that rob your life of depth and richness.

. . . .

MORE TO THINK ABOUT

How do you know if you have soft addictions? Check your pulse. If you feel it, be assured you have some. It's not *whether* you have soft addictions; it's *which* ones you do have.

. . . .

SOFT ADDICTION CATEGORIES

Soft addictions fall into four different categories: activities, avoidances, moods/ways of being, and things—edible and consumable.

Activities: Any activity can become a soft addiction if it is overdone or used to zone out or avoid feelings. Activity soft addictions tend to cluster in these areas: media, shopping, social, and other diversions. Think about the activities you may habitually overdo.

Avoidances: Where activities are the things you do, avoidances are the things you don't do. At first glance, it may be hard to see avoidance as a soft addiction. After all, avoidance involves *not* doing something. But not doing something, evading, or minimizing can be ways to keep you checked out and unengaged. Escaping can become a habitual response to upset and can feel just as compulsive as more active behaviors.

Moods/Ways of Being: Moods and ways of being can become soft addictions when they become habitual responses rather than genuine emotional responses to being upset. Think about the people you know who are habitually sarcastic or have high energy even when a situation doesn't warrant it. People who complain frequently, crack jokes, or act cool much of the time may be using that way of being as a habitual way to distance themselves from their deeper feelings.

Note: These mood soft addictions differ significantly from clinical mood disorders. The former are normal reactions that turn into numbing habits, while the latter are abnormal conditions that often require therapy and treatment.

Things—Edible and Consumable: Habitually overindulging in things from fancy chocolates to designer coffees can be a soft addiction. Consistently going for a "hit" when you are having feelings may signal a substance addiction. You may not have considered gadgets or designer clothing as being possibly addictive things, but if you must have the latest thing and feel incomplete without it, you may be vulnerable to this type of addiction. If you become anxious when your supply runs low or runs out, you're likely addicted. You may spend time planning on using a given substance. It might even take on the form of a ritual.

Some of the items listed below may strike you as odd, trivial, or silly. They are not so silly if you're one of those people who uses them instead of dealing with the issues in your life. In the workbook section of the book you'll find more tools to identify your own soft addiction routines and learn how to recognize if something is a soft addiction or just a harmless pastime.

Remember that at this point, you're really just increasing your awareness and allowing yourself to identify where soft addictions might be red flags for you. As you scan the list, you may think of others that are pertinent to you. Feel free to jot them down to keep track of them. As you'll discover, some of the items listed may sound relatively unimportant (nail biting) compared with others (television, the Internet). Remember, though, a soft addiction doesn't have to be anything monumental to constitute a spiritual roadblock.

ACTIVITIES

Media
- ☐ Watching television
  - *Channel surfing*
  - *Program junkie*
  - *Sports*
- ☐ Surfing the Internet
- ☐ Participating in chat rooms
- ☐ Checking investments
- ☐ Checking weather, statistics, news
- ☐ Reading magazines
- ☐ Reading only one genre of novels, such as romance or mysteries
- ☐ Listening to the radio
- ☐ Checking e-mail
- ☐ Playing computer games
- ☐ Playing video games
- ☐ Checking eBay
- ☐ Instant messaging
- ☐ Text messaging

Buying/Shopping
- ☐ Shopping
- ☐ Cruising garage sales
- ☐ Collecting
- ☐ Antiquing
- ☐ Bargain hunting
- ☐ Hanging out in the mall
- ☐ Perusing catalogs
- ☐ Clipping coupons

Maintenance
- ☐ Overeating
- ☐ Overexercising
- ☐ Glamorizing
- ☐ Hygiene
- ☐ Housekeeping
- ☐ Being a pack rat
- ☐ Caregiving
- ☐ Sleeping too much

Physical Mannerisms
- ☐ Hair twirling
- ☐ Twitching, jiggling, picking
- ☐ Gum chewing
- ☐ Nail biting

Sexual
- ☐ Flirting
- ☐ Sexual obsessions
- ☐ Phone sex
- ☐ Pornography
- ☐ Masturbating compulsively
- ☐ Being a voyeur
- ☐ Babe or dude watching
- ☐ Being promiscuous
- ☐ Leering
- ☐ Fantasizing

Work
- ☐ Overworking/keeping busy
- ☐ Overscheduling
- ☐ Overcommitting

Risk Taking
- ☐ Speeding
- ☐ Gambling
- ☐ Seeking danger
- ☐ Making deals

Social/People
- ☐ Name-dropping
- ☐ Following celebrity news
- ☐ Gossiping
- ☐ Storytelling

- [ ] Cell phone conversations
- [ ] Fantasizing/daydreaming
- [ ] Lying

Other Diversions
- [ ] Checking sports stats
- [ ] Doing crossword puzzles
- [ ] Playing card games
- [ ] Fantasy sports leagues
- [ ] Crafts
- [ ] Sports

AVOIDANCES

- [ ] Procrastinating
- [ ] Isolating
- [ ] Being late
- [ ] Playing dumb
- [ ] Living in clutter
- [ ] Acting helpless
- [ ] Playing the victim
- [ ] Hypochondria
- [ ] Phobias
- [ ] Stonewalling
- [ ] Being too busy
- [ ] Oversleeping/napping

MOODS/ WAYS OF BEING

- [ ] Being sarcastic
- [ ] Being cranky/irritable
- [ ] Indulging in self-pity
- [ ] Being "in the know"
- [ ] Being a drama king or queen
- [ ] Always being happy; always "on"
- [ ] Being a Pollyanna

- [ ] Chameleonlike behavior
- [ ] Acting like a sad sack
- [ ] Moping
- [ ] Blaming
- [ ] Looking good
- [ ] Complaining
- [ ] Constantly trying to please people
- [ ] High energy
- [ ] Jokester
- [ ] Perfectionism
- [ ] Fanaticism
- [ ] Being argumentative/ conflictual
- [ ] Acting cool

THINGS—EDIBLE AND CONSUMABLE

Edible
- [ ] Sugar
- [ ] Chocolate
- [ ] Fast foods
- [ ] Carbohydrates, high-fat foods, etc.
- [ ] Coffee
- [ ] Snack foods

Consumable
- [ ] Cigarettes
- [ ] Gadgets
- [ ] Electronics
- [ ] Designer clothes
- [ ] Shoes
- [ ] Collectibles
- [ ] CDs
- [ ] DVDs
- [ ] Brand-name merchandise

SOFT ADDICTION QUIZ

If you're wondering if something is a soft addiction for you, read through this quiz. How many yes answers indicate that you have a soft addiction? Even a single yes answer might qualify! Use each one as a prompt to look deeper. Of course, the more yes answers you have, the more likely a given activity or mood qualifies as a soft addiction.

1. Would you be unlikely to go on national television and say, "You, too, should do this" about your behavior?
2. When asked why you do this thing, do your reasons sound like excuses or rationalizations?
3. Do you do this activity or retreat to a mood compulsively or habitually?
4. Is there a particular routine that you follow, almost like a ritual, for this behavior?
5. Do you have difficulty imagining life without it (or even with less of it)?
6. Do you want to change this behavior, resolve to do so, but then find yourself unable to keep your resolution?
7. Do you feel scared or stubborn when someone suggests you stop or reduce this behavior?
8. Has the time you spend doing the activity or being in the mood increased without providing the same level of satisfaction it once did?
9. Have you been teased, mocked, or criticized because of how you're wasting a great deal of your time on trivial pursuits?
10. Has someone close to you become annoyed or angry with you about the amount of time, money, and/or energy you devote to a given activity?
11. Have you canceled or turned down positive opportunities in order to indulge an activity, substance, or mood?
12. Has your particular activity, mood, or avoidance caused you to get in trouble on the job?
13. Is this something that you would be embarrassed about if others were to learn of it? Does it feel like a secret you're ashamed of?

GROWING IN AWARENESS

There are three questions that you can ask yourself to raise your awareness and identify your addictions. *How much time do I spend? What is my motivation? What are my feelings?*

For example, a simple diversion can become a soft addiction when you spend twenty hours a week on it. Or watching TV to enrich yourself might be a great motivation, but if you are watching the same old program to check out and avoid your spouse, then it's likely a soft addiction. Or if you feel excited and motivated after something you do, it might be a great activity for you, but if you feel a false buzz or are spaced out afterward, then it's likely a soft addiction. The workbook at the end of this book has a variety of exercises and tools you can use to help identify and really distinguish between soft addictions and pastimes.

Note: Keep in mind that our concern is soft rather than hard addictions. This book is not designed to help individuals whose addictions are at clinically significant levels, such as people with an eating disorder like anorexia or bulimia. In these instances, psychotherapy or counseling is an appropriate resource.

MORE TO THINK ABOUT

Soft addiction or passion and pastime? If you are doing something and you are in a zone, buzzed, high, agitated, can't remember what you did/said/saw/bought, feel foggy, or drained—then chances are it's a soft addiction. On the other hand, if you are learning, growing, feel more of your feelings, are closer to yourself and others, feel clear, awake, alive and vibrant, then it's a passion. Just don't confuse the two.

How Much Time Do I Spend?

This is a simple but telling measure. Approximately how much time do you spend on each of your soft addictions during a given week? Make some guesses where you are uncertain, especially regarding moods and avoidances. The key is to give yourself a sense of whether you spend a lot, a middling, or just a little time on each activity or mood.

To further illuminate your time use, think about them with the following categories in mind:

Doing: Time spent physically engaged in an activity.

Thinking: Time spent mentally engaged in an activity. This includes preparing for it (thinking about what you need in order to participate in it), fantasizing about it, and worrying about it.

Frequency: How often you engage in the behavior throughout a day or week.

MORE TO THINK ABOUT

A student at the Wright Institute, a chief executive officer of a nationally recognized actuarial consulting company, calculated that he spent one thousand hours a year worrying. This is an actuarial estimate by an expert—not a mere guess. Realizing that a full work year is two thousand hours, he now spends his time planning and talking things out instead of just worrying.

As you think about the hours you've invested on your soft addictions, do certain ones stand out because of the amount of time expended on them? Do you engage in some behaviors fairly frequently?

What Is My Motivation?

Beyond what you do and how much time you spend doing it, there's the issue of why you do it. Examining and understanding your motivation is critical. Some people listen to music for distraction, while others listen to be uplifted or educated. Or there's the difference between someone who shops to fill time, escape emotions, or because she can't resist a sale versus the individual who is looking for personally expressive clothing or budget-appropriate furnishings.

Think about the soft addictions you've determined so far and consider your motivation for doing them. Is it high, low, or middle? High represents a spiritual or otherwise meaningful motivation, such as a desire to learn and grow. Low means your impulse is escapist, unconscious, unexamined, or aimed at fulfilling a surface need. Middle connotes an ambiguous or uncertain purpose.

As you examine your motivation for the checked items, pay attention to the ones that receive low marks because they are most likely to be soft addictions.

What Are My Feelings?

This last variable indicates how you feel around an activity or mood. It's important to consider how you feel at three points: before, during, and after the activity or mood. Think about the soft addictions where you devote time and have low motivation. Be alert for the following words (or similar expressions of the same sentiments) because they often reflect the feelings of people in the grip of soft addictions.

Before	During	After
Anxious/jittery	Zoned out	Embarrassed
Bored	Numb	High
Driven	Glazed	Shameful
Sad	Unconscious	Glazed
Excited	Buzzed	Continued
Compulsive	Getting high	numbness
Angry	Increased	Agitated
Self-pitying	agitation	Buzzed
Afraid		Forgetful (can't remember what you've done/seen/ heard)

If you find that you experience at least some of the feelings listed, you likely have a soft addiction. The most common soft addiction–induced feelings are the numbed, zoned-out state, or a kind of neutered emotion, such as a mildly pleasant buzz. This is a very different experience from a sense of joy or transcendence, states in which feelings are intensified rather than muted.

Tim, the founder and CEO of a successful and burgeoning accounting firm, knew that overworking and people-pleasing were soft addictions for him. He made his One Decision to be genuine and connect with others, and that started to really shift his activities and bring more meaning to his life. But Tim was shocked by what else he discovered as he used his identification tools to look at all areas of his life.

A closer look brought him face-to-face with his early morning routine. On a typical day, Tim would rise a few hours before the rest of the world to "to get a jump on the day," he claimed. His coffeemaker set by timer would beckon him downstairs, where he'd pick up the two or three newspapers he got every morning. He'd read all the papers front to back before getting ready and heading to the office.

Armed with his new awareness, Tim started looking at his time, motivation, and feelings in this routine. On the surface, his motivation for reading the papers was to stay up on the news of the day. In reality, he found out he was using them to avoid the anxiety he felt about his workday. It was one thing to scan headlines, but another to spend more than an hour reading the same news in several papers. He would wake up energized and motivated to hit the ground running, but after reading the papers, he felt sluggish, drained of all motivation, and very unsettled. Rather than fueling his sense of preparedness, he would be more zoned and full of nervous anxiety. And although it wasn't a lot of time he spent, an hour every day did add up, especially when he realized he could use half the time to scan the paper and the other half to strategize his day, even seeking support from his wife.

His coffee, he discovered, wasn't really a soft addiction to him. He enjoyed the aroma and savored drinking it during his morning routine, but he was also fine going without it. He didn't feel buzzed afterward and didn't really use it to check out. For Tim, raising his awareness has been very powerful. Now he's more able to quickly discern the activities that empower him, and those that distract him from having MORE.

UNMASKING AND ACKNOWLEDGING THE COSTS OF SOFT ADDICTIONS

One of the harder aspects to identify—and to face—are the costs of soft addictions. While there are exercises in the workbook at the back of the book to help you calculate costs when you are ready to do so, what we've uncovered at our Soft Addiction Solution training has been shocking. The average participants, when they really break down all the costs of each of their soft addictions, find that they are spending on average somewhere between $5,000 and $30,000 a year on soft addictions. And that's just the average on straight costs. This doesn't account for the opportunity costs or the nonfinancial costs of soft addictions—loss of intimacy, relationships, productivity, consciousness, motivation, as well as not getting your deeper needs met in satisfying ways. The good news is that when you release a soft addiction pattern, these resources are available for you to invest in much more productive ways.

....

"At the Soft Addiction Solution training I added up the costs of my gadget addiction, and I was shocked to see it was at least $5,000 on just the small stuff. I have phones and PDAs that I have only used a couple months because I had to have the newest one."

—Bill

....

(MORE TO THINK ABOUT)

Businesses lose about $3.5 billion each year in worker productivity because of March Madness, the NCAA basketball tournament, according to a survey by outplacement firm Challenger, Gray, & Christmas, U.S. When you think about all of the time spent on office betting pools, filling out brackets, and online gambling or Internet surfing, it's not very much of a surprise.

MORE ALERT

Beware the costs of your soft addictions: how much money do you spend a year on soft addictions? How much time? What are the costs in your life from lack of awareness and consciousness? What about opportunity costs—of what could have been? These are resources you can use toward having MORE instead.

By now, you probably have a good idea of what your soft addictions are. Your awareness will continue to grow. You might start by saying them out loud: "I am a daydreamer." "I watch way too much television." "I obsess about my hair." "I can't stop complaining about my life."

As difficult as it might be to verbalize your soft addictions, saying them out loud can be cathartic. While saying them doesn't mean you're rid of them, it can give you a sense of relief and release. Talking and sharing are parts of the process of living a highly conscious life. They help turn soft addictions from dirty little secrets into honest acknowledgments of how you've been spending your time and energy. The sharing can feel great.

A WEB RATHER THAN A LIST

As you identify your soft addictions, you'll discover that a mere list doesn't do them justice. Soft addictions aren't linear; they're more like a web of interconnecting strands. As you identify your addictions and do the exercises in this book, you'll start to see how your soft addictions interconnect, and how one leads to another. For instance, you drink a ton of coffee and get jittery. So you bite your nails and nosh on pretzels. You try to calm down, and end up zoning out in front of the television. In other instances, the connection between addictions is subtle. For example, you may identify the following as addictions: dieting, going to clubs nightly, playing card games like solitaire, reading escapist novels, feeling self-pity, and avoiding making a serious career choice. In and of themselves, these items do not seem like anything to be alarmed about. It's only when viewed in totality—an interconnected drain on time, energy, and spirit—that their power can be glimpsed.

The analogy to a web is appropriate because, like a web, soft addictions entice and lure the unwary, the various strands are connected, and once you're trapped, it's difficult to extricate yourself. On the other hand, because these soft addictions are all connected, once you shift one soft addiction, you'll find that others naturally begin to shift.

....

"I didn't realize how much my soft addictions had cost me until I made my One Decision and stopped my Internet gaming addiction. Not only did I gain back at least twenty hours a week, I gained my self-respect, the love I had almost lost, and my health. I easily lost fifty pounds and am healthy for the first time in my life. I started spending more time with my kids. I'm closer to my wife than I have ever been. I applied for a promotion that I would never have imagined for myself before—and I got it! I am making more money, but maybe even more importantly, I feel good about myself. I'm growing in my career, in my marriage, and as a dad—much more exciting than throwing away hours on the Internet."

—Alan

....

Think about your soft addictions from this holistic viewpoint. They're not just things you do or moods you have but a web of daily routines that hold you back from experiencing the life you want.

You've begun to identify this web and your particular brand of soft addictions. In the next chapter, you'll discover how your mind creates this web of soft addictions in the first place and what you can do to break free of them.

4

Minding Your Mind

"Change your thoughts, and you change your world."
—NORMAN VINCENT PEALE

Minding your mind harnesses the power of your errant thoughts to lead you to a life of MORE—more time, satisfaction, money, energy, and love. Like monitoring a playground full of lively children, minding your mind means that you keep tabs on your thoughts as they skip, leap, ramble, and twirl, always keeping an eye out for problems and staying aware of when you need to set limits. By minding your mind, you train your thoughts to align to your One Decision and channel their energy toward the life you want.

Clarity of thinking is crucial if we want to live the life we've always dreamed of. If we are better able to understand our mind and its penchant for unruly thinking—if we're able to spot what we call stinking thinking and denial—we can better identify the thoughts that lead us to MORE and avoid those that lead us to less.

The point isn't just to stop a soft addiction but to manage the thinking that triggers the behavior and even perpetuates it. We all use excuses, rationalizations, denial, defensiveness, cons, and cover-ups to perpetuate our less-than-desirable behaviors. These are evidence of our stinking thinking. Without understanding our thinking, we are likely to just replace one soft addiction with another. Minding our mind may be difficult, but it's also a liberating and exhilarating learning experience. By harnessing our thoughts, we experience a sense of clarity, integrity, and authorship of our own life—some of the greatest rewards for overcoming soft addictions. The degree to which we learn to mind our mind and rein in our stinking thinking and denial is the degree to which we can lead a life of MORE.

WHY MIND OUR MIND?

Our mind uses our thoughts and beliefs to maintain the status quo. That is because a basic function of our unconscious mind is to preserve our organism by maintaining homeostasis. Soft addictions can be seen as mechanisms of the status quo. They are proven, familiar, and safe. When risk and unpredictability threaten our mind, the mind responds with attempts to thwart change and uses our soft addiction routines to dull and protect us.

Stinking thinking is like the little devil on our shoulder, spewing negativity about ourselves, tempting us with mindless diversions to escape those bad feelings, making us feel justified for indulging, and rationalizing our behavior after we've indulged. To live the life we want, we must learn and grow, taking risks that challenge our security. By shifting our stinking thinking, we release the thoughts that trigger our soft addictions.

Let's see how Sam's thinking was keeping him locked in soft addictions and away from a life of MORE.

Sam was a night owl. He hated going to bed and would either watch television until he fell asleep or log on to the Internet to shop for books, music, and DVDs, meet his cyberfriends, peruse travel sites to plan his next vacation or check his investments. Hooked on late-night programming, channel surfing, and Internet browsing, he often didn't get to sleep until the wee hours of the morning. Not only was he tired most of the time, his sales were lackluster, his performance reviews were mediocre, and his love life was stagnant. His manager suggested that he come to the Wright Institute for sales training.

As far as Sam was concerned the problem was his job. *Who can try to sell day after day and not be burned out? My customers want more and more, but they never seem able to make a decision. How am I supposed to sign any deals if they didn't know what they want?* All of these stinking thoughts went through Sam's head on a daily basis.

When he met with the other participants in the sales course, he was shocked to discover the sales they generated, the rate at which they made new contacts, and how they were constantly improving their income. Rob, one of the top producers in the course, told him where his success came from—he took the early morning train into the city and got a jump on his day, planning his calls. As a result, his business hours were a lot more productive and he enjoyed his days more. He said he loved talking to people and making friends every day. He had even met his wife that way.

Challenged by Rob to start his day earlier, Sam insisted, "No way! I can't get up that early," as he defended his late-night routines. "I need to watch television at night. It's important to watch the news. I have to know what's going on in the world. I need to watch more TV to wind down after a hard day at work and get my mind off my annoying customers. Late-night TV is relaxing for me. And surfing the Internet is great! I find great deals, plan exotic vacations, and meet some interesting people at night on the Internet. I've made some really good contacts, and they count on hearing from me each night."

Undeterred, Rob countered, "Do you want to have cyber friends you'll never meet, or get to know clients and increase your sales?" Rob shared more about his own success, in his sales and in his life. "I'm getting to know my clients. It's a gas to solve their problems and really serve them. I'm not just focused on closing deals. I'm even improving my relationship with my wife—it's like I am really *with* her instead of running my agenda and thinking of the next thing I have to do."

Inspired by Rob's example and success, Sam made his One Decision. He decided to be genuine and tell the truth in all his relationships. As a result, he started to tell the truth to himself. He stopped rationalizing his soft addictions and began to clean up his stinking thinking. Rather than justifying his routines and hiding from his problems, he admitted he was conning himself.

The more he focused on his One Decision, his old habits were less attractive. He started to limit his Internet surfing and television viewing and even moved his television out of his bedroom. He started reading at night, talking with friends, and meditating. He was able to get up earlier in the mornings and get to work before others got there. He felt the extra hour or two in the morning was like getting an extra day. His sales manager was thrilled with his sales performance, and Sam felt more satisfied, too. He even had more satisfying dates. By making his One Decision and noticing his stinking thinking, Sam not only shifted his old behaviors, but he began to create a life of MORE.

STINKING THINKING AND DENIAL: WHAT THEY DO

Like Sam, we all use stinking thinking and denial to justify our behavior, avoid feelings, and con others as well as ourselves. Denial, defensiveness, overgeneralization, minimizing, blaming, and jumping to conclusions are just some examples of the stinking thinking to which we are vulnerable. When we don't think clearly and cleanly, we are likely to minimize or even deny that our soft addictions pose problems. Stinking thinking prevents us from viewing our routines objectively and honestly.

Stinking thinking is so pervasive we often don't realize it exists. We think our stinking thoughts are facts, not arbitrary decisions based on faulty beliefs. Our distorted thoughts normalize our soft addiction routines. Stinking thinking becomes like a sea we live in. We're like fish, not knowing water exists around them until they're caught. Stinking thoughts lead us to indulge in soft addictions, defend the behavior, and deny any problem with our actions. Stinking thinking becomes a sort of soft addiction in itself—a habitual thought pattern that we return to repeatedly for diminishing returns.

Soft addictions function as a filter of our experience, screening out useful input. As we enmesh ourselves in shopping, gossiping, and daydreaming routines, we fail to feel the pain that could guide us toward right action. Without feeling our pain, we more easily deny that anything is wrong. The vicious cycle, of course, is that we engage in soft addictions precisely because we don't want to feel pain. Without the ability to see our lives clearly and feel the pain completely, we can convince ourselves that our soft addictions are harmless or even that they are good for us.

That's why we deny with comments like: What problem? What pain? What do you mean this is a problem? I can't see it as a problem.

Rent *Monty Python and the Holy Grail* and watch the infamous bridge scene. In true Python fashion, the lone guard depicts denial clearly. Significantly outnumbered, he asserts he can win the battle even as he loses limb after limb, claiming they are "merely flesh wounds" and can cause him no pain.

We might intellectually know that spending hours on the Internet or buying and reading every gossip magazine are problems. We might know that there is a better way to nourish ourselves than mindlessly shoving a candy bar in our mouth or perching at the kitchen counter while loading up on takeout food from cardboard containers. Yet without our pain available to us, we don't grasp that something profound is happening beneath the surface. We eat, shop, or watch TV in place of taking effective action. We can't feel our spiritual hunger or our yearning to be loved, to matter, and to make a difference.

> MORE-SEL
>
> *"Our life is shaped by our mind;*
> *we become what we think."*
>
> —THE BUDDHA

Fortunately, we can learn to catch ourselves when we overgeneralize or use bizarre logic. If we notice stinking thoughts, we won't fall into the denial trap. When we become aware of our faulty thought processes, we can change our thoughts; when we change our thoughts, we can shift our feelings and behaviors in a more productive, meaningful direction.

HOLD YOUR NOSE: STINKING THINKING

What does stinking thinking sound like, especially as it relates to our soft addiction routines? Let's look at some of Sam's stinking thinking:

I don't have a problem.

I can't get up early.

My customers are never satisfied.

Joe stays up later than I do, and he doesn't find nearly as many bargains on eBay.

I only surfed the Web for half an hour last night.

I'll work on getting to bed earlier after I close this big account.

That customer is not going to pay on time—I just know it.

It's not my fault the sale fell through.

I can't fall asleep without visiting the chat room to see what is happening tonight.

I need to watch all the news every day.

....

(MORE TO DO)

Which of Sam's thoughts are like yours? How often do you or your friends express these or similar types of thoughts?

....

When we become defensive or use the above rationalizations for any of these purposes, chances are we are in the grip of a soft addiction. If we weren't in a mood, thought, or behavioral addiction, we wouldn't defend or rationalize so stubbornly. We would talk freely about the behavior or mood, ask questions about its source, and consider changing the way we're thinking or acting. Ultimately, we might decide not to change but we would be truthful about the addiction.

Consider the following two responses when someone is confronted about how much time they spend reading the newspaper each day.

A. Yeah, I see that my reading the newspaper cover to cover every day is taking a lot of time—plus the time I spend doing the crossword puzzle. I probably could use the time better.

B. I need to read the newspaper every day. I have to keep up. It is important to be an educated citizen. I might miss something otherwise. I think it's weird that other people can get through the day without knowing about what's going on around them; I don't know how you can stand to be uninformed. In fact, if there were more people like you, it would be easy for dictators to gain power because there's nothing they like better than an uninformed populace.

The second quote has a defensive tone and communicates, "Back off, I don't want to discuss this." The speaker goes on the offensive to throw off the questioner. He also denies any possible cost of his behavior and sees no other possibility. While being an educated citizen is certainly important, this person uses the argument as a defense rather than a truly thoughtful examination of the best ways to be informed.

> ### MORE-SEL
>
> *"Thought is the sculptor who can create the person you want to be."*
> —HENRY DAVID THOREAU

When you're locked into soft addiction routines, these excuses, justifications, defensive remarks, and rationalizations become verbal reflexes. When threatened with exposure of your soft addiction, you respond with some form of denial. In many instances, your response is so convincing that it's difficult for anyone to refute. It serves its intended purpose of backing people off, stopping any exploration, and preventing you from examining your attachment to something that limits you.

Recognizing our stinking thinking unblocks us and moves us in the right direction. When we identify these counterproductive patterns, we're in a better position to change them so they're in alignment with our One Decision. We open our eyes to all aspects of MORE—all the life, love, and meaning—that exist in the world.

STINKING THINKING: A FILTER

Why would anyone think the way Sam does? Stinking thinking stems from mistaken beliefs we have about ourselves, our feelings, and the world around us. Deep down inside, we often believe that we are not worthy or that others don't want the best for us. Some common sentiments:

> *I am not okay.*
> *It's not okay to feel my feelings.*
> *I'm different.*

I can't have what I want.
I don't deserve more.
I don't have what it takes to get through a rough situation.
Nobody cares.

Acknowledging our soft addictions means confronting these fears and doubts. If we really want MORE, we need to invite others to give us truthful feedback, catch ourselves in convoluted thinking, and identify the negative impact it has on our lives.

Instead, we rationalize, deny, and defend our soft addictions. Stinking thinking prevents us from mindfully assessing our behavior in light of our higher values and goals. In fact, we don't question our behavior, ignoring the niggling voices at the edges of our consciousness that question how we're acting. Because our feelings and consciousness are muted, we don't realize that we are doing things that are not productive or things that are even harmful.

MORE ALERT

Stinking thinking can be costly. Perhaps you've talked yourself out of asking for a promotion, postponed career moves, assumed people would reject you and don't make the sales you could, or blamed others for your situation rather than doing what you could to generate and receive more abundance. Notice how stinking thinking creates less, not MORE.

Kelly, an attractive woman inside and out, has what her friends call a good heart, and is known as a straight shooter in the advertising agency where she's employed. Kelly originally took her current job because of the company's reputation for good business and the value it placed on developing its employees. She was particularly impressed by her boss's reputation as a fair businessman. When a promotion opportunity came up, Kelly applied for it but was very upset when her boss informed her that her coworker had received the promotion. He also told Kelly how much he believed in and appreciated her: "I want you to know you're definitely on track for another promotion. We're impressed by your integrity and the way you're able to get the best out of your employees. I want to help develop you for another job that I think is much better suited for your career path."

Kelly, though, only saw that she didn't get this immediate promotion. She thought, *I'll never get that promotion. He was just stringing me along. He doesn't value my work. I should never have taken this job.* As a result of her stinking thinking, Kelly started to show up late for work, take long lunches, and spend long periods zoning out, poring over fashion magazines, and reading newspapers from cover to cover. She shifted her life away from a path toward MORE and headed into her soft addiction routines.

Rather than face her hurt, insecurity, and disappointment or discuss the situation with her boss, Kelly indulged her stinking thinking and her soft addictions. Fortunately, a coworker noticed her self-sabotage and recommended she get coaching before the potential promotion became a pipe dream.

Kelly began to recognize her stinking thinking for what it was, thoughts based not on the truth but on her faulty perceptions. She adjusted course and did eventually get her promotion, not just for any job, but for a job that was perfectly suited to her.

....

MORE TO THINK ABOUT

Recall a time when you failed or messed up badly (i.e., you received a failing grade, got a poor performance review, hurt a valued relationship). With hindsight, can you see how your thoughts were distorted by this failure?

....

MIND MANEUVERS

As we learn to recognize the many forms stinking thinking takes, we understand how it justifies and perpetuates soft addictions. Identifying our thought patterns helps us analyze and counter them. Because so many people deny their stinking thinking, it's only fitting that we start with denial.

The Many Faces of Denial

Refusal to admit that something exists or that it has a negative impact is denial. For instance, we don't recognize our soft addictions or

stinking thinking as a problem. To keep our denial intact, we resort to defensiveness, rationalizing, lying, minimizing, postponing, and comparing to explain, justify, or put off what we deny.

MORE TO DO

Rent the movie *The Devil's Advocate* to see the slippery slope of soft addictions and denial in action. (Al Pacino plays the devil and seduces Keanu Reeves's character using soft addictions as a lure.) Use it to recognize your own stinking thinking and break your denial by identifying similarities with all of the characters. See it with friends and discuss it afterward.

Defensiveness crops up when someone mentions our soft addiction routines and we reflexively defend whatever activities or moods have us entangled. Even if someone isn't accusatory but simply questions if we do too much of this or that—we respond as if we were indicted:

"Don't even suggest that my Tom Cruise fantasies aren't good for me. They're what I look forward to and I don't think it's fair that you're questioning me about them."

Rationalization involves creating superficially convincing and often ingenious arguments about why soft addiction routines aren't bad, and even why they are good. It explains and justifies.

"Maybe I do shop a lot, but I've got to have the right look to get ahead in the business world."

To pick up her daughter at day care every day, Kirsten, a busy executive mom, often couldn't find a parking spot and used the local doughnut shop parking lot. She rationalized, I *have* to buy something. I can't just park there without being a patron. So began her justification for a doughnut-a-day ritual that kept her from dropping her last few post-pregnancy pounds. It wasn't until her daughter, in her early stages of learning to talk, began to say, "Mommy, doughnut!" when Kirsten picked her up for the day, that she realized she truly was busted. "Out of the mouths of babes," she laughed in sharing her story at a weekend Soft Addiction Solution training. She broke through her denial and officially filed her habit as a stinking thinking ritual, making the first move to create a new and more nourishing greeting ritual for her and her toddler.

Minimizing is when we act like a soft addiction really isn't a problem, or if it is, it's not a big one. Trivializing the activity or downplaying a common mood is a sure sign of minimizing.

"It's only a little bit of gossip. It's not as if that's all I do."

Lying is an extreme form of minimizing. Fibbing about the scope and depth of our soft addiction routines keeps our denial going. When we lie to ourselves, we usually lie to others. We insist that we only shop one day a week when we know perfectly well that we go to the mall at least three times weekly, or we tell a friend or spouse that we don't enjoy wallowing in self-pity when in fact we take a perverse comfort in these "woe is me" moments.

"I don't watch a lot of television."
"I haven't done that since we talked last month."
"No, that couldn't have been me that you saw at the mall."
"I didn't take the last piece of cake."

....

"I feel like there is a computer chip in my head that is programmed to tell me, 'I need coffee.' But it's a lie. I don't need coffee. The 'I need' is a lie. Once I realized that I don't need coffee, I simply want it, it helped me look behind the lie and see that there was something else motivating me. Now, I'm more likely to take a better

break—like take a quick walk, call my wife, stand up and stretch, or walk down the hall to talk to my coworkers. "

—James

....

Postponing generally goes hand in hand with minimizing. It involves admitting our soft addictions aren't good for us, but putting off resolving the problem. We excuse current soft addictions by making a vague promise to do something about them in the future.

"I know I'm wasting a lot of time reading catalogs, but when I quit my job next year, I'm going to change what I do in my spare time."

Comparing is a particularly subtle form of denial. To put ourselves in a better light, we excuse our routines by comparing them more favorably to others who have even worse soft addictions.

"I may go to the health club a little too much, but that's nothing compared to that guy who is there every single day from open to close."

....

MORE TO THINK ABOUT

Which denial categories have you used to justify and maintain your soft addiction routines?

....

SNIFFING OUT OTHER STINKING THINKING

Denial and its many forms are the most formidable stinking thinking gambits. Denial keeps us from putting our One Decision into action. It must be overcome if we are to truly live the life we want, MORE.

More subtle—and sometimes more difficult to detect and neutralize—are the other forms of stinking thinking. They often seem so

> ### MORE-SEL
>
> *"The pursuit of truth shall set you free— even if you never catch up with it."*
>
> —CLARENCE DARROW

reasonable and their seduction so appealing that we can counter them only with extreme clarity and vigilance. Learn and beware.

Overgeneralizing

We often miss possibilities because we view a negative event as a never-ending pattern. Instead of seeing a negative situation as a unique event, we view it through a trick mirror that produces infinite images. We magnify and blow things out of proportion, imagine things are impossible, have hopeless thoughts, and think in extremes often characterized by all or nothing terms like "always" and "never."

> *This* always *happens.*
> *I blew it. I ate a hot fudge sundae, so my diet is ruined. I might as well* ———.
> *I won't be able to limit my television watching no matter what I do.*
> *I'll never lose weight.*

Jumping to Conclusions or Irrational Conclusions

Deciding that things are bad without sufficient evidence leads us to jump to conclusions. Instead of focusing on desired outcomes and how to achieve them, we may use a mental filter, ignoring positive or contradictory information in order to stick to our negative predictions. We mind-read and assume negative reactions or fortune-tell negative outcomes. We project things we are feeling onto others. We also use magical thinking, imagining connections where none exist.

> *They are going to fire me.*
> *She doesn't like me, so why bother to look nice.*
> *This isn't going to work out, so I should just quit and go shopping.*
> *I'll never get that raise.*
> *You don't like me. (In reality, I don't like you, but I am addicted to playing nice with you.)*
> *I did a horrible job. I answered that last question totally wrong. I flunked the test.*
> *I'll retire by winning the lottery.*

Emotional Reasoning

This form of stinking thinking involves reasoning based on how you feel without comparing it to reality. It occurs when people think that because they feel a certain way, that is the way it is. Then they overgeneralize or jump to conclusions.

I feel stupid, therefore I must be stupid.
I feel upset, so I must be a mess.
I don't feel good, so there must be something wrong with me.

I am the queen of emotional reasoning and using a mental filter to screen out anything positive. This type of stinking thinking continues to be one of my biggest personal challenges. In fact, my staff has learned not to trust my answers when they ask, "How did it go?" after I do a speech or a TV interview or lead a training. Because I feel vulnerable, or can only think of all the things I could have said or done differently, or simply because I feel raw, I get stuck in emotional reasoning. I'll tell them how poorly it went and how badly I think I did right after walking off the stage to a standing ovation that I didn't even see!

Should and Shouldn't

When we criticize ourselves or others with should, shouldn't, must, ought, and have to, we moralize the behavior. Shoulds and shouldn'ts reduce behavior to simplistic values like good or bad. This form of thinking often leads us to affix blame or avoid responsibility.

He should have fixed that.
I ought to have that handled by now.
I have to have that.

Blame/Shame

Blaming is often linked to overgeneralizing and should/shouldn't. You blame yourself for something you weren't entirely responsible for, or you blame others and disregard what you contributed. You overlook accurate attribution of responsibility and actually keep correction from happening with thoughts like:

It's all my fault.
You ruined it!
I didn't do it.

....

(MORE TO THINK ABOUT)

What stinking thoughts have you had while reading this section?

....

Labeling

This form of stinking thinking occurs when you name-call or when you attribute limited qualities to yourself and others. When relating to yourself, instead of saying, "I made a mistake," you tell yourself, "I am a loser," "I am stupid," "I am a jerk." When categorizing or name-calling others, we think things like, *He's a fool. What do you expect from a capitalist?* This keeps you from learning and taking effective, corrective action.

The mind is infinitely creative in developing categories of stinking thinking. Stay alert and see how many others you can find. A few others that I find amusing include:

Irrelevant excuses: *I hadn't had my coffee when that happened.*
Silly rules: *I already went to the bank. I can't retrace my steps today.*
Funny logic: *If I eat peanut butter and jelly on toast, it is not the same as having a peanut butter and jelly sandwich, so the calories don't count as much.*
Limited thinking: *I can't do it; It's never been done before; I'm not capable.*

Scarcity thinking: *It's because I don't have enough time, money, or resources to change; If I only had more help, I could do this.*

....

"I have this very strange logic I use to beat myself up in the morning. When I have a stressful meeting coming up, I think, 'I'm fat. If I just lost these extra pounds, the meeting would go better.' It doesn't even make sense, but that's what goes through my head."

—*Elise*

....

LIGHTEN UP TO THINK MORE CLEARLY

You don't need to get rid of your stinking thinking; you need to moderate it with humor and compassion. With a sense of humor and compassion for our personal flaws, we find it easier to see and accept how our behavior is misaligned with our dreams. Humor gives us the distance and space necessary to admit that there's something wrong with our soft addiction routines.

None of us likes to feel stupid or looks forward to admitting a mistake. It's doubly difficult to admit these feelings or mistakes when we can't laugh at or forgive ourselves. Maintaining a sense of humor promotes the compassion that facilitates questioning, examining, growing, and changing our behavior. With compassion and humor, we admit less than desirable things about ourselves and still know that we are okay human beings. We don't have to lie or deny to protect ourselves. We can face the unattractive parts of ourselves—our flaws and unflattering needs—with greater equanimity.

(MORE TO DO)

Need help minding your mind? Just follow the advice of the International Man of Mystery, Austin Powers, and tell your mind, "Oh, behave!"

"Stop it. I'm going to wet my pants!" Sue was laughing so hard at Bart's soft addictions trials and tribulations she was practically crying.

Bart had made a conscious effort to have a sense of humor when it came to his soft addictions—a far cry from the old days where he'd avoid telling the truth or hang his head in shame and embarrassment. Bart had Sue in stitches as he talked about his babe-watching soft addiction. He had developed a rating scale from 0 to 5, with 0 as "look away fast" and 5 being a panting drool akin to that of Pavlov's dog. He regaled his MORE group with stories about the number of five-glance women he spotted over the summer that sent him to the chiropractor for neck adjustments because of abrupt rubbernecking. We began to look forward to hearing these absurdities from him. Making fun of himself gave Bart the distance to look at himself objectively and begin dealing with his soft addictions. He even took improvisation classes and had some success at stand-up comedy. Though Bart still falls back on his soft addictions at times, he sees them for what they are and jokes about them. With humor and compassion, Bart moved himself away from his addiction routines and toward MORE.

DEVELOPING YOUR SENSE OF HUMOR

Transitioning to a life of MORE is a huge challenge for any of us. It can be especially challenging for those with perfectionist personalities. Without humor, living your One Decision can feel like an impossible challenge rather than an invitation. Most of us, though, will benefit if we make a conscious effort to ease up on ourselves and laugh at the things we do. In the workbook at the back of this book you'll find techniques for developing self-acceptance, compassion, and a sense of humor like keeping a humor journal, finding creative ways to express your humor, and practicing daily forgiveness.

> ### MORE-SEL
>
> *Be inspired by someone who has a sense of humor about herself: "When choosing between two evils, I always like to take the one I've never tried before."*
>
> —MAE WEST

(MORE TO DO)

Read *Confessions of a Shopaholic* by Sophie Kinsella or *Rachel's Holiday* by Marian Keyes for a humorous view of stinking thinking. See if you can relate to the main characters' hilarious rationalizations and loopy thinking.

THE SOFT ADDICTION TEMPLATE

Another powerful tool you'll discover for minding your mind is the Soft Addiction Template. We use this template throughout our curriculum at the Wright Institute with some amazing results. For now, you'll be exposed to the first part of the template that primarily addresses stinking thinking, but with the chapters that follow, we'll add to the template to incorporate additional skills. You'll find a blank copy of the template you can use in the workbook at the back of this book. For now, just review and read the template below. Keep in mind that any time you are having stinking thoughts, you can use the following template to reprogram your thinking. Students at the Institute often use this to clean up their thoughts. You can find an interactive version of this template on our Web site, www.judithwright.com.

1. What event or situation triggered your stinking thinking? What soft addiction(s) did you turn to?
2. What feelings were you having?
3. What thoughts were going through your head during or after this event? How do those thoughts keep you from pursuing MORE?
4. What positive thoughts could you think instead (thoughts reflecting the reality of the situation, or thoughts that are humorous, compassionate, or forgiving)?

As you look over your responses, can you see your soft addictions with greater clarity? Can you see how stinking thinking prevents you from recognizing the routines that cause you to get less out of life?

....

"I had a particularly stressful business presentation to prepare for at work, and my stinking thinking was right there with me. 'It's going to be terrible. My senior manager will never like it. I'll be lucky to just get through this one.' Luckily, after learning about stinking thinking, I was able to recognize it quickly. I just took it as a sign that I was having some strong feelings. I noticed I was afraid and angry and decided to make a different choice. Instead of staying rooted in my stinking thinking, I thought about my vision for the meeting and how I wanted it to turn out. Rather than beat myself up, I reassured myself that I had prepared well and was doing my best. It really shifted my attitude and my presentation. My proposal was accepted, and I really saw that my boss wasn't so different than I was, sharing many of my same fears. Noticing my stinking thinking has given me a whole new template for how to address my challenges at work."

—Wynona

....

Use this template in the back of the book as a powerful, life-changing exercise that can help you track the thoughts that prompt indulging in your soft addiction. Again, the template will help you learn to replace that stinking thought with a compassionate or more positive and accurate thought. Not only will you overcome your soft addiction, but you will also learn to communicate to yourself with clarity, love, and compassion. With each chapter, you will discover new skills to apply with this template.

Stinking thinking stems from our need to explain to ourselves and to others why we live with less, fulfilling our surface wants and never really feeling satisfied. These thoughts keep us from really knowing ourselves. Being aware of your stinking thinking can lead you to discover the mistaken beliefs you have about yourself and the world, leading to more self-knowledge and understanding. In the next chapter, you'll learn to appreciate your more essential self by unearthing the deep-rooted reason for your soft addictions: the Why.

5

DISCOVER THE WHY: CRACKING YOUR OWN CODE

"The basic principle of spiritual life is
that our problems become the very place
to discover wisdom and love."

—JACK KORNFIELD

Beneath each soft addiction routine, a treasure awaits our discovery. Decoded, every aspect of our soft addictions—the substances or activities we turn to, the triggering situation, and even the feelings we flee—reveal key information. All soft addictions have a positive intent because they spring from a desire to take care of ourselves. Ironically, though, these addictive routines prevent us from actually taking good care of ourselves because they mask the underlying problems that make us feel unfilled, empty, lonely, uncomfortable, or unloved. Soft addictions stuff down the feelings we need to feel and prevent us from reading the information that our system tries to send.

The Why of our addictions often lies just beyond our conscious reach. We may recognize the urge to indulge a soft addiction, accepting superficial analyses (*I'm bored, I need a break*) as if they really explain our behavior. We respond to our stinking thinking and miss the deeper Why. *Why do I want a soft addiction at this moment? Why do I have this soft addiction routine? Why did I develop this pattern?* Often we don't see the deeper needs—yearning for comfort, hungering to matter, and longing to feel significant— underneath the surface urges. In fact, as we saw in the preceding chapter, our stinking thinking functions to buffer us from those powerful stir-rings deep within us. Yet, when we finally embrace our underlying needs and fears, we are better able to have the life we truly want.

In this chapter, we will be looking at two types of Why—the historical Why and the functional Why. The historical Why is why, in the past, we developed our soft addiction (or its precursor) in order to deal with certain situations. By tracing this historical Why, we can understand how we developed our soft addiction patterns as children as creative, adaptive response to challenges—doing the best we knew to do with the resources and abilities we had available at the time. The functional Why, on the other hand, is why I am turning to my soft addiction right now? Why, for example, do I want a candy bar right now when I didn't want one fifteen minutes ago? Both of these Whys play a strong role in keeping us locked in our ruts and routines. But by cracking our code and unlocking them, we can begin to release the habits and routines that have been holding us hostage.

DIRECTING THE FLOW

When you unearth the Why—the underlying needs—beneath your soft addictions, prepare to uncover a powerful emotional force. Deep feelings are embedded in those needs, which until now have gone undetected.

MORE ALERT

You may be taking the damper off emotions as you discover your Why. Go toward your feelings and experience them fully. As powerful as they are, you are stronger. If you run away from your feelings, you'll fail to harness their power and be likely to slip back into your routines. There are no bad feelings, only underdeveloped skills in dealing with them. Get support and build the skills to become more you.

Soft addiction routines are a way we have of regulating our energy or the flow of life through us. Our emotions comprise a big part of our life energy. If we don't like our strong emotions and desires, or think we must contain them, we try to manage that flow through soft addiction routines. Soft addictions function like the resistor in a sound system or other electronic device, which channels and damps down the electrical energy flowing in. It takes in and at the same time it resists the full 110 volts arriving at the system, letting in only the level of electrical charge that the device can work with.

In a similar way, when we don't have the capacity to handle the flow of emotions and desires pouring through our bodies, we "resist" our life energy by numbing ourselves with a soft addiction routine. The result is a "checked-out" state of low emotion that we accept as normal. But it's not normal. Look at young children; they aren't checked out. They have lots of emotions, which they express freely. The checked-out state is a behavior we've learned in place of developing the ability to direct our life energy. When we acknowledge the hungers beneath our routines, then we can expand our capacity to let life flow through us.

As I learned to live my One Decision to be awake, alive, and to feel my feelings, I began to choose activities that helped me feel more vital rather than numb. I began to allow my feelings rather than stuff them. It was only then that I realized how much I had been using my soft addictions to regulate the flow of my emotions. As I explored my historical Why, I realized that since I hadn't known how to deal with my emotions as a child, I had done the next best thing—I anesthetized them. As I accepted my emotions, I felt more sadness, hurt, fear, and anger, but also discovered more joy, healing, success, and even love. I stopped striving to be comfortable and accepted my discomfort. Ironically, that acceptance allowed me to be comforted and nourished. I not only allowed my feelings, but I realized that I actually needed my feelings to feel satisfied. My emotions made me feel more me, more genuine, more real.

WHY THE WAITRESS IS STUCK IN HER NUTTY ROUTINE

While sitting in a restaurant working on this book, I noticed that my waitress, Donna, kept retracing her path in and out of the kitchen, emerging each time with a handful of nuts. Donna had only a few customers in the restaurant, so I started a conversation with her. She mentioned that she was eating handfuls of nuts out of boredom. "I'm not even hungry yet I can't seem to stop. I keep grabbing them every time I go into the kitchen," she explained.

This instance of Donna's behavior alone doesn't signal a soft addiction; we would need to know more about Donna and her various routines. However, Donna's actions tell us a lot about why we fall into soft addiction routines. Donna may have been upset or feeling anxious about any number of things—the empty time, the lack of business or tip money—yet all she registered consciously is that she was bored, so she kept returning to the kitchen and the nut bowl.

MORE TO DO

Try analyzing the Why behind a friend or loved one's soft addictions. Write down this person's addiction routines and speculate about the deeper reasons he or she is drawn to those particular routines.

Fritz Perls, the founder of American Gestalt Psychology, saw boredom as withheld anger.* I believe it can result from other repressed emotions, too. Donna told me that she loved her job but found it difficult to focus when it was slow. She said, "It's hard to feel like I have meaning on a day like today. I'm just filling time." Clearly, Donna was afraid of feeling worthless and of feeling broke, of not making enough money to pay her bills. She attempted to numb her fear with boredom and by raiding the nut bowl.

Donna's Why isn't boredom—that's just a surface explanation. By looking deeper into her routine, we find that she's hungry for security, to make a difference, to feel useful and engaged. By understanding what she's really hungry for, Donna could create more ways of meeting her deeper needs more directly. To feel engaged or to make a difference, she might choose to make deeper contact with her customers even when it's slow, or make better friends with the staff, or even ask for more responsibility—all of which would give her a deeper sense of security.

*Frederick S. Perls, *The Gestalt Approach and Eyewitness to Therapy* (Palo Alto: Science & Behavior Books, 1973).

Who knows, by engaging more fully, she might even receive a promotion, become a manager, and learn to deal with her own employees' boredom.

The Origin of Soft Addiction Routines: Mistaken Beliefs

Most of our soft addiction routines can be traced back to aspects of our youth. These are the behaviors or attitudes we learned in order to deal with the world, which were reinforced by our mistaken beliefs about ourselves and the world around us.

As children we learn to do things like push down our tears, deny fear, repress anger, and even restrain joy and love in the face of family disapproval or discomfort. To deal with the feelings we learned to hold back. We might reach for a candy bar or a book, go off and hide, or collapse in self-pity—the beginnings of our soft addiction routines. Back then, our routines protected us or brought us much needed comfort. We did not believe there were alternative ways to act.

From our childhood experiences we formed beliefs about ourselves and the world. We decided whether we were lovable or not; if the world was safe or dangerous; and if others were interested in our satisfaction or not. We often formed mistaken beliefs from our limited viewpoint. From these mistaken beliefs our stinking thinking grew, and in turn spawned our soft addictions.

As young children with few available resources, our soft addiction routines were creative adaptations to challenges or tough situations. As adults, we have other resources for coping with comparable difficulties. Yet we tend to fall back upon those deeply ingrained habits from childhood and blow right past other choices. It's as if, in some ways, we still see the world through the eyes of a child. We try our softly addictive behaviors again and again, unconsciously thinking

> ### MORE-SEL
>
> *"Your past forms you, whether you like it or not. Each encounter and experience has its own effect, and you're shaped the way the wind shapes a mesquite tree on a plain."*
>
> —LANCE ARMSTRONG

they will eventually work. We create an addictive routine by applying ineffective solutions to undefined, unrecognized problems.

Had we all grown up in situations that fostered direct expression of our feelings and provided comfort and encouragement, we would express ourselves more directly and effectively today. We would have learned to talk through our feelings and concerns and receive appropriate guidance, feedback, or comfort instead of turning to soft addiction routines. As adults, we have the power we lacked as children to understand our deeper hurts and longings and address them directly. But we're also fighting deeply ingrained behaviors. And, in many ways, our society promotes soft addictions by discouraging dealing effectively with our emotions. We are rewarded, indirectly, for hanging on to our stinking thinking.

Let me share stories with you from my life and other people's to help you discover the breeding ground for your soft addictions. You can see how childhood experiences evolve into adult soft addictions. The stories also explain how it's possible to extricate ourselves from our routines by linking early experiences with specific soft addictions.

THE HISTORICAL WHY STORIES

As I looked more closely at my own soft addiction routines of zoning out with reading, television, and snacks, I discovered myself as a chubby little girl idly watching television after school, eating bags of chocolate chip cookies, drinking cartons of milk, and scribbling homework. When I looked even closer, I saw a lonely girl with upsets she couldn't share or express. Going back to that time in my mind, I could sense distress and tension within and around me as if there were an undertow lurking below the seemingly calm surface. I didn't want to add to the tension or upset in the house, yet there were feelings and situations I couldn't stomach. I began to eat to fill my tummy so that I didn't feel the churnings inside. I effectively numbed myself from the upset. In my loneliness, I hungered for connection and more relationship with people. I didn't find it in the world around me, so I sought it in the world of books and television. These patterns continued into my adulthood. I now know when I have an urge to indulge in a soft addiction to look inside for the little girl who is longing for reassurance and comfort. I know she deserves attention and company, the kind that God and I can give her.

Bob's Why—Tension and TV Dinners

"I can't have a television in the house. I'm too addicted," my husband, Bob, emphatically stated when we got married. Slow to learn that my husband always meant what he said and didn't tell me this lightly, I made the mistake of keeping the television in our home. I finally woke up to reality after seeing Bob completely lose himself while flipping constantly between two and three programs, shutting me out even as I struggled to make conversation with him in thirty-second bites during commercials. (We no longer have a television in our house, except one we store and pull out to watch movies.) When Bob asked his mother about the origins of his television addiction, she responded, "When you were little, your father couldn't tolerate the messes that little kids make. We got our first TV when you were four and your sister was one and a half. I noticed that when we snacked in front of the television, your father didn't fuss over you kids. So, I began serving dinner on TV trays. Your father's silence was a relief." Bob's mother didn't realize that soft addictions begin as a misguided attempt to deal with unwanted emotions. Rather than letting meals be a time for the family to talk or for children to receive attention, at Bob's childhood home they became a time to manage their father's upset and anxiety by putting everything into a haze. Bob learned to eat away anxiety. Wanting to zone out at mealtime is still a much greater issue for him than for me. He has learned to manage it, but the urge to merge with the television still pulses strongly within him.

Heather's Why—Dressing Up to Cover Up

"Shop till you drop!" Heather shouted out her battle cry. Anything she could purchase to look good, even if it meant overspending on designer clothing, she did. But after maxing out credit cards and hiding purchases from her husband, Heather decided she wanted to make some changes. As she looked more deeply at her urge to shop, she realized that, as a child, she had received a lot of positive attention for being pretty. Whenever she felt insecure or unloved, she would dress up to get attention. Heather concluded that it didn't matter how well she did things; what mattered was how she looked. Since Heather couldn't satisfy her hunger to be understood and valued by her mother, she accepted the substitute of becoming her mother's little doll, literally. Looking back, she realized her mother had laid out her clothes for her at night until she was twelve years old. After looking at the Why and making her One Decision to be a substantive woman who makes a difference in the world, Heather turned her life around. She still sometimes overshops or places too much importance on how she looks, but seeing the Why under her soft addictions now helps her to ask directly for attention and seek contact in positive ways, such as calling a friend or asking her husband for a hug. She's even gone back to college as an adult, realizing that she values her mind, not just her appearance.

Discovering the deeper needs and lifelong patterns underneath soft addiction routines creates self-acceptance and compassion. When you are closer to understanding the Why, you develop empathy and understanding for yourself. Soft addictions stop looking like some moral flaw or manifestation of a weak will. You reveal them for what they are—misguided yet often creative attempts to meet a very real and legitimate hunger. I am aware of my hunger to express and make contact. Bob can see his deeper hunger to be positively affirmed, to feel safe and secure, and to talk through things. Heather now sees her hunger to be accepted and loved. Recognizing the Why—the situations that bred our beliefs and behaviors—we gain increased understanding and empathy for ourselves and others. Aware of these deeper hungers, we can begin to develop strategies to meet them. With this knowledge we can make different changes in alignment with our One Decision.

CONNECTING PAST WITH PRESENT

The Why stories you have just read offer a glimpse into the links between our experiences as children and our soft addiction routines as adults—but only a glimpse. It would take many pages to do justice to the complex web that links the events of our pasts to the routines of today. But the first step is to understand that we formed mistaken beliefs about the world as children. For instance, I decided isolation was the only way to protect myself. In response to his father's upset, Bob concluded that expressing himself fully was bad. Heather made up her mind that her real self was unacceptable and only her appearance mattered. Looking back, we can all identify the points at which we mistakenly decided our feelings were bad and unwanted; we can pinpoint incidents that communicated that people didn't want to hear us; we can see how we might have come to the conclusion that the world was an uncaring place.

Once we gain this perspective on our soft addictions, we're better able to challenge our limiting assumptions. We can accept that we're not bad, weak, or stupid for doing what we do. We can see the positive intent behind our behaviors, the ways in which we created the patterns as a kind of self-care. This perspective helps us develop compassion for ourselves and create comfort, healing, and a fuller life.

....

"As a kid, my dad was never around for dinner, and I just thought that was the way it was. I hated those lonely dinnertimes. When I became a dad, I avoided meal times as much as possible. I didn't even realize that I was in my avoidance soft addiction until my kids starting complaining about it. I realized that I didn't want to feel up-set, like I did when my dad wasn't around. Now that I uncovered this Why, I realize that I don't need to feel upset, because I am no longer that child, and now I am doing things differently. I'm learning to create a nourishing, connected dinner with my wife and sons. In fact, we often make dinner together. It feels great and I love feeling close to my wife and children."

—Ben

....

Take a moment and consider the Whys in your past. Perhaps you dealt with the tension in your parents' relationship by tuning out fights, or fought loneliness with an active fantasy life, or trying to please everyone in the family to avoid upset. It may have been that watching hours of sit-uation comedies on television or voraciously reading science-fiction novels helped you deal with pain, anger, or fear.

Whatever your experiences as a child, your behaviors were an adapta-tion to your environment. Today, you're still responding reflexively to that childhood environment, even though you're no longer in it. There is nothing wrong with these responses when they're consciously chosen. The problem is when they are unproductive, habitual, and unconscious responses. The key, therefore, is to make the responses conscious. Even though many of us have multiple soft addictions to different things, it is likely that a coherent, underlying pattern drives them. As we begin to discover those patterns, we can unlock the errors of our thinking.

Dean's wife was furious about the way he tuned out any time there was conflict between the two of them. As soon as she raised her voice, he was gone. "It's like he's not even in the room anymore," she complained. Dean had made his One Decision to live life as an adventure, and part of that meant having the courage to go back and see where his patterns came from. He expected to have a lot of feelings about what he found, but he never dreamt he'd have more compassion for himself.

"When I was little we lived near a train," he explained. "My parents would fight like cats and dogs, screaming at the top of their lungs. I was so relieved when the train would come by because I couldn't hear them anymore." Dean had used the train to learn how to tune out conflict or raised voices. Eventually he no longer needed the train sound, because when anyone raised their voice he literally didn't hear it. Realizing where this came from, Dean had compassion for the child he was, the child who had no better way to deal with the conflict in his home. Now as an adult, he had gained some perspective on the origins of his soft addiction, developed compassion for himself, and learned better ways to meet conflict more directly.

THE WHY OF YOUR MOODS

So far, we have mostly discussed soft addiction routines related to activities, avoidances, and things. But soft addictions also take the form of habitual moods and ways of thinking. Just as Donna the waitress persisted in a physical activity (visiting the nut bowl) to avoid her true feelings, we develop persistent mental habits to escape our emotions and avoid responsibility for our lives.

Maybe the following list can help you identify some of your mood addictions. Do you see yourself in any of these ways of being? (Think about patterns from your childhood and family, too.)

Avoiding or Minimizing: You put your head in the sand, isolate, or pretend things aren't as important as they really are.

Attacking and Feeling Superior: You criticize, point out other people's inadequacies, or put others on the spot.

Self-Pity/Shame/Inferiority: You act like a sad sack, beat yourself up, put yourself down, sink into hopelessness and despair, indulge in self-pity, whine, or feel like a hapless victim.

Passive-Aggressive: You procrastinate, say yes without meaning it, or punish people indirectly by withdrawing from them.

Manipulation: By making indirect requests, you shift the focus but never ask directly and forthrightly for what you need and want.

Defensiveness/Lying: You rationalize, justify, distort the truth, deflect, lie by omission, or lie outright.

Obfuscation: You're vague, act spaced-out, divert attention from yourself, bring in irrelevant information, or make mountains out of molehills.

None of us wants to see ourselves as manipulative or false or hostile. But remember, our mood addictions have the same positive intentions as our addictions to things; namely, we developed them as coping mechanisms in response to our environment.

To help you find the Why behind your addictions to certain ways of being, read what Cindy and John had to say about their discoveries.

Cindy's Passive Aggressiveness

"A lot of my addictions revolve around negative attention, whether it's lying, being messy, avoiding, procrastinating, or being passive-aggressive. When I look at my childhood, I realize that when I was about six or seven years old, I received what I would now call 'mindless attention.' It appeared to be positive, but it came off as insincere. My parents would toss off a statement like 'nice job' and then would move on. They were more engaged with me when it came to negative attention. So, I learned to have people connect with me by calling me out, criticizing me, and noticing my bad behavior. I hungered for connection and expressed that by being messy, passive-aggressive, and procrastinating, all of which became a pattern."

John's Self-Pity

"An addiction of mine that I uncovered is complaining to my wife. I realized that I gripe to her when I want to get her attention. I believe I know in some way that she'll work harder to please me and pay more attention to me if I am unhappy. She expects less, too. That's the payoff—just as it was with my mom when I was growing up. I got the most attention from my mom when I was unhappy. No one in my family joked or talked pleasantly. We all complained and only listened to each other's complaints. When I think back, it was a rotten way to get attention! It sure held us back."

THE FUNCTIONAL WHY: WHY NOW?

As we've seen, you can find lots of clues to your soft addictions by looking at your past. There's also another way to help spot your unmet needs and adaptive responses: that is to notice what you are feeling in the moment, right before you start heading into one of your soft addiction routines. By observing yourself in the here and now, you'll find triggers—situations, unmet needs, and other factors—that spark certain patterns. Something happens, and you feel a sudden desire to watch television, surf the Internet, daydream, or eat. By following that behavioral trail back to its starting point, you can start to spot the Why under your soft addiction routines. You can answer the question: why am I reaching for my soft addiction in this moment?

I wonder where she slept last night? Look at her ratty coat. Get a haircut, will ya? These are the thoughts that skittered through Rosa's mind as she checked out her fellow passengers during the elevator ride from her forty-fourth floor apartment to the ground floor.

Rosa rode the elevator every morning, but she always avoided talking to people. She was too engaged in talking to herself, in her head. Besides, who would want to get to know the bunch of losers she made them out to be? At the same time, Rosa didn't feel good about herself when she had these thoughts. While she got a little cold comfort from her superiority, her judgments made her feel even more cranky and alone.

After becoming aware of her pattern of attack and superiority and making her One Decision to be genuine and truthful, Rosa cracked her soft addiction code. She had made a commitment to tell the truth as fully as possible at all times. As she began to tell herself the truth, she recognized that her judgmental thoughts were red flags—signals of underlying upset and fear. Rosa put others down to give her ego a boost and mask her own sense of inferiority.

Now when she indulges in gossipy thoughts and negative judgments, Rosa understands that she's really feeling insecure about herself and scared about her day. She faces her fear—planning for obstacles and problems that might come her way—and soothes herself in the process.

Rosa turned her soft addiction into a friendly cue to help her look at her feelings and name her "demons" of the moment. As Rosa treats herself more kindly, she finds she also has more compassion for others. Now, instead of mentally criticizing everyone, she wishes them a good day or says a silent prayer for them. Rosa is starting to feel nourished by being part of the human race, not separate from or above it

CRACKING YOUR CODE

Like Rosa, you can begin cracking your soft addiction routine code. There are tools in the exercises at the back of the book that will help you to figure out why you do everything from fantasizing to overshopping to slinking into self-pitying moods. By thinking about the issues raised earlier—your childhood experiences, your patterns of behavior—you have already cracked some of the code. Just becoming aware of how your soft addictions correspond to events and actions in your past and your present may have started you thinking in the right direction. You're catching glimpses of the Why. Here are two examples of exercises from the workbook that will help you crack your own code.

Breaking Up Is Hard to Do—
Addressing the Historical Why

A powerful and fun way for affirming and releasing the historical Why of your soft addiction is to actually break up with it by writing a Dear John letter. Writing is a great tool to discover facets of yourself and your soft addictions. When our Wright Institute students write letters to specific addictions as if they were people, they often understand why they are drawn to them and are able to affirm their positive intent and let them go. They acknowledge the negative effects of the addiction in their life and use humor and compassion to explain why they are breaking up. I'll guide you to write your own Dear John letter in the workbook at the end of the book, but here's a sample of a letter to inspire you.

> *Dear Ms. Cigarettes,*
>
> *Thank you for providing me with years of service as a pacifier and an icebreaker.*
>
> *Back when I first started dating you, I was just a kid—anxious and dying to be cool. You were my way to calm my fears, give me something to do, make contact (it's easy to ask for a match), and fit in.*
>
> *Over the years you've continued to comfort me. Now, when I suck in smoke, it's like sucking on a pacifier or my thumb.*
>
> *I'm finding that I can no longer afford this relationship. Not just that you're no longer a cheap date, but you're really not good for me. I don't breathe as well, I cough more, and my endurance is less. Not only that, I smell bad.*
>
> *Worry not for me, I'm finding other ways to soothe myself and give myself some-thing to do with my hands. I'm not saying I'm leaving you totally just yet. But it won't be long.*
>
> *I've loved you a long time and it's time to say good-bye.*
>
> *Love, adieu,*
> *Charity*
>
> *P.S. Mr. Java, I really can't see you as much, either. I want to say a slow good-bye. You and I have seen a lot of each other. But I want to play with Mr. Tea and Ms. Juice now. Thank you.*

The Soft Addiction Thesaurus— Translating Soft Addictions into Feelings

You will find that your various soft addictions, whether behaviors such as overeating or moods like being a chronic sourpuss, consistently relate to underlying feelings. Once you become aware of what feelings trigger your behavioral or mood soft addictions, you can start to translate your addiction into the underlying emotion. You can find the Why behind your soft addictions in the moment. You'll know *why* you feel like you *have* to check your e-mail right now because that's what you do when you feel anxious about a new work project or you realize you are being judgmental because you are feeling insecure.

A powerful and helpful way to become aware of these feelings is by creating a Soft Addiction Thesaurus. You can identify your soft addiction or behavior on the one side, and then try to identify the corresponding feeling beneath it. You'll find an exercise for this in the workbook, but here are some examples of a soft addiction thesaurus.

Soft Addiction Behavior	Feeling/Mood
Judging others in my head	Insecurity/feel bad about self/scared about my day
Gossiping	Loneliness
Working out excessively	Anger/resentment
Fantasizing about movie stars	Feeling unloved
Constant complaining about work	Fear of change

....

"There I am standing in front of the vending machine, stuffing in quarters as fast as I can. I don't even know how I got there. All I know is I have to have some chocolate and I have to have it NOW. Then I used my Soft Addiction Thesaurus to look up the behavior or mood and realized that I often reached for chocolate when I was scared. I remembered that I was just about to dial the number for a possibly big sale and the next thing I knew, I was at the vending machine. Now I know what's going on with me, why I had to have that candy bar right now. I can face the fear and reassure myself, ask a colleague for tips, rehearse the call or a million other things to deal with the fear—and get the sale."

—Luke

....

Carrying around a thesaurus can be helpful as a reference to the underlying feelings when you catch yourself in a soft addiction. When you find yourself indulging in your soft addictions, you can pull out your thesaurus. It will remind you of the feelings that lie beneath your soft addictions.

MORE TO THINK ABOUT

Jungians say that alcoholics drink spirits because they crave spirit. Perhaps you gobble up sweets because you crave more sweetness and treats in your life. What other possibilities do you see?

You can think about what you could do to tend to your feelings, comfort yourself, or better prepare for a situation rather than turning to your soft addictions. Remember, you and your emotions are valuable and deserve to be treated with care.

"I had a soft addiction of snacking on bowls of cereal in the afternoon or in the evening. The problem is that I have two small daughters who were starting to see this example as the way to eat a meal, so they would beg me for cereal all the time. As I looked in the past, I remembered that as a child mealtimes were always a little out of control. Rather than deal with the unspoken quiet conflict and the feelings we were stuffing down, my parents would let me and my siblings do whatever we wanted and so I would eat cereal and cold hot dogs for my meals. Once I realized this, I saw that these unhealthy snacks were how I tried to comfort myself when I was feeling anxious as an adult. I had never really learned to eat nourishing meals as a child, so it was no surprise I was feeling challenged as a parent. With this compassion for myself, I decided to treat myself, as an adult, the way I would have liked to be tended to as a child. I have now learned to make nourishing meals for myself and my family, and when I'm feeling upset and want to reach for the cereal, I know I need to talk to my husband or a friend before I eat. I'm proud to say my daughters are growing up now with a much better model for taking care of themselves."

—Eve

To crack the code of your soft addictions, you've explored the Why— the mistaken beliefs, ingrained habits, mood addictions, personal history, feelings, and present-day pressures. Cracking the code of your soft addictions provides powerful clues to understand where your patterns come from and what triggers them in the moment. This self-knowledge gives you power to direct your life, rather than being at the effect of your unconscious motivations. Rather than accepting your stinking thinking and rationalizations as explanations for your behavior, you'll know why you are doing what you are doing, and you can begin to find satisfying ways to address your needs. Deeper hungers and yearnings lie beneath every craving for your soft addictions. In the next chapter, you will learn how to identify and fulfill these deeper hungers to lead a life of MORE.

6

FULFILL YOUR
SPIRITUAL HUNGERS

*"It seems to me we can never give up longing
and wishing while we are alive.
There are certain things we feel to be beautiful and good,
and we must hunger for them."*
—GEORGE ELIOT

Spiritual hungers are the essential desires that drive our quest for the life
we want. They are the deepest and most important needs we have. Yet,
paradoxically, they are also the needs we are least trained to meet. We remain relatively unaware of our deeper yearnings, confusing them with
our surface cravings. We then try to sate these unmet hungers with our
soft addictions, but no matter how hard we try, they can never assuage
these deep needs.

How we relate to our deeper hungers and needs defines our lives.
The degree to which we are aware of our hungers determines our degree
of satisfaction and fulfillment, our contribution to life, our impact, and
our experience of joy, suffering, peace, and love. If we deny our
hungers, we miss the opportunity to feed the deepest parts of ourselves.
We become anxious, frenetic, distracted, and unfulfilled and fail to live
the life we want. When we identify our deeper hungers and seek to fulfill
them directly, we create a life of MORE.

LEARNING THE LANGUAGE OF SPIRITUAL HUNGERS

Meeting our spiritual hungers takes skill. We are surrounded by messages through magazines, television, and advertising that tell us the answer to life's great challenges can be solved instantly by meeting our surface cravings—get this gadget, buy this wrinkle cream, drive this car. Unfortunately, these soft addictions only lead us away from our deeper needs. To combat this programming, we need to learn to recognize our hungers in the moment and make the right choices to meet them. And when we do, our soft addictions melt away.

Learning to meet our spiritual hungers is like learning a new language. It's easy to memorize vocabulary words but more difficult to speak the language fluently. Even knowing the words doesn't guarantee that we fully understand their meanings. We don't gain full facility with them until we steep ourselves in their culture of origin.

Most of us are far more adept at speaking the language of our wants—our cravings for our soft addictions—than we are the more poignant language of our inner hungers. It's easier to say, "I want ice cream" than "I hunger for connection and to make a difference in the world."

As I began to crack the code of my soft addictions, I discovered the deeper needs I had been covering up and numbing with my soft addictions. I hadn't realized that my voracious appetite was actually my hunger to feed my soul, not just my body. That big empty yawning hole inside was my hunger to be filled with spirit. I hadn't recognized or honored my hunger to matter, to make a difference, to love and be loved, to be part of something bigger than myself.

> ### MORE-SEL
>
> *"To desire God is the most fundamental of all human desires. It is the very root of all our quest for happiness. Even the sinner, who seeks happiness where it cannot be found, is following a blind, errant desire for God which is not aware of itself. So that, from one point of view, it is impossible not to desire God."*
>
> —THOMAS MERTON

As I began to live according to my One Decision and chose activities that helped me to be conscious and to feel my feelings, I finally started to feel satisfied and fulfilled. I was filling my life with nature walks, good talks, big cries and belly laughs, inspiring books and music, sacred travel, spontaneous fun, biking along Lake Michigan, and so much more. I was actually meeting my deeper needs to be, to feel, to express myself, to open myself to spirit, so I didn't have the cravings for my soft addictions. I didn't have to fight them off with willpower. By meeting my deeper needs, the compulsive cravings dissipated. I had discovered the power and beauty of fulfilling my spiritual hungers.

In this chapter, you will be introduced to the vocabulary, as well as the culture, of spiritual hungers. You'll contrast that with the culture of wants and the language of soft addictions. You'll even begin to learn to translate from one language to the other. You'll become more and more adept at recognizing your spiritual hungers and meeting them in the moment, and you'll begin living the life you truly desire.

EXPERIENCE THE DIFFERENCE: SPIRITUAL HUNGERS V. WANTS

Spiritual hungers are the deepest longings of our hearts, a feeling of emptiness that yearns to be filled, a desire for beauty, love, hope, contribution, and a sense of the divine. If we didn't have this hunger, this emptiness, we might not be compelled to find God, higher purpose, or meaning. This yearning leads us to open ourselves to love, to aspire to greatness, to serve, to contribute, and to worship.

Throughout millennia, people have felt deep spiritual hunger: an urge that compelled them to build stone circles and cathedrals, to chart the movement of the heavens, to search for meaning, to explore the rhythms of nature, to lift

> ### MORE-SEL
>
> *"It was when I was happiest that I longed most. . . . The sweetest thing in all my life has been the longing . . . to find the place where all the beauty came from."*
>
> —C. S. LEWIS

their heart in song, to offer thanksgiving in worship, and to believe in a force greater than themselves.

This is the universal yearning of the human heart. Beneath our differences, cultures, creeds, nationalities, belief systems, and race runs the undercurrent of spiritual hunger that unites us all. We all hunger to be seen, to be loved, to be touched, to matter, to be part of something greater, to be one.

This spiritual hunger fuels our desire for and pursuit of MORE.

....

"I was addicted to overworking. I would find little things to do at work right before I was supposed to leave—an extra e-mail here, a phone call there, one last piece of paperwork, etc. I would end up getting home later than I had promised, and my husband would be angry and upset. As I dug deeper, I realized that I had a very deep hunger. It felt like it lived right at the core of my being. I uncovered this spiritual longing or hunger to matter, to make a difference in the world. I thought that if I just did a little more work, then I would count, then I would matter. In truth, I was avoiding my husband and the intimacy our relationship promised. As I started to recognize this hunger, I made shifts to my routine to feed my hunger directly. I would call a friend at the end of the day and talk about how I was feeling. When I came home, my husband and I would take time with no distractions just to talk. I'd share about my day, my challenges, and most importantly, my feelings. The more we added this ritual to our days, the less I puttered at the office and the more I met my deeper hunger to matter to him, but most importantly to me. I still work hard, but I also feel a sense of belonging that I never felt before. I feel like I matter—not because of my extra hours—but just because I am."

—Alexia

....

The Little More v. the Big MORE

You know the difference between the big MORE of life and the little more: more "stuff," gadgets, shopping, etc. But it is helpful to hone the distinctions, both in definition and how you experience them. It isn't enough just to intellectually understand the difference; you need to be able to distinguish in the moment what you are feeling. You will be less likely to deceive yourself that some soft addiction you crave is the same as hungering for the real MORE.

For instance, we don't *hunger* for a plasma-screen TV, the latest computer, or tracking our favorite celebrity's every move. We *want* these things. We *hunger* for love, beauty, transcendence, and the opportunity to make a difference. Simply put, we *want* more. But we *hunger* for MORE.

....

"I have the things; I have the gadgets, the house, the cars, the family, and the job. But what I really want is the contact and relationship. I want someone to know me, see me, and hold me."

—*Rob*

....

You wouldn't think differentiating between the two would be that difficult. Unfortunately, our soft addictions blur the line. We feel an urgency about both our wants and our hungers. We're convinced that we can't possibly be happy or satisfied unless we possess a certain object or indulge a certain mood. At the same time, we ache for a deeper connection with others.

What's the difference?

Hungers are cravings of the soul; wants are demands of the ego. Fulfilling a hunger leads to a deep sense of satisfaction, while fulfilling a want just leads to more wanting. As our wants are satisfied, we become addictively attached to their objects and routines. We experience the short-term rush of obtaining the new car or the new gadget, but it doesn't last. When we seek the small more, we sense scarcity and feel threatened no matter how much we have. What if we can't have the object in the future or can't get more of it?

We feel anxious and don't want to let go. We are caught in the Want Cycle.

MORE-SEL

"Odd, the years it took to learn one simple fact: that the prize just ahead, the next job, publication, love affair, marriage always seemed to hold the key to satisfaction but never, in the longer run, sufficed."

—AMANDA CROSS

Riding the Want Cycle

Never underestimate the power of wanting. Our wants may be superficial, but they drive us powerfully. Why? Because they help us escape our deeper hungers. Precisely because our hungers are so deep, we shy away from the abyss, not knowing that true happiness waits for us in the descent. Spiritual hungers are never superficial, but their power may seem negligible compared to the drive of wants because we're so good at pushing hungers away.

> ### MORE-SEL
>
> *"Buddah's doctrine: Man suffers because of his craving to possess and keep forever things which are essentially impermanent. . . . This frustration of the desire to possess is the immediate cause of suffering."*
>
> —ALAN WATTS

Read the following list of wants. Note how falsely compelling they are. Say them out loud and think about what might be the real hunger that resides beneath each.

"I want an Armani suit."
"I want a BMW."
"I want that dress in the window of Bloomingdale's."
"I want to win the lottery."
"I want a sexy girlfriend."
"I want a rich boyfriend."
"I want space."
"I want a Krispy Kreme doughnut."
"I want to play a video game."
"I want to surf the Net."
"I want you to leave me alone and get off my back."
"I want to escape."
"I want to veg out."

Notice how these wants feel like "I gotta." While there is nothing wrong with these wants or with satisfying them, the intensity of them is the problem. We get caught in the Want Cycle: *I have to check my e-mail right now. I want to play a computer game immediately. I need a cup of coffee.* We feel like our happiness depends on getting what we want, even though getting what we want doesn't fulfill us. The slight high or numbing sensation we get doesn't last, so we start craving or wanting again and the cycle continues.

NAMING YOUR SPIRITUAL HUNGERS: THE VOCABULARY OF MORE

Spiritual hungers speak to something deeper and more essential than our wants. They reflect the longings of our hearts to know that we exist, to express our essence, to experience connection with others, to make a difference or to be part of something greater than ourselves.

Hungers might be harder to name than wants, but that's only because we're not taught to look for them. Below is a list of different kinds of spiritual hunger. Contrast the feel of this list with the list of the Want Cycle.

I hunger . . .
To exist
To be seen
To be heard
To be touched
To be loved
To be affirmed
To express
To experience fully
To learn
To grow
To trust
To develop
To be known
To matter
To know another human being
To be close
To feel connected
To belong
To be intimate

To love
To do what I came here on earth to do
To make a difference
To please God
To fulfill my purpose
To unfold my destiny
To feel connected to the greater whole
To be one with all
To know God

This is a general list. You can customize it and make it yours. The following examples show how people who attended one of the Wright Institute's trainings customized their hungers.

Juan: "I hunger for respect and admiration from my family, my coworkers, and people in my community."

Mickey: "I hunger for satisfaction, affirmation, and validation, both what I can bring to myself and also receive from others."

Catherine: "I yearn to have deep contact with others, to really see others, and for them to see me."

Rick: "I hunger for caring and nourishment, to see myself as a blessing, to respect myself. I hunger for joy, spontaneity, freedom of expression. I hunger to feel alive and free."

When we acknowledge our hungers, we might feel vulnerable. It can be painful or moving to express our longing for love or God or connection to the universe. Don't close your heart if pain surfaces—the pain of unfulfilled yearnings or forsaken hungers. When you open your heart to pain, you also open it to love and comfort.

ACCEPT NO SUBSTITUTES: DISTINGUISHING BETWEEN WANTS AND HUNGERS

Hungers and wants often seem similar on the surface. But the distinctions matter. Let's start by looking at wants.

Wants are more visual, easier to picture, and more specific than hungers. We want very explicit things: the exact type of gadget, a certain designer's

MORE-SEL

"If I had known what it would be like to have it all, I might have been willing to settle for less."

—LILY TOMLIN

clothing, a distinct model of car, a brand of snack food, or a particular version of a computer game, or even certain people, moods, or fantasies. A want must be met exactly as it is pictured (the precise item, a particular rendition) to fully satisfy. Typically, this specificity makes wants harder to fulfill than hungers.

It's not that we shouldn't have preferences for what we eat, buy, consume, play, think about, or work with. It's that sometimes this preference turns into an obsession that limits our freedom.

Hungers, on the other hand, are easier to fulfill because they are deeper, more essential, related to emotions, and therefore more general than wants. That means the options for fulfilling hungers are almost unlimited. Moreover, fulfilling any one hunger can also fulfill other hungers. By feeling loved, for instance, we may also feel known. And as we feel known, we may also feel self-respect, feel seen, and feel alive. Any spiritual hunger, once addressed, spreads a sense of fulfillment throughout our whole being.

Hungers point to a direction or a possibility. Any movement in that direction will address the hunger. Even better, the very acknowledgment of our hunger satisfies us, because we are no longer running from ourselves or hiding our deeper yearnings. We begin to understand ourselves and to find compassion. We feel and sense ourselves more deeply. We have met ourselves at a deeper level.

Unlike wants, fulfilling hungers is limited only by our own creativity. If I hunger to be loved, for example, I can call a loved one. I can reread a heartfelt thank-you note. I can recall how someone once did something nice for me. The possibilities are limitless.

The following story about Anna shows how indulging in a soft addiction limits our opportunity for satisfaction until we admit what it was we really craved all along.

Anna was hooked on instant messaging. A college student majoring in computer science, she was in the study room, shooting off instant mes-

sages back and forth with her
friends when she realized, *Wait a
minute. We are all sitting in this same room!*
Anna recognized she was deep in
her soft addiction, not her deeper
hunger to connect with others.
Suddenly the lightbulb went off
inside her—she and her friends
were creating a false sense of connection by having superficial conversations via computer. Once she
remembered how hungry she was for real connection, she called out to
her friends sitting in the room. "What are we doing typing messages back
and forth when we're so rarely together in person?" she asked. "I say we
turn off our messaging programs and get caught up." Although her request seemed straightforward, it was a scary step for her to take with her
friends. They responded beautifully and ended up having a very meaningful conversation. She learned that one of her girlfriends had been
struggling with some challenges in her life but had been too shy to say
anything, and Anna herself got some support on bigger dreams she was
pursuing. The simple act of noticing her hunger shifted not only her
evening but the course of her friendships.

> ### MORE-SEL
>
> *"We are meant to be addicted
> to God, but we develop secondary
> addictions that temporarily appear
> to fix our problem."*
> —EDWARD M. BERCKMAN

SATISFYING YOUR SPIRITUAL HUNGERS MOMENT BY MOMENT

Indulging in a soft addiction is so reflexive, we have to be quick on the
draw to shift from responding to a want to fulfilling a hunger.

Life bombards us with challenges, pressures, and tough situations all
the time. Our habit is to use soft addictions to manage the emotions that
result. And it happens in the blink of an eye, because that's how quickly
our stinking thinking jumps in to lead us away from MORE and toward
numbness.

It doesn't have to work that way, though. By the time we get to a soft
addiction, we have actually bypassed many deeper hungers that we could
have met in the moment. Satisfying your spiritual hungers doesn't
require long stretches of time for quiet contemplation. Our deeper

hungers can be met quickly: it is a matter of awareness and intent, not just time.

....

"I started a new soft addiction in the last month of picking my cuticles horribly. We had just moved into a new house that we had worked hard for, and I thought that the new house was going to make us closer as a family. When this didn't instantly happen, I became more anxious, afraid, and upset. My magic solution hadn't worked out, and out of anxiety, I had begun picking at my cuticles. Once I realized that I was hungry to be more connected with my husband and my boys, I could do something about it. Looking at this soft addiction was a gift. Now I ask my husband and boys to hold my hand when they see me picking my cuticles. I get the connection I am hungering for without having to get attached to this new addiction."

—Diane

....

MORE-SEL

"I cannot count the good people I know who to my mind would be even better if they lent their spirits to the study of their own hungers."

—M. F. K. FISHER

It takes practice to notice and respond to the spiritual hungers that arise moment by moment. But it can be done. Just as a tennis player can hit the ball harder by moving the racket faster, some people are more practiced in differentiating their hungers from their wants and going out to meet them. These people fulfill their hungers more rapidly.

To the extent that you can rapidly sense the difference between wants and hungers, sort through them under pressure, and go directly toward meeting your hungers, you experience MORE and attain the life you truly want.

As I have learned to identify and respond directly to my spiritual hungers, the quality of my life has shifted dramatically. My One Decision compels me to pursue my spiritual hungers. I don't need to go through the layers of soft addictions, stinking thinking, and mistaken beliefs. Instead I can go directly to feeling connected, or loved, or to being touched. Naturally, I do give in to my soft addictions at times. But I know I have a choice and I am getting better and faster at it all the time.

CONNECTING YOUR WANTS TO YOUR HUNGERS

There is a deeper hunger underneath every craving for a soft addiction. Every *want* has a corresponding *hunger*. As you learn the language of your hungers, you can learn to translate your wants to discover the deeper need underneath—and learn to meet that hunger directly. If you *want* a big bowl of ice cream, chances are you *hunger* for comfort. And you can seek that comfort in many different satisfying ways—get a hug, call a friend, cuddle your puppy. If you *want* to share a juicy tidbit of gossip, you probably *hunger* for connection and belonging. And you can't get a real sense of connection from talking about other people, but you can by talking about yourself and the person you are with.

Learning to translate your wants into hungers, and then fulfilling those hungers brings you the life you want. This powerful skill guides you to fulfillment, satisfaction, and love.

You'll get even more help to do this in the chapters to come, but you can start to develop your awareness of spiritual hungers and how you short-circuit them through the following exercises. You'll find these and other exercises in the workbook at the back of the book. Also, don't miss playing the computer game on my Web site (www.judithwright.com), where you can test your skill in matching hungers with the surface want of soft addictions (just don't get addicted to it!).

ARE YOU GOING FOR MORE OR LESS?

The more practice you have in distinguishing between deeper hungers and soft addictions, the better. Your proficiency can make the difference between living a life of MORE or one of less. Following are three steps to follow to exercise your awareness muscle.

Identify your wants. It's okay to have wants. The value is in knowing them for what they are. You can even have fun developing your awareness of what you want. You can list all of your wants—from the concrete to the fanciful and from the small to the big—from coffee to reading the paper to your dream car to your salary to fantasies. Enjoy the act of wanting without having to act on your impulse. Picture a store filled with every kind of thing you have on your list. Imagine you are a small child running through the aisles saying, "I want!" Little children enjoy the act of wanting, without feeling they need to possess everything they admire. Mimic their ability to just want. You can even take it to the next step as you practice pursuing your wants. There's nothing wrong with wants, providing they don't start limiting or harming you or others. Your wants will have less power over you if you entertain them in moderation.

> MORE-SEL
>
> *"America is a country who is starving, but not for food, as much of the world is. America is starving for love."*
>
> —MOTHER TERESA

Identify your hungers. Learning to identify your hungers is a deeper and perhaps more difficult assignment. One way to start noticing your hungers is by reviewing the list of hungers earlier in this chapter to see which ones feel true for you. Focus on the ones that strike a chord in your heart. Revisit your One Decision and see what hungers it reflects. If you haven't formulated your One Decision yet, you'll move closer to it by recognizing and claiming your deeper hungers. If you discover that you are hungry to connect with others but your pattern of lying or avoiding the truth is distancing you from them, then you might make this One Decision: *I am genuine and real.* Or if you hunger to be loved, your One Decision might simply be *I love and am loved.*

Connect your wants and hungers. Once you've learned to identify your wants and hungers, the next step is to connect them. By raising your awareness, you will start to see how a specific want is merely a substitute for a deeper hunger. One way to think about it is by completing these two sentences.

I am hungry for ____.

What I do instead is ____.

If you're having difficulty thinking about how you'd complete the sentences, consider the following examples:

I Hunger . . .	What I Do Instead Is . . .
To be seen	Crack jokes Gossip Wear outrageous clothes Overspend on clothes Buy the latest gadgets Manipulate for attention
To matter	Buy expensive gifts for others, outside my budget
To be important	Be in the know—voraciously read newspapers, study data, scan the Internet obsessively for data Fantasize and daydream that others find me irresistible
To be touched	Act out in sexually inappropriate ways Compromise my standards of relationship in order to be touched
To connect	Gossip Overdo celebrity news Watch tons of television and talk about people in TV programs as if they are real acquaintances

HUNGER FOR A SENSE OF DEEP CONNECTION

The benefits of focusing on hungers will show up everywhere—including your relationships. So often we make the mistake of sharing only our surface wants. As a result, we end up with partners who share our soft addictions instead of our spiritual hungers! But when we share our hungers with another person, we attain true intimacy, a deep sharing of soul to soul.

When my husband, Bob, and I talk, we've learned to be pretty direct about expressing our spiritual hungers and deeper yearnings, so our conversations are very fulfilling. We don't spend the bulk of our time talking about our surface wants or our soft addictions. Instead of discussing television programs or celebrity news or gossip, we share what matters most to us with love, truth, lightness, humor, and emotion. To be sure, we still have our soft addictions and off moments. But we know how to reorient to our deeper hungers and desires.

Don't waste your time, energy, and resources in the safety of "small talk." Don't wait until you already know someone well to reach out and connect through deeper hungers rather than wants. You'll miss out on great possibilities for relationships. Just imagine a first date where you discuss your deeper hungers rather than your superficial preferences.

When I was leading a pilgrimage in France, we had arranged to meet and learn about the Jerusalem monks, an urban coeducational order, in the heart of Paris. There we met Sister Edith, whose first words to us were, "All my life I have been searching for God." We loved the simplicity of her statement and how it directly revealed a universal hunger. We knew so much about her from those words. The ensuing conversation was blissfully uplifting. There was no small talk or beating around the bush. She established a powerful connection both with us and with herself when she articulated her hunger.

MORE TO DO

Read through the singles ads in your newspaper. How many of them reflect surface wants? How many reflect spiritual hungers?

Our ability to identify our spiritual hungers or deeper needs and differentiate them from our soft addictions truly does define our lives. It is probably one of the most powerful skills we can develop if we want to release our soft addictions and pursue a life of MORE. By identifying these deeper needs we can meet them directly. The rewards are exponential because as we satisfy one hunger, we satisfy many. In the next chapter, you will develop a vision of a life in which you fulfill your spiritual hungers and implement your One Decision. As you'll discover, we are all visionaries at heart.

7

Develop a Vision

"A vision is not just a picture of what could be;
it is an appeal to our better selves,
a call to become something more."

—ROSABETH MOSS KANTER

By this point, you have probably realized that a life of MORE is not just about quitting soft addictions. In fact, addressing soft addictions isn't the real focus—meeting your spiritual hungers is the key. Just getting rid of a substance or an activity doesn't solve anything. Releasing one soft addiction often just makes space for another. Our deeper hungers persist because they're still unfulfilled. This is the point where the power of Vision comes into play. Inspiring and uplifting, your Vision can help you resist the allure of your soft addictions. Your Vision guides and propels you to a life of MORE.

Many people succumb to soft addictions because they don't have a Vision. They think, *This is as good as it gets* or *This is how it is.* They settle into a life not realizing that they could want more and envision and achieve greater possibilities. They lose their motivation and succumb more easily to their soft addiction routines.

Vision reflects what is really important to you, what matters deep in your heart. It gives you the momentum to move through the barriers of your soft addictions. Your deeper hungers provide fuel to power your vision. Think of the compelling power of the yearnings and vision held

MORE-SEL

"I have a dream that one day this nation will rise up and live out the true meaning of its creed, 'We hold these truths to be self-evident, that all men are created equal.' This is our hope. . . . With this faith we will be able to work together, to pray together, to struggle together, to go to jail together, to stand up for freedom together, knowing that we will be free one day. . . ."

—MARTIN LUTHER KING, JR.

by Mahatma Gandhi or Martin Luther King, Jr. Gandhi hungered for connection, justice, and unity. These hungers defined his vision and carried him through immense barriers toward his dream of a unified, free India. Similarly, we are still moving toward the vision of Martin Luther King, Jr., fueled by his passion for justice, equality, and love.

Time and time again, we have seen the power of Vision at the Wright Institute. People come to us to achieve a goal or perhaps to solve a problem. We are usually able to support them to gain those results fairly soon. The harder part of our job is to help them envision a bigger, more satisfying life, beyond solving a problem or reaching one goal. Yet once they do, the quality of their lives expands exponentially. They start to see their soft addictions and stinking thinking as impediments to their Vision. They have something to strive for that really matters to them, and it's worth resisting temptation and reaching for their Vision instead.

FANTASYLAND OR VISIONS THAT ARE GRAND?

Our vision is our One Decision in action. Without a One Decision, we don't have a reason to let go of our soft addictions, and without Vision we aren't able to picture what our life will be like without them. In fact, we usually spend far more time planning and visualizing our soft addiction routines than imagining the possibilities of fulfilling our heart's desires. We are often more adept at fantasizing and filling wants than envisioning and filling deeper hungers. Vision helps us cultivate our capacity to see beyond the surface to what could be.

"I thought that if men gave me expensive gifts, it meant I was valu-

able," shared Suzanne, a gregari-
ous cosmetics representative. "I'm
embarrassed to admit it but getting
a man's attention, and going from
one short-lived relationship to
another, become soft addictions
for me."

In her job, Suzanne had plenty
of engaging contact with women,
but she craved men's attention.
She had elaborate daydreams and

> ## MORE-SEL
>
> *"A rock pile ceases to be a rock pile the moment a single man contemplates it, bearing within him the image of a cathedral."*
>
> —ANTOINE DE SAINT-EXUPÉRY

fantasies where she was escorted by the hunkiest celebrities and courted
by royalty. She dreamt of romantic scenes over gourmet meals, being
showered with flowers, and being sent presents from her favorite designer store. Suzanne had planned every detail of her wedding hundreds
of times yet had never been engaged. She flirted outrageously, dressed
provocatively, and couldn't seem to stop herself from making eyes at
every guy. She showed little discrimination in whom she dated. Without
a man around, she felt empty and worthless. Suzanne had a picture of
what she wanted, but not a Vision of what she hungered for.

Once she admitted her soft addiction, she went on a journey that led
her to her deeper hungers to be seen and loved. She made her One Decision: "I am a woman I respect. I am loved and draw my security from
my inner resources, my capacities, and my relationship with spirit."
From her One Decision, she developed her vision: "I express myself fully
and honestly. I am recognized, acknowledged, and appreciated by myself
and the world around me. Strong and independent, I support myself
financially and emotionally. I respect myself and am well treated by myself and others. I date men whom I respect and who respect me."

Suzanne felt inspired and buoyed by this image of herself as an independent woman who feels comfortable without a relationship. Not only did
she dress differently—to please and express *herself,* not just to attract men—but
she also found new strength in doing things by, and for, herself. Rather than
be dependent on men's attention to feel better about herself, Suzanne began to draw on the support of her circle of women friends. With Vision as
a beacon before her, Suzanne completely transformed her life. She still
dates, but her dates are meaningful. She dates better quality men. Rather
than waiting for Mr. Right to give her the things she wished for, she uses her

MORE-SEL

"Vision is common to those courageous people who dream and make their dreams reality."

—BOB WRIGHT

financial and emotional independence to give her what she wants. No longer waiting for some fantasy future, Suzanne is enjoying her life tremendously. She knows now that if she does choose to marry, it won't be to fulfill a fantasy, but rather to have a full partner who is empowering her to have the fullest life possible.

WHAT IS VISION?

With Vision, you see more clearly how to create the life you always wanted. Vision is the projection into the future of a fulfilled life based on your One Decision. It is a picture of your One Decision in action. Your One Decision is your guiding beacon for the quality of your life, but Vision empowers you to picture living that way in every area of your life. Vision may shift with the evolving changes in your life, but its intent remains constant.

Vision differs from goal setting. A goal is measurable with a specific time, space, or quantity. In the next chapter you will learn to create goals to help you implement your vision, but Vision is the starting place. For instance, a Vision related to your body might be, *I am lithe and flexible. I enjoy being in my body.* Your goal, then, might be to be able to touch your toes within a month's time. Your specific action might be to take a yoga class.

Living with Vision, and its accompanying goals and action steps, has opened up whole new vistas for me. Being married to Bob has been a constant training in the power of

MORE-SEL

"Cherish your visions. Cherish your ideals. Cherish the music that stirs in your heart, the beauty that forms in your mind, the loveliness that drapes your purest thoughts, for out of them will grow all delightful conditions, all heavenly environment; of these, if you but remain true to them, your world will at last be built."

—JAMES ALLEN

vision. Bob sees possibilities where I see roadblocks and limits. He holds a large vision for me—seeing me doing things I never imagined, accomplishments that seemed beyond me. His vision is so compelling that it gives me a reason to be my best, to avoid my soft addictions. There is no indulgence that is worth losing a dream come true. Every year Bob and I envision our year, in every area of life. We think about our One Decisions, our spiritual hungers, and our aspirations and we come up with a vision for each area, a plan for our year. There are no empty goals, only steps to make our dreams come true. When I remember my vision, my work isn't a duty. I am less likely to indulge in procrastination when I remember that my tasks are part of living into my Vision.

....

"I work at a large bank going through a major merger. The previous mergers were 'work hell,' with endless meetings, tedious details, and lots of work on top of our regular work. But this merger was so much more fun. We had the same meetings, the same level of detail, and the same extra workload. But this time, I created and held a different Vision. I decided I would have fun myself and create fun for my coworkers. The only thing different in the equation was me. I kept my eye on the bigger picture of why we do all the work, holding Vision for the job and for the larger scope of our work. I didn't just focus on the details and the jobs that I didn't like to do. The outcome? I didn't slip into my mood addictions of self-pity and complaining because my vision was to provide the best experience for our clients. My superiors are thrilled, and my employees are having a great time."

—Krista

....

What We See Is What We Get

Vision guides all our lives. Whether you know it or not, your life has been formed by some sort of Vision, positive or negative. Sadly, it is too often an expression of our negative thinking, unconscious belief systems, and poor self-esteem. Our negative visions often lead us to try to numb our pain or gain false comfort by succumbing to soft addictions.

A positive Vision helps us avoid cycling through limiting self-fulfilling prophecies driven by unconscious beliefs and get true nourishment and comfort instead. Often, we're not even conscious of this cycle. For instance, if we believe that we cannot fulfill our spiritual hungers, then we unconsciously act in a way that confirms and reinforces that belief.

"See, I knew nothing good could ever happen to me," Peter repeatedly says to just about anyone who will listen. Peter, an IT project manager, holds an unconscious belief that things in his life are never going to work out well for him. He lives in fear, waiting for something bad to happen; he imagines bad endings to conversations and being rejected. Peter repeatedly pictures himself in disastrous situations, humiliating outcomes, and unsatisfying results. His vision is a negative vision, based on false beliefs and an addiction to pessimistic moods. His mind is more focused on planning problems than developing solutions. Feeling discouraged and hopeless, he overindulges by watching television late into the night, eating sugary snack foods, and wallowing in his pessimistic moods. His addictive routine feeds his negative worldview and vice versa. This cycle keeps him from acting in positive ways.

At a Soft Addiction Solution workshop, Peter uncovered his deeper hunger to matter and to make a difference. He made his One Decision to be a potent force on the planet, and to live as if anything is possible. Out of his decision, he developed a positive Vision. "I take actions in spite of my fear. I live as if others are here to support me and I interact with them in positive ways. I treat myself lovingly in all that I say and do. I reach out to others for support. I consistently speak up and generate ideas and discussion where I am because I know I have something to contribute." Peter created a picture of fulfilling his spiritual hunger rather than indulging his addictions. Orienting to Vision helped him to change his actions, challenge his faulty belief system, and compel him to overcome his fear. Since shifting from a negative to a positive Vision and applying the other skills for breaking free of his soft addictions, Peter was promoted several times at his company

> ## MORE-SEL
>
> *"When I dare to be powerful, to use my strength in the service of my vision, then it becomes less and less important whether I am afraid."*
>
> —AUDRE LORDE

and has most recently learned to partner with his wife of ten years in a way that has brought an intimacy and closeness that others envy.

Where Visions Come from . . . and How to Access That Place

A key aspect of our work at the Wright Institute is to help people create a powerful Vision to inspire their work—often far beyond what they dreamt possible. I have learned, from working with hundreds of people who on the surface don't seem like visionaries, that Vision is not something available only to a select few. People I talk to claim that they are not visionaries, and yet they've developed Visions and made them come true. I am constantly inspired by the fact that we can all discover the uplifting, loving dreams flowing inside each one of us when we listen to our hearts, rise above our soft addictions, and align to our One Decision.

MORE TO DO

Make a list of visionaries throughout history, like Walt Disney, Hildegard von Bingen, and Martin Luther King, Jr. What do they have in common?

"I want to lose weight," Sarah proclaimed as she waltzed into my office and shook my hand with her powerful grip. A new coaching client, Sarah was a force to be reckoned with. When I asked her why she wanted to lose weight, she responded, "Isn't it obvious?" Not to me, it wasn't. While certainly not model thin, Sarah was attractive, well groomed, and creatively and colorfully dressed. I couldn't understand why this solid success in the competitive world of advertising should be focused on her weight. Without a bigger Vision, her weight loss seemed to me to be nothing more than an empty goal.

I asked her a few simple questions: What is it that you hope losing weight will give to you? How do you want to feel about your body? How do you want to relate to your body? What do you want to use your body for? What would you feel like if you lost the weight? Within moments, this imposing woman's entire demeanor shifted. Her faced softened, her eyes glowed, and she shared a potent and inspiring Vision about her body.

She talked about how she envisioned herself completely relaxed with her appearance, feeling secure in her body, with the grace and physical expressiveness of a dancer. This is the vision she formulated: "I am sensuous and supple and surround myself with sumptuous self-care." By answering these questions and looking more closely at her soft addictions, Sarah was able to articulate her higher Vision—one that revolved around physical health and creativity, not just thinness. This Vision, along with her One Decision to be guided by her heart, gave her a reason to shift her routines. She enrolled in a dance class, pampered herself, and eventually stopped hating her body. As she began to revel in her body, she easily lost the weight she desired, but more importantly, she fulfilled her vision of being supple and sensuous.

> ## MORE TO DO
>
> Be inspired by the visionary, and my hero, Jacques Lusseyran. Read *And There Was Light* for a deeply moving, challenging, exhilarating example of a life of MORE.

DESIGNING YOUR LIFE: CREATING YOUR VISION OF MORE

Now you can think about creating your own vision. Below, you'll find questions to guide you, as well as some Dos and Don'ts that have worked for thousands of others we have worked with who have created their visions. Allow yourself to dream of the life you want—where you fulfill your spiritual hungers and are guided by your One Decision.

Your Designer Life

Imagine you have just arrived on this planet. You can review and choose from all ways of being in all walks of life to design your life any way you want, from scratch. What activities, feelings, and experiences will you choose? What values will you select to guide you and how will you incorporate them? If you proactively designed your life, what would it look like?

Most likely, you wouldn't design a life based on your surface wants. You wouldn't actually plan on watching nineteen hours of television a week. You wouldn't stipulate twelve hours of daydreaming weekly or insist you really need to surf the Internet until your eyes water and your brain becomes bleary. Compulsive shopping, worry, and self-pity routines wouldn't be high on your list, either.

What we all desire is a life following our highest values, pursuing and satisfying our spiritual hungers. Think about how you would design your ideal life. What would you put into this ideal life design? Jot down your ideas, if you wish. You'll find them useful when you create your vision in the workbook part of this book.

Vision Dos and Don'ts

A powerful vision is one you can almost taste, feel, and hear. Wording it in the present tense gives it the most power because you imagine yourself doing, not planning. Remember, it is not a reaction to a particular problem or situation. The following Dos and Don'ts will help you create a strong vision.

Do	Don't
Do fulfill your spiritual hungers	Don't just feed your surface wants
Do have a proactive vision	Don't settle for a reactive vision
Do feed your soul	Don't just cater to your ego
Do write your Vision in present tense	Don't write it in the future tense
Do create a Vision that deepens your life experience	Don't fantasize an escape from life
Do picture your One Decision in action	Don't picture your soft addictions in action

Do	Don't
Do inspire yourself	Don't numb yourself
Do picture how you will feel, what will be, what your life will be	Don't settle for a vague wish
Do go for MORE	Don't go for more "stuff"
Do be sure it is yourself you please	Don't worry about pleasing others
Do keep your wording positive and affirmative	Don't use "not" in your Vision
Do envision MORE	Don't limit your possibilities
Do apply Vision every day	Don't just wait for the future to use your Vision

....

"Procrastination is my soft addiction of choice, and when my boss asked me to organize a small storage area, I got nervous about completing it. He had given me a clear time frame by which I needed to be done, but I found myself seeking out distractions. Finally, I remembered that I had a Vision for this space. I saw it as a beautiful and organized resource area for myself. I pictured myself being able to quickly respond to requests for materials because I would know right where they were. Every time I started to notice my procrastination, I stopped, closed my eyes, and pictured my Vision again. I ended up completing the project before deadline and it still looks great."

—Rachael

....

CRAFTING YOUR VISION

Crafting a Vision is not as hard and doesn't take as long as you might think. In fact, at the Soft Addiction Solution training, I give people two minutes to come up with a Vision for each area of their life, and they develop beautiful, inspiring Visions in this short time frame. Remember, the point is not to make your Vision perfect. The very act of imagining the life you want will serve you, so don't belabor it. Vision is in you, it just needs to be invited out.

A truly holistic Vision encompasses who you are in all aspects of your being. Picture yourself living your One Decision and fulfilling your spiritual hungers to create a life of MORE. You can develop an overall Vision for your life, or you can start by designing Visions for specific aspects of your life. You may find it helpful to use the areas of life that we use at the Wright Institute, drawn from Bob Wright's Comprehensive Model of Human Growth and Development, as you'll see below. You don't need to compose a Vision for every area of your life. Simply pick the areas that seem most important to you right now, or the ones you are most anxious to change. In the workbook section of this book, you'll find work sheets to help you actually write them, but for now just let yourself flow, imagine, and dream. What would you do? What would you feel like? Imagine the quality of your experience.

MORE ALERT

Potential obstacles to developing your vision:

- Being embarrassed about your deeper hungers
- Listening only to your head and not your heart
- Confusing Vision with vague wishes, such as "I want to be happy"
- Mistaking escapist fantasies for the potential realities of Vision
- Being afraid of change

Use the following questions to spark your imagination.

My One Decision: What is your One Decision? If you haven't created it yet, what One Decision would you like to test-drive? (You may want to refer to the One Decision chapter as a reminder.)

My Spiritual Hungers: What are your spiritual hungers, your deeper yearnings? Let them inspire your Vision. How would you live your life if you were oriented toward fulfilling your spiritual hungers in each of the following areas of life?

My Body: Think about your relationship with your body. Do you hunger for touch, to know you exist, to connect? What would your ideal relationship with your body look like? How do you feel about your body now and what would you like to be different? How would you like to use your body—to experience your life, to touch and be touched, to heal, comfort, or love? Most of us have a narrow idea of the potential in our relationship to our body, defined by surface-oriented media. Picture yourself in a healthy relationship with your body. Really stretch for the exquisite richness of sensation, fullness of breath, and experience of aliveness.

My Self: How do you want to feel about yourself? What deeper hungers do you wish to fulfill? To know you exist? To learn and grow, to develop? What is your Vision for your self-development, self-esteem, and self-respect? Picture what it might be like to have your feelings and emotions more available. Imagine a relationship with yourself that is satisfying, respectful, and loving. What might that look like? Consider the possibility of rich awareness, deep compassion, and support for your well-being, and reach for it in your Vision.

My Family: How do you envision your relationship with your family of origin and your family of choice? What hungers do you picture fulfilling—to be affirmed, to connect, to be heard? What would be different with your family? Do you envision more connection, support, truth, genuineness, mutuality, acceptance, or fun? What do you picture when you dream about your ideal family state?

With Others: What hungers do you want to meet with others—to be affirmed, to be respected, to connect, to belong? What do you hunger for in your relationships with friends, coworkers, acquaintances, neighbors? What would your relationships with these people look like? What would you do that you are not currently doing?

My Work and Play: What hungers do you long to meet at work—to express, to be seen and valued, to develop your talents, to make a difference? What do you hunger for in playtime? Envision recreation that refreshes you. Imagine how you could weave work and play together in your workday. How would your days look when defined by this Vision?

My Society: What do you hunger for in your relationship to society at large— to be part of something bigger, to make a difference, to contribute, to matter and have an impact on your community? What is important to you? How would you integrate your principles and values into your public life? How would your days be different?

My Spirituality: What do you hunger for in the realm of spirituality—to feel connected to something greater than yourself, to feel part of the whole? How might you feel if you were more satisfied in this area of your life? What might you do differently or shift in your daily routine? What if your spirituality infused all aspects of your life? How could the different areas of your life fit together synergistically to bring you spiritual fulfillment?

Other Areas: Is there another area of your life that these don't cover? Envision satisfaction and fulfillment in this area as well.

EXAMPLES OF VISIONS

Here are examples from our students' Visions for various areas of life. Let them inspire you to create your own. For more ideas on Visions, see the database of visions on our Web site, www.judithwright.com.

My Body: My body is pain free, and I feel good about it. I move with grace and I am strong. I have both muscles and feminine curves. I lovingly nourish my body and enjoy it.

My Self: I feel self-confident, and I treat myself with respect. I think in positive ways that help me succeed in relationships and work. I encourage myself and do not allow guilt or shame to hold me back. I am continually learning and growing and deepening my capacity to love myself and others.

My Family: My family is a source of strength, solace, and support. We value truth and genuineness. I challenge and support them to be their best and they do the same for me. We move through conflict honestly and openly because we value each other's experience.

With Others: I count on my friends and they can count on me. We tell the truth, share our feelings, and expect a lot from one another. Our lives are adventures of mutual support and celebration as we encourage each other to our highest.

My Work: I am a leader in my field, an excellent manager and salesperson. I am constantly learning, growing, and improving in my work, and supporting those around me to grow and be their best. I create value and serve: I am proud that those I supervise are valuable workers.

My Society: I contribute my time, energy, and gifts to people and causes that matter to me. I bring truth, aliveness, engagement, and service to my communities. I value the earth and volunteer at prairie restoration projects.

My Spirituality: I am a spiritual man. I am engaged in an active journey of faith. I focus on spirit throughout my day, to learn to live more sacredly. I follow a path of truth and love even in difficult times, supported by my faith and friends.

Overall Vision: Life is a great adventure of learning and growing and I live it fully. I care deeply about the world around me and am a "net giver" in all that I do.

Ewan, a young Internet marketing specialist, made his One Decision to love and be loved, after having spent much of his career—and his life—feeling very alone and isolated. Although this One Decision never wavered, his Vision changed and grew as he applied it to different situations in his life. He describes his Vision as follows: *I am a loving man. I show my caring through my actions. The people in my life who are important to me know that they are important to me. I show my caring through fairness, believing in others, and helping them to be their best. They do the same for me.* The wording and picture of Ewan's vision evolved over time, but its essence remained the same. Remembering his Vision helped him break his isolation addiction and take risks to reach out to people in his office, mentor a new employee, and ask out on a date an attractive, vibrant woman whom he would not even have talked to before. Ewan found

> **MORE-SEL**
>
> *"Go confidently in the direction of your dreams! Live the life you've imagined."*
> —HENRY DAVID THOREAU

that by allowing himself to keep his Vision fresh and in front of him at all times, he was able to gradually move closer and closer to it, and to the life he had always wanted—one of fulfillment and closeness.

A Vision is very powerful. Remember that a Vision is your One Decision in action. The combination of your One Decision and Vision gives you a reason to overcome your soft addictions. You have a bigger picture and a bigger reason for creating a life without your soft addictions. Creating a vision is empowering, and implementing it will truly change your life. In the workbook section of this book, you'll find the tools necessary to turn your Vision into daily action, as aided by a wonderfully simple, easy-to-use concept covered in the next chapter, "The Math of MORE."

8

The Math of MORE: Add and Subtract to Achieve Your Vision

"Dismiss what insults your soul and your very flesh will become a great poem."

—WALT WHITMAN

With your Vision as a guide, a deceptively simple formula for MORE will help you break through the grip of your soft addictions: add things that enhance your Vision and subtract things that take away from it.

In this new math, adding actually subtracts and subtracting adds. Adding real nourishment to your life naturally subtracts your soft addictions, pushing them out of the way. And when you subtract your soft addictions, you automatically add more time, resources, and consciousness to pursue the life you want.

You'll learn to add substance to your life, not fill your life with substances. In short, you will discover what I call the Formula for MORE.

MATH LESSON

I always thought that the way to get rid of a bad habit was to go cold turkey, use my willpower, and just grit my teeth and bear it. But I never really could get all that psyched up about letting go of the only things that I seemed to look forward to in life. I was already feeling deprived, which was why I was eating, shopping, watching TV, and engaging in all my other soft addictions in the first place. Even though I felt out of control and wasn't so proud of indulging in these habits, I wasn't so sure that I wanted to get rid of them, either. What would I do without looking forward to watching TV at night or without my snacks or shopping? Even when I used my considerable willpower and finally lost weight, where was the big reward? I was thin but still unhappy and obsessed with food— constantly thinking about what I would eat, when, with whom, how much, and how often, plus reading recipes like they were the answer to my happiness.

Then I made my One Decision and discovered the big secret. As I was doing things that added to my life, my soft addictions were melting away. They just weren't so attractive anymore. My One Decision was to be conscious, awake, alive, and to feel my feelings. So I sought out activities, people, and entertainment that helped me feel that way. I started reading better literature and found that I wasn't missing the daily newspapers I used to read from cover to cover to zone out. At the end of a long workday, instead of watching TV or drinking a glass of wine, I found myself out in our hot tub under the stars, or talking with Bob about our day, or going to a movie, or riding my mountain bike in the woods, taking a walk in the sunset, or cuddling up with a great book. The list was long, and the more I focused on adding things that were in alignment with my One Decision, the longer the list became.

I had discovered the Math of MORE! By adding things that really nourished me, my soft addictions were naturally decreasing. I had it all wrong before. It wasn't about subtracting habits from my life when I was already feeling deprived; it was about adding things so that I not only didn't feel deprived, I felt alive, nourished, fulfilled.

I cannot tell you the difference this has made in my life. Now when I want to indulge in a soft addiction, I use the other skills and ask myself, Why? Why now? What am I feeling? What am I really hungry for? I am much more able to add something that really nourishes me. If I do indulge, I can look at my behavior with compassion, as a signal that I really need something more. My soft addictions are simply reminding me that I have unmet hungers and that I need to add something yummy to my life to meet those deeper needs.

Throughout this chapter I'll share with you what I and others have done to use the Math of MORE in our lives, and how to determine your own Formula for MORE. I hope you will be inspired to add MORE to your life, too, and watch how much easier it is to subtract your soft addictions. And when you do subtract your soft addictions, see how much MORE there is.

LEARNING THE NEW MATH

Living according to the Math of MORE makes our dreams come true. You'll use this Math to generate your own formula for MORE, an action plan to realize your Vision. Like me, most people think that when they have a bad habit, they should just use their willpower to stop it. Think of all the people who have lost weight only to gain it again, or those who replace one addiction like smoking with another like overeating. Merely getting rid of a soft addiction doesn't lead to a meaningful, rich life. But addressing your deeper hungers does. The Math of MORE helps you clarify what to add to your life to meet these hungers. When you add to your life, you are less likely to replace one addiction with another.

> ### MORE-SEL
>
> *"One of the things that makes a dead leaf fall to the ground is the bud of the new leaf that pushes it off the limb. When you let God fill you with His love and forgiveness, the things you think you desperately want to hold on to start falling away and we hardly notice their passing."*
>
> —JAN KARON

Learning to Add

While you may need to curb some of your soft addictions and get rid of others, the main focus in the Math of MORE is to add nourishing things to your life. When you add more reading, socializing, or getting together with friends, you'll watch less TV. If you usually gossip at work, talking about yourself instead of others will shift the focus. Many more examples of these activities will be found later in this chapter.

Learning to Subtract

As we've discovered, with the Math of MORE, subtracting actually adds. Subtracting means decreasing the percentage of time, money, resources, and energy tied up in soft addiction routines. Subtracting does not necessarily mean

eliminating something completely or immediately. You don't need to subtract down to zero; just reducing the frequency, duration, or intensity of a behavior over time can create exponential results.

THE FORMULA FOR MORE

The Formula for MORE is simple:

Life + Spiritual Nourishment − Soft Addictions = MORE

The skills you have been learning throughout this book feed the formula by giving you ideas for each element of the equation.

ADDING UP TO A LIFE OF MORE

You don't have to invent the life of your dreams from scratch. In the rest of this chapter, you will learn the kinds of things you can add and subtract: activities of self-care and nourishment, personal power and self-expression, and life purpose and spirituality. Think about what you'd like to add to *your* life as you read. At the Wright Institute in the year of MORE curriculum, students use a method called the Assignment Way of Living to add things to their Formula for MORE. Students go through a full curriculum where they do assignments or homework to try new skills—adding different ways of being and activities to their lives so that they can more fully embrace and honor the full spectrum of who they are, not just who they were trained to be. Adding is a powerful way to transform your lifestyle and your life.

The ideas, additions, and subtractions in this chapter offer inspiration but not a prescription. This is about discovering what works for you and brings your Vision closer to fruition. It is not about following a recipe, but about following your heart. Dream about possibilities for your life as you discover the many ways to care for, develop, and discover your self—the ingredients for a great life.

ADD NOURISHMENT AND SELF-CARE

Nourishment and self-care are the foundation for any journey—just as a climber requires food and rest before beginning a hike, you need to learn proper nourishment of your soul to sustain your journey to MORE. Self-care means anything that maintains or feeds your body, soul, mind, and spirit and contributes to creating a meaningful, fulfilling life. Self-care is foundational. It starts with becoming aware of your feelings, needs, and hungers. It also means breaking any myths you might have about self-care and developing an enhanced relationship with your emotions. It can include anything from maintaining clean and neat surroundings, giving more hugs, being spontaneous, dancing, adhering to financial discipline, being organized, expressing your feelings, and stimulating your intellect. We often confuse soft addictions and self-care. True self-care satisfies our hungers, not our wants. A conscious renewal break is very different from indulging soft addictions. Morgan's story illustrates the difference.

A hardworking financial executive, Morgan was always impeccably dressed and immaculately groomed as she strived to make a good impression. Driven to succeed, she'd often find herself at the office late into the night. She put in long hours at work and spent every free moment networking to get ahead. Always wound up, she was often abrupt in her communications—curt and terse and urging others to get to the point. She focused entirely on getting ahead—unaware that she was really running from a deep fear of failure. Her father had a history of reversals of fortune, declaring bankruptcy more than once, and she had vowed early in her life that she would not be like him. She would have not only financial security but also abundance. In the rare moment that she did take time for herself just to be or to go to the art museum (which she loved), Morgan felt guilty and full of anxiety, like she was goofing off.

From the outside, it looked like she had it all handled. She kept her finances and her house in order and scheduled haircuts, facials, and massages as a regular regimen. But inside she was empty. She treated herself like a car that needed regular maintenance, not a woman deserving of loving self-care.

Morgan came to the Wright Institute because she wanted more intimate relationships in her life. As she looked closer, she saw she had a deeper hunger to love and be loved, and yet she was using her overworking soft addiction to distance herself not just from others but from herself. Through her courses and the support of other students, Morgan made her One Decision: *I love myself and treat myself as a unique gift to the planet, giving and receiving in a natural rhythm.* As she learned to treat herself as someone worthy and special, she applied her ability to be disciplined to real self-care. She began to attune to her true feelings, rather than pushing them away with overworking. She scheduled two breaks during each business day where she would take a walk or call a friend and just chat. She packed picnics for herself and took them to the park instead of eating at her desk. On Friday night, she was more likely to be at the opening of an art gallery in town than catching up at the office. Surprisingly, her productivity increased, and she found she had more energy and more creativity to give to her job. She began to enjoy her free moments and used them to restore herself. She allowed herself more nourishment, and a sense of peace pervaded her life.

The following are possibilities to help you increase your self-care. Consider building routines of self-care that increase your baseline of nurturance.

Add Nourishment and Maintenance

You may not be as disciplined as Morgan and may need to add regular self-care routines like exercise, regular massages, or dates with your spouse. Decide the frequency, schedule them for the year, and put them on your calendar. Then, do not cancel one without rescheduling it. Look for routines to support your physical, financial, and emotional health—from exercise and healthy eating to financial integrity and vacations.

Morgan needed to *experience* nourishment, not just go through the motions. You can take a moment to find nourishment in your daily rituals, whether it's purposeful stretching when you awaken, caressing your face as you wash in the morning, or lovingly rubbing lotion into your skin rather than slapping it on. Let your daily bath or shower be a time of sensory indulgence. Nourish yourself during the day with conscious breathing, stretch breaks, or calls to friends. Make mealtimes nourishing for your body and soul by eating lunch on a park bench instead of at your desk. Read something inspirational, jot in a journal, lunch by a favorite tree, write a poem, walk in the park, meditate, take a ten-minute nap, or take in a museum exhibit. Tuck yourself in at night rather than flopping into bed.

Consciously chosen self-care is not indulgent or extraneous. It sustains you in your Vision. You finish your day energized rather than drained. It creates a baseline for living a life of MORE.

....

"When my personal coach suggested I start adding things to my life that were more nourishing, I had no clue where to start. She gave me a great tip that I use every day. I made a list of everything I could think of that would renew and restore me— taking nature pictures, calling a friend, reading a good book—and then I wrote each of them on a piece of paper and stuck it in a jar. Now, every time my youngest goes down for his nap—and other times just for fun—I pull a slip out of my self-care jar, and away I go. It's been great and it's forcing me to keep thinking of new things I like to add. Having something fun and nourishing and easily accessible has made it so much easier to resist just turning on the TV or going online to shop—my former favorite diversions. And when I feel the urge to do my soft addictions, it's because I haven't been dipping into the jar frequently enough."

—Cindy

....

Add Ability to Be with Feelings

Emotions play the most important, and most often ignored, role in self-care. People are often surprised to discover that we have an entire feelings curriculum at the Wright Institute where we teach people, step by step, to break through their beliefs about their emotions, to learn to identify them, and then to learn to express them fully and responsibly. We developed this curriculum because we have learned, through working with our students over the years, that feelings are one of the most critical building blocks for a life of MORE.

MORE ALERT

The single most detrimental function and cost of our soft addictions is that they numb us from our feelings. Without our feelings, we will never know our full power, essence, and purpose. We will never live the lives we were destined to live.

At the very core, our soft addictions are attempts to move away from our feelings. Most of us have not been raised to honor or accept all of our feelings, so we turn to soft addictions to numb them. The formula is straightforward and powerful—the more you engage with your emotions, the less you will indulge your soft addictions. Whatever your Vision is, conscious, responsible expression of your feelings draws you to it. Your emotions hold immense clues about your concerns and hungers. If you learn to be with yourself and your feelings, you learn to draw on the wisdom of your heart. Your awareness of hurt will lead you to comfort; your anger will lead to greater effectiveness; and all of your emotions will lead to greater fulfillment. Give yourself permission to feel.

Jenny was a successful executive in a large manufacturing organization. At thirty-five, she was making a great salary and on her way to another promotion. Jenny credited much of her success to being able to be "one of the guys." The formula, she thought, was to stay tough and not let your feelings get in the way of the job. It was a great strategy, except it didn't work. Jenny spent much of her time repressing or ignoring her feelings. In the evenings she would turn to her soft addiction of snacking or zoning out on the Internet to mask her feelings, which eventually would build up enough that they would pop up at unexpected times. Sitting back at her desk after a particularly intense meeting, tears would suddenly well up in her eyes. Always the consummate professional, she would quickly make her way to the bathroom and lock herself in a stall. When she was sure no one else was in there with her, she'd cry as quietly as possible until she felt like the tears weren't going to surprise her again. Then she'd hurry to the sink where she'd splash her eyes with water so no one would have any idea she'd had feelings on the job.

Jenny's relationship with her emotions completely changed after taking a course at the Wright Institute. It was revolutionary for her to learn that emotions were not only okay, but a critical part of her self-care. As she started to let herself express her feelings, her biggest fear was that she'd turn into an emotional mess on the job. To her surprise, she found that the more she learned to let her feelings be expressed on a regular basis, the less likely they were to take her by surprise. Not only that, she discovered that as she learned to notice and become aware of her feelings, she became a better manager and leader. She had a more solid sense of who she was and could respond to challenges and strategies much more effectively. Rather than being a curse, her feelings end up being a blessing, not just to her career but to her life.

<hr />

MORE TO DO

Add space to be and feel. Stop. Right now. Take a deep breath. Stretch. Close your eyes. Spend a brief moment with yourself right this minute. Aahhhh. Whether you add ten minutes of quiet time or many hours, you will learn to appreciate the empty space inside and allow it to fill with spirit instead of "stuff."

<hr />

ADD PERSONAL POWER AND SELF-EXPRESSION

While self-care is foundational, self-expression and personal power are more advanced ways we can make positive additions to our formula. With a baseline of emotional nourishment, we're more ready to learn how to use our innate personal power. Developing and expressing ourselves means we honor and express our feelings and assert our will, we develop and share our gifts and talents, and we practice positive ways of being. We generate meaning by stepping into our fullest potential, by remembering the truest essence of who we are, and by expressing it with, to, and for others.

Kyle, a freelance creative writer, was humorless. Uptight and stoic, he reserved all his creativity and expression for his writing. Meeting him in person, you would never guess his creative profession. Despite his writing success, Kyle felt like he was wasting his life, which led him to make his One Decision: *I learn and grow in all that I do, sharing myself more and more with the world.* As Kyle began to let himself be more known, he developed a healthy acceptance for all parts of himself, and started to unveil a sly, sardonic sense of humor. Coming from this well-groomed, straight-postured man, it was charmingly disarming. Before, revealing his humor was an intimate act, and now it felt refreshing and freeing. He turned less to his mood soft addictions and more to positive modes of expression. "I hadn't realized how serious and out of touch with people I had become. By unearthing my sense of humor, I feel like I unearthed myself," he shared.

Kyle's artistic ability had been previously expressed in his writing, but he began to add other forms of creative expression. He enrolled in a printmaking class and journaled and wrote poetry like he used to in college. He even read one of his poems at an open-mike poetry evening at the local coffeehouse. At work, he remains assertive yet creates deeper contact with people. His organizational skills are now being shared with others. He even began writing poetic e-mail memos and joking with his division president about problems at work. The president told Kyle that he was really enjoying getting to know him and asked him to head up the quality of life task force. Not only was his quality of life improving, but he would also help others to that end.

Add Asserting Your Will

Many of us do not have good training in asserting our will. Either we ignore our desires altogether or we irresponsibly assert ourselves. Many of us have been trained to avoid risks, to refrain from telling people what we want or what we care about, or ask for what we need. In the end we turn to our soft addictions as a way to hide from ourselves. By learning to flex our assertiveness muscle, we will not only engage in conflict and challenges more easily, but we're also more likely to receive what we desire and ultimately have a more positive impact on our world. Asserting our will encompasses a broad range of activities, from learning to ask for what we want to engaging in conflict responsibly. Practice by identifying things that you want and then ask for those things from coworkers, family members, or even strangers. As you build your asking muscle, you can even request outrageous things. You might be surprised to discover how many things you receive. You can also practice asserting yourself by saying no. Perhaps when someone asks you to do something for them and you really don't want to, but you think the "good friend" response would be to say yes, say no instead. Eventually you can keep building your skills of engaging in conflict and even fighting responsibly. The more you assert yourself in the world and go for what you want, the less you'll unconsciously turn to soft addictions to numb yourself from your desires.

....

"I took a yearlong course in personal development and at the end of it, we had a special graduation evening for friends and family. There was a song that meant a lot to us as a group and we wanted to sing it, but with its varying vocal ranges and our lack of singing ability, we weren't likely to inspire our audience! I took a risk and asked a woman I knew through church if she would be willing to sing it into a recorder so we could play it for the graduation. 'Why don't I just come to the ceremony and sing it in person?' she replied. I was blown away. Her powerful voice resounded throughout the room and was the perfect end to our ceremony. I stood there with tears in my eyes, not just for the song, but also for my gratitude in having developed this new skill of assertiveness that had delivered a gift not just to me but to the entire graduation."

—Adrienne

....

Add Developing and Sharing Your Gifts and Talents

We all have undeveloped gifts, talents, and skills. Our Vision moves closer to reality when we nurture and develop these special attributes. Whatever wonderful picture you have of yourself in the future, it emerges from these authentic gifts and not from inauthentic soft addictions. Sharing your gifts with the world is something you can do no matter the level of your gift development, whether beginner or master. For example, you don't have to be a concert pianist to share your piano playing with friends, at a nursing home, or for your own enjoyment. Perhaps you are a good listener, play a mean game of tennis, bake great chocolate chip cookies, or can change the oil in any car. Maybe you are a great letter writer, picture hanger, computer whiz, or whirlwind house cleaner. Honor your gifts and be generous with them, no matter what they are.

Add Creative Expression, Humor, and Positive Ways of Being

Soft addictions are often reactive: you react to the discomfort of a feeling or to an event that stirs feelings you haven't even identified. Conversely, creative self-expression is proactive: you put something forward of your own accord.

Creativity does not just spring from artists, musicians, and craftspersons. We can all create in every mode of expression. Expressing yourself through conversation, work, song, decorating, making a great dish for dinner, and by voicing your opinion are just some of the possibilities. Anything that creates something new and expresses an inner urge is creative. The more you create and express, the more alive you feel and the less you will numb yourself.

....

"One of my soft addictions was living through my children. So rather than carting them off to violin lessons, I decided to take lessons myself. I had never done any creative lessons, and especially not music in my entire life. I not only learned something, but my daughters and I shared the challenges and victories in learning a new skill."

—Hannah

....

If you see the humor in your behavior, you can look at yourself with a more compassionate, objective perspective. Humor tends to diminish your perfectionism, allowing you to feel more motivated to create and take risks. Maintaining a sense of humor about yourself helps you fearlessly examine soft addictions and admit some of the nutty things you do. You can laugh about the hours spent scanning the papers for the best deals on jogging shoes or about how you drift into daydreams while people are talking to you. Adding a sense of humor helps you to feel genuine delight and get naturally "high" so you don't depend on soft addictions for an artificial buzz. More consciousness and awareness means more creativity, spontaneity, and flow—all of which help you experience more natural joy and delight.

....

(MORE TO DO)

Host a "foible fest" with your friends. Share your silliest moments.

....

ADD INTIMACY

Adding intimacy to our lives can feed us in ways that our soft addictions never will. The ability to forge deep, lasting relationships—both personal and professional—can provide us with much greater satisfaction, nourishment, and success. With a foundation of nourishment and personal power, we are more willing to become closer with the most important people in our lives. Learning to be intimate means being willing to recognize the limiting rules, myths, and beliefs we have about ourselves and the world. Often this means tracing back to our childhood and looking for where these beliefs were formed, as we did with our soft addictions when we explored the Why. As we become more aware of our family training and the attitudes we've developed, we can start living according to our own rules. This is a liberating experience, allowing us to create more honest and fulfilling relationships with the meaningful people in our lives as well as the opposite sex.

At the Wright Institute, I teach a course about intimacy and family beliefs, which I have found are the foundational pieces to creating the life we want. Start now by noticing where you are, or aren't, intimate with people. Who do you engage with? Who do you avoid? The more you learn to get closer to people in your lives and develop deep relationships, you will be meeting your spiritual hungers and your soft addictions will be less attractive to you.

ADD LIFE PURPOSE AND SPIRITUALITY

Whereas self-expression finds its outlet in creative activity, life purpose and spirituality infuse our being and inform our doing. It is conscious activity.

It is an awareness of our unity with the transcendent. It means identifying our life purpose, fostering beauty, love, aliveness, consciousness, nourishment, gratitude, and compassion. Making your One Decision is a powerful step on your journey with purpose and spirituality. Where your purpose may define the why of who you are, your One Decision teaches you how to live with purpose and spirit every day. And the beauty of the One Decision is you don't need to know your purpose to make it or live it.

So often, when people decide there must be more to life, their inclination is to start seeking spirit and life purpose in church, meditation, prayer, or even pilgrimage. Invariably, however, they've missed the opportunity in each moment of life and as a result are doomed to disappointment if they don't gain more nourishment, power, and intimacy first. As you start to add MORE to your life, you'll find that you get a greater sense of meaning, purpose, and spirituality. And at the same time, the more you can add meaning and purpose to what you are already doing, the less attractive your soft addictions become.

Who would have thought that a hard-driving sales executive would experience mystical union in a business meeting, but that is exactly what happened to Mike. In the middle of a presentation, he looked around the room and suddenly comprehended that everyone wanted the best for him. His heart opened and he felt a deep caring for everyone. He realized that he was not only presenting a sales strategy, but also supporting the overall spiritual development of himself and everyone in the room. It was as if all were gathered to fulfill a higher purpose far beyond the presentation.

While this might seem to be a flight of fancy, Mike began changing the nature of his client development process out of this understanding: "I started to realize there was something bigger going on in my life than just making my numbers. I had the opportunity to touch, and be touched, by many lives as I was on my sales calls." Guided by clear purpose and spiritual perspectives, Mike began to ease his soft addiction of being driven and remaining distant from people and instead sought to add an inspirational, uplifting element in every contact he made with customers or sales trainees.

Upon hearing of an illness or seeing someone struggle or suffer, he found himself automatically saying brief prayers at work. He felt that his life of faith was deepening as he moved into increasingly vulnerable and meaningful conversations with coworkers. He became intensely curious about everyone's spiritual life. By asking others about their spiritual practices, he felt that he was learning and expanding his own. He had never thought of himself as particularly conscious or compassionate until one day when his secretary asked him what he had been doing to become so caring and aware of those around him. Mike began to find everything he did fueled by the excitement and challenge of living to his highest potential every day, in every way.

Add Being Awake, Alive, and Spiritually Nourished

Adding consciousness and awareness to life allows us to be more present and available and to bring ourselves to every moment. Increased consciousness supported by spiritual nourishment allows us to emerge from the fog and feel life coursing through us and around us.

This process can be as easy as reminding yourself to wake up and pay attention; reading a book on the power of presence; or taking a dance, yoga, or meditation class. Spiritual nourishment boosts and maintains our baseline of consciousness and aliveness, and is akin to the new leaf pushing the old leaf—the soft addiction–related behaviors—off the limb.

A spiritually nourishing moment doesn't need to take time. It's hugging a friend, capturing a snowflake on your tongue, expressing feelings, walking in the park, meditating, or pouring love from heart to heart as we gaze into the eyes of our beloved. True spirituality transcends our traditional religious views and beliefs. It's a sacredness found in everyday moments and experiencing all of life as a sacred journey.

....

"There is a big part of being a dad I think I would have missed if I hadn't started looking at my soft addictions. I still read the paper and drink coffee, but I do so with more discernment, consciousness, and purpose. My One Decision to be engaged and present helps me remember that human contact and really being with each other is more important to me. My daughter knows me more now because of how I am with her and the things we talk about. I think that means the most to me. My daughter knows me in a way that I never knew my dad."

—Casey

....

Add Beauty and Inspiration

Adding beauty and inspiration to your life nourishes your spirit. Beauty has a power to move you and make you feel better about yourself. A flower at your breakfast table, a photo of your beloved on your desk, or a beautiful screen saver lifts your spirit. Organization itself possesses a powerful beauty. Creating clean, uncluttered spaces and orderliness soothes the spirit and helps you relax. Beauty in all its forms creates a powerful doorway through which inspiration and creativity can enter.

Inspiration includes anything that touches your heart or moves your soul, such as poetry, music, stories of courage, love notes, and sacred texts. Always keep something inspirational on hand so you have instant access during transition times (such as the end of the workday) or when tempted by your soft addiction routines.

Inspiration can be simple and portable—a small booklet in your purse, an uplifting CD, or a quote or photo in your wallet. I keep a "God bag" packed with a variety of ever-changing treasures: uplifting literature, a candle, a leather-bound journal, a fountain pen, rosewater spray, or even a joke book. Plus, my suitcase never leaves home without my traveling altar with lightweight fabrics to throw over any surface, a few candles, spiritual icons, and my iPod loaded with music I love. No matter where I go, I have customized, beautiful surroundings to inspire me.

ADD ACTIVITIES SPECIFICALLY DESIGNED TO FULFILL YOUR HUNGERS

Like a grocery store stocked with ingredients for your meals, the list that follows is a storehouse of activities to feed your spiritual hungers. At the Wright Institute, students in our learning laboratories use these activities as life assignments. They challenge mistaken beliefs, open new possibilities, and teach new behaviors. Adapt these assignments for yourself, and add ideas for activities that would feed your deeper soul urges. Then you'll have a ready list of additions for creating your Formula for MORE.

Spiritual Hungers	Assignments
To know you exist	Speak up when you feel ignored until you feel acknowledged Create a ritual to welcome yourself to your day
To be seen	Show up and express yourself Do something outrageous Practice stating your preferences Dress well and consistently in a way that reflects you
To be heard	Speak up in a meeting State an opinion clearly Argue with people and challenge ideas Sing out loud in public
To be affirmed	Be with people who believe in you Ask for feedback from a friend Get positive attention five times a day by doing a good deed or greeting someone warmly
To be touched	Get a massage or facial Give and receive hugs Do a relaxation meditation, tensing and releasing every area of your body Ask your lover to hold you or even rock you like a baby Cuddle your cat or dog

To be loved	Look for evidence of being loved, cared about, thought about, and held in other people's consciousness Keep a journal of kindnesses Acknowledge to yourself when someone does a caring act for you, and record it Be with people who understand and appreciate you
To be loving	Perform random acts of love and care Write love notes to loved ones Do something to further someone's dreams Be friendly everywhere you go
To express	Feel and share your emotions Express your creativity in dance, art, writing, problem solving, or crafts Learn and grow every day Share your opinions with others Debate an issue
To be known; to be connected; to matter	Share of yourself Keep no secrets from your spouse Join a group that values truth and honesty Seek out feedback Be a good friend Empower other people's dreams—believe in them, support them, encourage them, and keep them accountable

Spiritual Hungers	Assignments
To make a difference; to fulfill your destiny	Be value-added and make contributions in every gathering you attend Volunteer for a cause that matters Contribute to everyone
To be one with the greater whole	Pray or meditate to be with God Develop an active relationship with God or spirit Commune with nature Go on a spiritual pilgrimage Practice feeling like you belong to the brotherhood of mankind Look for the divine spark in other people. Live life as a sacred journey Visualize yourself as a beloved child of a loving God

ADDING TO YOUR FORMULA

Now that you have been exposed to the wide range of possibilities that you can add to your life, start thinking about your own formula. What goals do you have and what action steps do you want to take to move toward your Vision? What would be a few goals you could pick that would help you create a life of MORE? You can begin to enter them in the Formula for MORE template found in the workbook section of the book.

SUBTRACTING IN YOUR FORMULA

Now that you have planned what to add to your life, you can look at what you would like to subtract. At this point in the process, identifying soft addictions to subtract should be easy. Think about the ones you identified previously, and add any that you've thought of since.

Subtracting might begin with your soft addiction to zoning out in front of the TV or surfing the Internet late at night. Instead, you might add a self-care routine that includes tucking yourself into bed. Or you might reduce a soft addiction to overworking when you add lunch with friends and planned more activities for after work. Subtracting self-critical thoughts and negative moods may perhaps be the most difficult, but you'll find that by expressing them to others and asking them for reassurance, you will reduce their occurrence.

Subtracting is easier when you add something compensatory first, but it can still be difficult to break long-ingrained habits. Here are a few tactics that have been helpful for others.

Subtract Temptation: Identify the Initial Step in the Cycle

What tempts you to lapse into your listless state? What activity precedes sitting down and watching lots of television? What happens right before you start a marathon gossiping session? Whatever it is, identify it and try to avoid it. Change your route to work so that you don't pass the shop where you habitually overspend. Cancel your cable subscription for your television, remove the computer games from your computer, or clean your cupboards of tempting sweets. Any change helps disrupt the soft addiction cycle. We are creatures of habit, and changing even one step of the routine decreases the temptation to indulge in it. The initial step in the cycle can be an especially important item to subtract.

Subtract in Stages

One of the most common mistakes people make in learning to subtract is trying to eliminate activities all together. Subtracting in stages, or making one small doable step, has power beyond what you realize. You

"Habit is habit, and not to be flung

out the window, but coaxed

downstairs a step at a time."

—MARK TWAIN

can start by placing doable limits on soft addiction routines. Rather than swearing off spending, limit the amount of time you give yourself to shop or establish arbitrary parameters, like refusing to eat dessert on any day starting with a T. You're changing the routine and reducing the habit gradually.

For example, you might add a comforting bedtime ritual to help you subtract your nighttime television watching. But you would also want to subtract your television watching overall in stages, starting small and increasing the limits as you go along.

Staging the limits in this fashion is often easier than setting an ambitious goal right from the start. If you are going to subtract television watching, you might first move your television out of the bedroom. Then you might limit your television watching to two hours each day. Later, you could consider canceling your cable service. The exact formula is not important; what is important is that you choose something that feels doable for you.

"When I began letting go of my soft addiction to TV, it was still a big part of my daughter's life so I let her watch when she was with me. But as a divorced dad, my time was limited with her and the TV was keeping us apart. I gradually limited her time in front of the TV, not all at once but in small stages. At the same time we added more fun activities together. Now she's taking the lead. Last month she asked me to start playing my guitar with her and now we've decided to write a couple songs together, which is much more fun than watching a concert on TV!"

—Peter

Subtract Negative Thoughts

Curbing self-deprecating thoughts and eliminating rationalizations is one of the best things you can do for yourself. This pervasive force of negativity justifies soft addiction routines and undermines your Vision. Subtracting these negative thought patterns creates room for MORE—more loving, affirming, encouraging, truthful, and empowering thoughts. You might want to revisit the chapter "Minding Your Mind" for a refresher course in countering your stinking thinking.

Subtract Clutter and Confusion

It is easier to stay conscious without distractions. Think about what's on your kitchen countertop, dining room table, or your desk. When it's clean and clear, you think twice before messing it up. A vision, by definition, is something we need to see clearly. Without clutter, important things stand out in relief.

Reduce clutter and confusion by cleaning surfaces, organizing drawers, and creating a quiet setting. Start by cleaning one drawer or a small section of countertop. Rather than turning on the television as background noise when you come home, play some inspiring music. Enjoy five minutes of your commute in the quiet, without the radio or CD playing. Get used to being with yourself.

....

MORE TO DO

Focus on what is being naturally added to your life—time, money, resources, consciousness, energy—as you subtract your soft addictions. Create a balance sheet with what you're adding next to what you're subtracting. Use this sheet as a reminder of all the good things you are bringing into your life.

....

HOW IT ALL ADDS UP TO A PLAN

We can all make our dreams come true by living according to the Math of MORE. There is no wrong way to do it. Any movement in one area influences another area. The important part is to choose a place to start and then do it.

Your Formula for MORE includes your One Decision, your spiritual hungers, and your Vision, and also helps set goals and activities to make your Vision a reality. You design it both with the activities you add and those you subtract. As you work on your formula, describe your goals in terms of measurable results rather than wishes or vague desires. Action steps should be concrete and doable, and you should choose steps that you are fairly certain you can accomplish. Keep in mind that any step toward your Vision, no matter how small, generates MORE.

Pick a time period for your goals of anywhere from a year to a month. If you set a goal for a year, break the goal down further into smaller goals you can accomplish in a month. Action steps hold the most power when they cover no more than three to four weeks. If you choose action steps that only take a day or a week to accomplish, you'll recommit, inspired by your small successes.

With all this in mind, you are prepared to create your own Formula for MORE whenever it feels right for you. There are templates and more instructions available at the back of the book to help you.

Tyler's Formula for MORE

To see the Formula for MORE in action, let's look at Tyler's approach to living his Vision using the Math of MORE. You can use this example when you create your own Formula for MORE in the workbook section of this book.

Tyler was tough. His military background had taught him to be organized and disciplined, but no matter how neat his home was or how organized his project desk was, he felt like he was missing out. He wanted MORE out of life. He watched others around him having a sense of joy, spontaneity, and intimacy he had never touched. His military background didn't provide him with tools to get the warmth and connection he realized he hungered for. Growing up on an army base, the fourth of six children, he learned early on the importance of hard work and discipline. His adult life became a series of non-nourishing yet practical routines that had become soft addictions for him. He worked out too much and ate sparsely, like he was always rationing. He dutifully upheld all of his responsibilities but took little pleasure in them. While he valued hard work, his career success meant little to him. He didn't really enjoy his achievements.

Underneath, Tyler was a caring, vital, and energetic man, but on the surface all you could see was his stoic veneer. He hungered for more human connection, flexibility, and spontaneity. He yearned to use his military training for higher purposes and to apply his fierceness to causes that mattered to him.

Tyler used the Formula for MORE to reinvent his lifestyle. First, he reviewed his One Decision and his overall Vision. Next, Tyler wrote down the soft addictions that were in the way of achieving his Vision and the spiritual hungers that he most wanted to address. Then, Tyler applied the Math of MORE to implement his Vision. He developed long-term goals and action steps, the concrete activities that would get him to his goals. For both goals and action steps, he planned what he would add to his life and what he would subtract.

EXECUTING YOUR PLAN IMPERFECTLY

Do not concern yourself with perfection or think that you have to make the choices Tyler did. The point is to align your life in the general direction of your Vision. You want the opportunity to learn, adjust, and experience an abundance of life, and that is not possible if you're frozen in some idea of perfection.

Think of it this way. If you fly on a plane from Los Angeles to New York, the pilot follows a flight path, but he does not fly directly on an exact straight line at every moment. He continually corrects course from moment to moment, turning left, then right, and back again, dealing with different flight and weather conditions. His flight plan doesn't need to account for all the different conditions that come up. View your formula in the same light and allow course corrections on your journey.

A Formula for MORE shouldn't be focused on eliminating all soft addictions. Simply getting rid of an addiction isn't that big a win. Adding more spiritual nourishment into our lives and releasing the hold of our soft addictions is what matters. We are adding sacredness to our lives and creating space for more of everything we hunger for.

Your Vision can become reality, and the good news is that you don't have to do it all by yourself. You need and deserve support in this quest, and in the next chapter I'm going to share with you the many ways you can enlist this support and draw sustenance from it.

My One Decision

I commit to a life of loving truth. I live life fully, manifesting gratitude and joy in everything I do and pursuing love and connection.

My Vision

I am a robust and vital man, a man of consequence in my world. I live strongly and fiercely, giving freely of myself. I am alive and engaged, learning and growing with excitement, constantly orienting toward higher principles and my One Decision.

My Soft Addictions

❒ Mood addiction in the form of gloomy thoughts
❒ Solitary excessive workouts and weight training
❒ Sparse, utilitarian meals
❒ Caffeine and sugary drinks
❒ Television, especially late-night viewing of violent action shows

My Spiritual Hungers

❒ To be affirmed and acknowledged
❒ To matter

What I Will Add

My Goals

❒ Increase nourishing, sustaining meals by 50 percent
❒ Add more playing: softball, biking, playing at the park with my daughter, at least once a week
❒ Increase flexibility by working out and experimenting with other ways to be in my body (tai chi, aikido, yoga) at least twice a week
❒ Provide intellectual stimulation and alternative entertainment by reading at least one good book a month
❒ Increase self-respect by increasing self-care, acknowledging my successes, seeking positive feedback from others, and bragging at least once a week
❒ Generate my own excitement and adventure instead of watching it on television by taking a risk a week and stretching myself

My Action Steps

First three weeks:

- ❏ Enjoy a three-course dinner once a week with my wife
- ❏ Get bike tuned up
- ❏ Go to bookstore
- ❏ Take a class in aikido or tai chi

Next three weeks:

- ❏ Begin reading a book
- ❏ Go on a bike ride
- ❏ Ask my wife to tell me what she admires about me
- ❏ Keep an acknowledgment journal to track my successes and the positive things others say about me
- ❏ Watch a "chick flick" with my wife (rather than another violent adventure movie) and try to find some redeeming value in it

WHAT I WILL SUBTRACT

My Goals

- ❏ Decrease soft drinks by 50 percent
- ❏ Limit workouts to one hour, and three times a week
- ❏ Limit television viewing to no more than two hours a night

My Action Steps

First three weeks:

- ❏ Drink two caffeinated sodas per day instead of four to six
- ❏ Work out six times per week instead of seven
- ❏ Move television out of the bedroom

Next three weeks:

- ❏ Drink one caffeinated soda per day
- ❏ Work out five times per week
- ❏ Enjoy one night per week without TV

9

GET SUPPORT AND
BE ACCOUNTABLE:
A LITTLE HELP FROM YOUR
FRIENDS AND YOURSELF

*"In order to fight the good fight, we need help.
We need friends . . . we need the help of
everything around us in order to take the
necessary steps toward our goal."*

—PAULO COELHO

No visionary in history ever achieved his or her Vision in solitude. Realizing a Vision and releasing your soft addictions demands more than one
person alone can supply. This is a good thing, because it forces you to
discover the comfort and joys of support as well as the certainty and direction that accountability can provide. The support of others enables
you to bring your Vision to life, while the mirror of accountability provides feedback to keep you going in the right direction.

Without support and accountability, the insidiousness of soft addictions will lure even the strongest among us. Soft addictions are so thor-
oughly woven into our society and the temptation to unconsciousness so
strong that it is only with a strong support network that we can resist pre-
vailing trends and choose a life of MORE instead. With support, we are

inspired and encouraged. And with accountability, we gain checkpoints to keep us on track.

The accountability process explained in this chapter will guide you to choose the right action steps and to establish timelines that include periodic assessment of your progress. It teaches you to build in rewards and consequences. The support system helps you surround yourself with people to guide you, to encourage you, and to celebrate you as you move toward the life you want.

....

"I'm a maverick. I don't ask for help and don't want people checking up on me. I thought support was for wimps and accountability was for uptight accountants. But somehow I joined a MORE group. I lost forty pounds, stopped eating sweets, let go of TV, and got into a regular workout routine. For the first time, I am able to consistently move on things I say I'll do. I trust myself to start and finish projects, and I have more faith in myself as I become more consistent. It was because I realized that I actually could make things happen—OK, I admit it, with some support that I am starting my own business.

—*Laura*

....

ACCOUNTABILITY

Accountability means simply that— taking account. Many people mistakenly believe that it means punishment for failure. Accountability merely suggests assessing where you are in relationship to your goals. Below you will find concrete ways that you can add support and accountability into your Formula for MORE worksheet you learned about in the last chapter and that you can find in the workbook section of the book. Building assessments into your Formula for MORE will help you avoid sliding back into your soft addiction routines.

> ### MORE-SEL
> ....
> *"If you're climbing the ladder of life, you go rung by rung, one step at a time. Sometimes you don't think you're progressing until you step back and see how high you've really gone."*
> —DONNY OSMOND

Tell People About Your Vision

As soon as you tell someone about your new Vision, you automatically make yourself accountable. Knowing that someone else knows your plans keeps you more aware and honest. Giving words to your Vision helps you to focus on what you're accomplishing and makes you more eager to live up to your declaration. Sharing gives others permission to be committed to your success.

For example, I've told many people that I am writing this book. They've responded by sending anecdotes about their soft addictions and telling me about their deeper hungers. Others send me quotes and articles and wish me well. As I wrote this paragraph, one of my students sent me an e-mail with a great quote on spiritual hungers; my niece e-mailed from Italy asking me how the writing is going; and my husband called to check in on me and remind me to have fun with the book. I am happy to be asked, "How's the writing going?" I appreciate being in other people's thoughts. Their knowledge of my goal keeps me moving toward it.

(MORE TO DO)

Discover a new kind of "Tell-a-vision." Tell someone your Vision today. Drop it into a conversation or even send an e-mail. If some asks you what's up, tell them!

Add Time Frames to Goals and Action Steps

Putting action into motion is difficult if you don't make it concrete with commitments like, by next month, I'm going to spend ten more minutes every day on this truly meaningful activity that connects to the Vision I have for myself.

All of your goals and action steps, therefore, should be assigned a time frame. Goals should

> MORE-SEL
>
> "A goal is a dream with a deadline."
> —NAPOLEON HILL

cover longer periods of time—quarterly, by season, or within a year. Action steps can be planned anywhere from a week to a month in advance. Consider them alive-lines, rather than deadlines.

When setting time frames, be realistic and don't make too big a leap from where you are now. It's generally not realistic to go from a life filled with soft addictions to one filled with nourishing activities overnight. Unrealistic time frames discourage us and cause us to abandon our plans. When you meet an alive-line, you'll feel rewarded and keep moving forward. So keep them simple and incremental to assure your success.

MORE TO DO

What are some of your goals and action steps? Put them in your Formula for MORE in the workbook section of this book. And assign yourself alive-lines. Put the steps in your date book or calendar. Keep your list with you and check your progress weekly.

Assess Progress with Another Person

Ask someone to check in with you regularly so you can report your successes and defeats. Based on the feedback you receive, you can decide to renew your plan or to readjust it. If you aren't making progress, then adjust your steps. Your buddy can help you strategize.

"I have always avoided commitments and timelines, but I finally decided I wanted to stop complaining and start living the life I really want. I joined a MORE group that would help keep me accountable from week to week. My soft addiction is clutter, and I would always make grandiose promises about what I would do, none of which I ever completed. In the group, I made a realistic goal—spending fifteen minutes working on my clutter each day for three days in the next week. I ended up doing way more than that, but it felt so good to set a goal that I intended to keep and have accountability to do it."

—Denise

Design Rewards and Consequences

Accountability encompasses both rewards and consequences. Rewarding yourself when you meet your goals gives you positive incentives for moving toward your Vision. For example, treat yourself to that new play you wanted to see when you successfully curtail your television watching for a month. Read a chapter of that great book you've had your eye on or take a luxurious bubble bath to relax after completing a task that you had been putting off. Plan conscious breaks for yourself and use them to celebrate the completion of your action steps.

Ashley had a soft addiction routine of watching a home shopping channel late into the evening. She would often fall asleep in her clothes in the living room in front of the television and wake up rumpled and confused in the middle of night. So, she set a goal of creating a bedtime ritual that was much more nurturing. If she went a whole week without falling asleep in front of the television, she rewarded herself with a treat to support her bedtime routine—a nice pair of pajamas, a sweet bedtime story, a new candle to light, a calming CD to lull her to sleep. The choices she made not only motivated her to continue working toward her Vision, but also helped provide her with more sweetness, more beauty, and more peace.

By adding rewards to your action plan, you learn to celebrate your successes. People in soft addiction routines tend to have black-or-white thinking—*Either I completely give this up or I have failed.* Celebrating the success of each small step helps reinforce new behavior and reminds you that every step counts despite back-and-forth movement. Rewards can include breaks, entertainment, or any activity you enjoy.

Be creative and set encouraging, not punishing, consequences for when you fall short of your goals. Plan realistically so one failure does not cause complete abandonment. Take a moment now to write out ideas so that you have a ready list. A consequence could be to journal about your resistance to change, or to call a friend for support. You might also design consequences that keep you aware of the costs of your behavior. For instance, you might write a check to your favorite charity to manifest the financial loss you experience when you are irresponsible with money. Design your consequences to lead you toward your Vision.

....

MORE ALERT

Beware of rewarding progress with a soft addiction!

....

....

"I work for a manufacturing company where I manage many employees. I am responsible for a monthly report that sums up where we are each month in our deliverables and productivity. Every month, I dread it for three weeks and then leave it to the night before it's due to complete—my soft addiction to procrastination! My life coach supported me instead to do a little bit of it each day and plan a reward for myself. I did just that, rewarding myself with the first massage I've ever had. It was great. I got my report done on time with no drama!"

—Rick

....

SUPPORT

Remember that part of living a great life means having more support—more people vested in your success, more encouragement, connection, resources, partnership, intimacy, and inspiration. Getting and giving support is a beautiful way to meet our spiritual hungers. The universal hungers that we all have are fed through the compassion and honesty of other people.

Kicking any sort of addiction is easier when you have support. With a circle of insightful friends to talk to, you'll find it infinitely easier to resist the allure of soft addictions. A support network provides real, meaningful relationships as opposed to surface satisfactions. Find people you can trust to give you honest feedback. They'll help you strategize and overcome obstacles as well as engender possibilities to help you achieve your Vision.

The following section provides a myriad of ideas on how to solicit and accept support for the life you want. Gather ideas as you read, then put some of them into your Formula for MORE worksheet in the workbook section of the book.

Recall a time when you received emotional support from another person. Remember how you felt when that person listened, offered advice, or demonstrated his or her care for you. Hold the positive feelings of support in your mind to motivate you to reach out to others for help.

HOW TO CREATE SUPPORT

Like many people, you may find the idea of having support attractive but the prospect of finding it challenging. How do you convince your fellow soft addictees to support you in your search for MORE? How do you meet new people who see the value in a spiritually nourishing life and recruit them to join your support group? There are many ways, and here are some of the most beneficial.

Clear your barriers to support. Many of us learned not to use support in our families of origin. Learn to recognize limiting family patterns and beliefs to open yourself to the possibilities of new types of support.

Discover supporters through new activities. Using the Math of MORE, you decided to add a variety of nourishing behaviors and activities to your life. It stands to reason that you're likely to meet people involved in these new activities who resonate with your Vision. Perhaps your formula includes going to plays, performances, lectures, or book signings. That could lead to participation in literary clubs, art museums, or a foreign affairs club. You could take up quilting, fly airplanes, or practice tai chi. All these activities will generate a new pool of people to draw support from.

> ### MORE TO DO
>
> Become a student of life. Students are curious, ask questions, and are ready to learn. Assume everyone around you has something to offer you or teach you. You'll be surprised how much support is available when you ask.

Solicit support from family and friends. Not everyone will automatically support the changes you make as you try to create this new life. In fact, people may make fun of you or treat you with disdain, disbelief, or disrespect. Don't be surprised if some actively undermine your efforts to change. Perhaps they feel threatened by the changes or are in denial about their own soft addiction routines.

Nonetheless, don't keep your desire for a more meaningful life a secret. In addition to resolving your family patterns, explain to your family and friends that you are undertaking something that has meaning for you and that you want their support. Tell them about your One Decision and share your Vision. Let them know you are creating MORE in life. From your heart, include them in what you hunger for.

Come to terms with your decision to change. When you are at peace with your decision and maintain great resolve, you'll naturally generate more support and avoid the naysayers. If, on the other hand, you're ambivalent about changing, people sense the uncertainty. They may then reflect your doubts and ambivalence in their comments and attitudes. When you feel more secure about your choices, other people's comments and opinions bother you less. The strength of your One Decision becomes stronger than anyone's negativity. However, prepare for comments like:

"Why are you doing that?"
"What do you think you are doing?"
"What makes you think you can change that?"
"What difference does that make?"
"What makes you so high and mighty that you think you're better than us?"

"You don't hang out with us anymore; do you think you're too
good for us?"

"You're such a dreamer."

> ## MORE-SEL
>
> *"Keep away from people who try to belittle your ambitions. Small people always do that, but the really great make you feel that you, too, can become great."*
>
> —MARK TWAIN

To empower yourself around your commitment, it is critical that you allow yourself to feel hurt, angry, or afraid when others don't want to change with you. Remember to express your feelings responsibly, but be sure to express them. Trust that you will find people to support you or that they will find you.

CREATE FRESH SOURCES OF SUPPORT

Anticipating negative reactions, you may have a stinking thought like, *Everyone I know is an Internet junkie; I'm never going to get them to approve of what I'm trying to change.* If you can't look to your immediate circle for support, you need to create new relationships with a different circle, whose beliefs and values are more aligned with your own. This isn't as difficult to do as you might think. Here are some easy-to-use tactics to create fresh support.

Talk to People

When most people think of support, they imagine that it has to come from a good friend, spouse, or therapist. While these are great sources, don't overlook the power of talking to anybody and everybody. The universality of soft addictions makes it a natural conversation topic. I have talked about soft addictions with complete strangers, having had stimulating discussions with waitresses, entrepreneurs, flight attendants, CEOs, housewives, ministers, priests, rabbis, tradespeople, beauty contestants, children, grandparents, high-powered advertising executives, homesteaders, home schoolers, and high schoolers. They all immediately shared their struggles or at least said, "I have a friend who . . ."

Almost every person has wrestled with soft addiction routines. Some have overcome them and now lead a life of MORE. Others may have a strong desire to overcome them. Most people are likely to be highly receptive to a conversation revolving around the subject and will provide you with verbal and emotional support as you work to change the way you live.

Give Support

When you give support, you see interactions with others as opportunities for mutual support rather than as chances to gossip or indulge in other superficial exchanges. By consciously reaching out to others, you'll encourage others to reach out to you, creating mutuality.

My husband is a master of mutual support. A very intentional man with big dreams, he is acutely aware of his Vision and goals. He also keeps the Visions of others in his consciousness all the time. Follow him for a day and here's what you see. Between coaching clients he stops at the local coffeehouse, greeting the servers behind the counter, most of whom he knows on a first-name basis—this one he's supporting on getting a degree, that one he's encouraging to use his degree. Or later, after supporting people in back-to-back coaching appointments, you might follow him to pick up his car for an afternoon appointment. On the way, he greets a neighborhood homeless person and asks him how he likes his bike—the one that Bob had arranged for someone to donate to him, only to find out that he sold it. Then on to the garage where his car is parked, he greets the valet whom he knows well because he has encouraged him to get out of drug dealing and get into making some real estate investments. Bob assumes any conversation is for the purpose of creating value for both parties. As he talks to people—anyone from the UPS delivery person, his seatmate on an airplane, a close friend, a salesman for copying equipment, a taxi driver, or a CEO he coaches in leadership training—he engages them in conversation about what is important to them and helps them identify and clarify their dreams. He delights in finding ways to support each person he comes into contact with. He'll solve problems, find resources, and inspire them with possibilities. Through these conversations, he discovers talents or resources that facilitate his own Vision or the Vision of someone in his life. Not only does he create mutual support, but he also creates a larger resource network that spirals outward, weaving a web of connection and possibility.

Participate in a MORE Group

While you can create support in many ways, don't underestimate the power of a group of people all going for MORE. Encourage the people around you to join you on your path. Look for connections at every gathering: book groups, neighborhood meetings, work teams, Bible study, committees, play groups, family holidays, sports teams, writers' groups, spiritual groups, and members of your car pool. Post a note in your neighborhood grocery store, health club, or coffeehouse.

> ### MORE-SEL
>
> *"Never doubt that a small group of thoughtful citizens can change the world. Indeed, it is the only thing that ever has."*
>
> —MARGARET MEAD

If you'd like to join or even start a MORE group, or just receive support and inspiration, log on to my Web site (www.judithwright.com) to find what you need to start a group of your own, be part of an online community, register to start a group in your area, attend a training, or even become a trainer yourself. Or, you can join the ongoing MORE groups our coaches lead by telephone or in person. You can ask questions, share victories, strategize recovery from defeats, be inspired, and find even more ways to MORE on our Web site. You'll also find a forum, quiz, soft addiction computer game, teleclasses, and more to encourage and support you on your path. Click on "Soft Addictions Solution Special Offer" and enter the code 4M6R3 to receive a special offer of support.

CONTRACTING WITH OTHERS: TAKING SUPPORT AND ACCOUNTABILITY TO THE NEXT LEVEL

While you will want to talk to as many people as you can about your Vision and plan, contracting with a few key people will provide a higher level of support and accountability. A formal contract will ensure that you both enter into the relationship with a high degree of commitment. It will keep you focused and provide more specific ways to stay accountable.

In the ongoing MORE group from the Soft Addiction Solution training at the Wright Institute, students contract with each other, monitor assignment accomplishment, share their plans, provide feedback and encouragement, trade battle stories, and report in on what has happened in their quest for MORE.

Like them, you can use various types of contracts and assignments to help you achieve greater support and accountability.

Equal Trades: Creating Support Buddies

An equal trade contract involves finding someone who is working on the same issue and making a formal commitment to each other. Talk to people to discover who is interested in what interests you. It might be someone at the gym, in your book group, or at the coffeehouse. Look for someone who has the same soft addiction routines and is interested in decreasing dependence on them. Or, you may find an individual wants MORE even if his or her routines differ from yours.

"I am an entrepreneur and my primary income really depends on my sales. But I was getting off track with too much coffee, procrastinating, and a million other diversions. Through an organization I belong to, I met another entrepreneur in the same position. We started just by sharing successes and challenges but then decided to formalize our relationship and decided we'd become primary support for each other. That was over three years ago. It's a rare day that goes by that I don't call him or he calls me to think through a complex business situation, to be cheered on for a success, or to be listened to when we've hit a roadblock or failed at something. It started out more formally and we would schedule calls with each other. Now we both contact each other naturally as part of our normal flow. I know he has saved me from some major business errors, and I've supported him to take some risks he needed to for his business. Having an agreement to mutually support each other has reaped huge rewards for both of us."

—Richard

One-Way Contracts

Realistically, you may not know someone who shares your soft addiction routines, or you might not be able to find a person interested in entering into an equal trade contract where you both support each other. Don't be shy about asking someone to hold your contract for you. Many people will gladly lend you support and feel honored that you chose them. Select someone who will be encouraging, compassionate, and caring, but who will also firmly hold you to your agreements. Tell them your Vision, goals, and action steps, as well as the timeline you created. Check in with them on a periodic basis to account for your progress, to problem-solve when blocked, and to recommit. To let them know the importance of the matter, set up a regular check-in time.

Let's Make a Deal: Trade Strengths and Gifts

You can also contract to trade strengths and resources. This type of contract works best when you ask for support and establish a clear trade agreement. Make it official and it will work much better for both of you. It is really a barter arrangement, and it's important to be clear on the specifics of the trade. If you treat it casually, so will your trading partner, and neither will hold the other accountable. Set a time limit on what you're trading and be willing to renegotiate the deal's terms at the end of the designated time.

This "let's make a deal" strategy is especially effective for married couples or other loving partners.

Nag, nag, nag. That's how Scott viewed his wife Chris's prodding him to get in shape and eat better. And Chris resented his complaints about how controlling she is, thinking, *Stop telling me how uptight I am. It's just that you are too loose!* After joining a couples group at the Wright Institute, they started to explore their relationship and realized how much they were missing the innate synergy in their couple. In many ways, they were a perfect blend and well matched to support each other. They each made their One Decision—Scott committed his life to aliveness, and Chris chose to live her life as an adventure. As a result, they contracted with each other for support.

Scott hadn't worked out since he played sports in high school and wants to be more physical. Chris is savvy about nutrition and exercise, so he asked her for support with his diet and workouts. Rather than living the adventure she craves, Chris tends to overclean the house and indulges in busywork and too much TV. She asked for Scott's support in letting go of her cleaning obsession, having more fun, and being more spontaneous. Chris promised to support Scott by cooking at least three low-fat meals a week and to plan outings like biking or hiking. Scott committed to help her take breaks and loosen up at least three times a week. He tells her jokes, brings home comedies, and sends her funny e-mails. They have a meeting over breakfast every Saturday morning and discuss their Visions and goals for the week and design their plan to support each other. They've become closer and appreciate each other, rather than irritate each other. Chris is having more fun, and Scott is in better health. Now they're also leading a group of other couples who are learning to partner with each other.

SUPPORT IS MORE THAN A TEMPORARY TOOL: THE MANY USES OF YOUR SUPPORT NETWORK

Support isn't limited to someone to talk to when you're tempted to fall back into a soft addiction routine or to hold you accountable for your new goals. People who get MORE out of their lives have a circle of support that they use in various and creative ways. They're open to help from others, whether it's a friend who's willing to lend them an ear or a professional who is able to help them deal with complex feelings. Let's look at ways in which you can use support throughout your life.

MORE-SEL

"Nothing is more powerful than a great network of support. In fact, you will not be able to break out of the grip of automatic living without the help of other people. Find new friends who are also willing to stand out the wild winds. Create a group of friends dedicated to supporting one another to make the entire group's dream come true."

—NICHOLAS LORE

Support for the Feelings that Change Brings Up

As you break free of your soft addictions and start to create the life you always dreamed of, the feelings that you have been suppressing will start bubbling up. Expect to experience feelings—all of them. Positive change is still change, and change is scary. You may feel angry from time to time as you become frustrated. You may feel more exposed and vulnerable as you strip away your soft addiction routines and become more genuine. Accept your sensitivities and see your feelings as positive. Others who understand what you are going through are invaluable. Seek other people who are comfortable with talking about and experiencing feelings and who won't be shy about telling you how they feel.

Marta, a teacher in her thirties, had made her One Decision to be nourished in everything she did. As a result, she lost a significant amount of weight and felt more energized and alive. Being more present and in touch with her body, Marta had more intense feelings than she had in years—whether joy, fear, anger, or love. Not only that, men started paying more attention to her. Though she felt flattered, she also felt more vulnerable than ever. She was so threatened by her feelings and this new attention that she started to eat more and put back on the weight she had lost, unconsciously trying to discourage men from asking her out.

Fortunately, Marta recognized that a better alternative was to seek support. She talked to people who also had gone through these changes and all affirmed the feelings that she was having, sharing their own experiences. Instead of gaining weight to protect herself from her feelings, Marta slowly began to accept that there was nothing wrong with her and in fact, there was a lot right with her. Her feelings were paving the way to her being more real and more satisfied.

Vision-Keepers Help You Keep the Faith

As we journey toward our Vision, we naturally question our decision. Most people have doubts, second thoughts, and concerns about what they are doing. Frequently, doubt rears its ugly head: *Why did I say I wanted this, anyway? It's too hard. What's so hot about making conscious changes, anyway? I* call this a "chump" conversation. In the clarity of a moment, you make the One Decision and start to create your Vision. Then you run into a difficult moment and have second thoughts. Your resistance comes up in the form of derogatory thoughts about yourself: *What was I thinking? I'm a chump. I actually believed for a second that I could have MORE in my life.* This is a critical time for reinforcements.

> ### MORE-SEL
>
> *"Sometimes our light goes out but is blown into flame by another human being. Each of us owes deepest thanks to those who have rekindled this light."*
> —ALBERT SCHWEITZER

Enlist a Vision-keeper for yourself. Ask a friend, coworker, family member, or even a boss to be your Vision-keeper. Give her your written Vision and ask her to read it to you regularly. Ask her to randomly e-mail it to you and remind you of it when you are faltering. Call her when you are having doubts. This type of support is essential, especially when you have a big dream and you start doubting it precisely because of its enormity.

I had a dream of creating a retreat and conference center where we could work with people in greater depth without the distractions of everyday life, while supported by beautiful, natural surroundings. I envisioned people growing and mutually empowering one another to transform their lives in this setting. I searched for land for more than three years, looking for something that felt right and was within two hours of Chicago, where we lived. We finally found a beautiful property replete with rolling hills, forests, and native prairie situated around a lake. The buildings, however, were a mess. There was beautiful architectural design, but no one had ever finished the buildings. They were rotting from neglect and water damage. Animals had burrowed into the buildings, mice ran rampant, water poured in the walls. Most of our friends told us we were crazy when they saw the property. They said if we did buy the place, we should torch the buildings. They shook their heads in disbelief.

....

(MORE TO DO)

Volunteer to be a Vision-keeper for someone you know who is making positive changes in his or her life. Feel the sanctity and honor of holding a Vision for another.

....

At the time, we also had a lovely home in an exclusive suburb that we had just redone and decorated. Why would we give that up for this ramshackle place? One of our friends, a founding member of Findhorn, the famous intentional spiritual community in Scotland, knew what could happen when people followed and built from spirit. She believed in what we were doing and could see our Vision clearly. She became our Vision-keeper. When we became discouraged and wondered whether we were doing the right thing, we would call her. She reminded us of the importance of our Vision and her belief in us. She never faltered in her belief and her stance. She played an essential role in making the big leap to establish the Prairie Spring Woods Conference and Training Center, which is now a flourishing, successful enterprise, serving many people.

Creating a Life Team

Support isn't just for the present, but also for the future. Creating the life you want isn't about crossing a finish line and winning the race. It's an ongoing process, and though it's important to have people supporting you as you move toward your goals, it's just as important to have people helping you after you've achieved them.

For this reason, creating a life support team makes sense. In essence, the team consists of committed people living MORE. Purposeful, growth-promoting, and inspiring interactions with your team will be the norm. Your interactions will be relaxed, but never casual. Mutual purpose defines all you do.

Most of us, however, don't consciously pick our friends and actively decide who might best help us achieve our vision. As a result, we don't naturally create a life support team. Instead, we surround ourselves with people who like to do the same things we like, which often means we hang out with our soft addiction partners. Celeste is someone who has gotten past this and built a life support team in a highly conscious manner.

Celeste, an entrepreneur in her early forties, owns a beauty salon whose client roster includes television stars, harried professionals, and others who view her salon as an oasis of calm and care. The value she provides reaches far beyond the services she offers. People may stop in for a facial, but walk out talking about their dreams and feeling renewed in the very core of their spirit. She views the services she provides as part of a larger spiritual mission to serve others. In addition to her thriving business, she's a mother of two, devoted wife to her husband and now a student who is taking college courses on the side to complete her degree. Originally from Eastern Europe, Celeste appreciates the opportunities she found here and wants to take full advantage of them. Life is a rich experience for Celeste, and yet she constantly hears her family and friends saying, "Slow down, you do too much. Why are you so busy? How come you don't come to all the family gatherings? Who do you think you are?" Their lifestyles are very different, and they feel threatened and judge her for all she is doing.

MORE ALERT

Be prepared for jealousy and resentment from unsupportive people who may try to make you feel guilty about doing so many positive things. They may even mask this jealousy as concern. Having the support of others who are not threatened by your success is essential.

Though she loves her family, Celeste has had to make a conscious choice not to allow them to hold her back. Despite their feelings about it, she picks and chooses family events to attend, and prefers deep contact with the individuals in her non-family circle. She has recognized that she needs people who truly support her mission, who will cheer her on in what she's doing, who don't belittle her accomplishments. Socializing and just hanging out aren't enough for her. She wants to connect deeply with people, share goals and encouragement, and talk about things that matter. Rather than getting stuck with the built-in support her family has provided, she's now chosen to surround herself with other people who are going for their dreams. She loves to be with entrepreneurs making a difference in the quality of their world, and her husband has become her greatest cheerleader. Celeste's One Decision is to make the world a better place for having been in it, and she is working toward building a team who will help her leave her mark.

Like Celeste, you can assemble a similar life support team. This doesn't mean that you exclude everyone from your life who remains stuck in a soft addiction routine, but it does mean you form a group you can rely on to keep you focused on the MORE for years to come. To build this team, keep the following guidelines in mind:

Pick supporters. Look at candidates for the team as supporters rather than just socializers. Fun people are great, but that is not the criterion for membership.

Make conscious choices. Be conscious in your choices; don't just fall into relationships or blindly accept someone for your team just because you grew up with her or have worked with him for years.

Expect more. Insist that people bring their gifts to the party.

Go for depth. Look for interactions with depth, a deeper sharing of life goals, inner yearnings, and strategies to live MORE.

Change your filters. Be aware of how you screen out people you deem inappropriate or not your type. Using different filters can open you up to new possibilities.

Seek Role Models and Inspiration

As you become more aware of conscious living and get more involved in meaningful, soul-inspiring activities, you're bound to encounter people who serve as models for a life of MORE. They are the people who treat life as a sacred journey and have learned to manage their soft addictions. Finding these role models—who provide the support of "I did it, and you can too"—is not as difficult as it might seem. When you open your mind as well as your eyes, you'll see that role models surround you.

Look for people who are alive, vital, and who make a difference. Watch for emotionally available individuals who possess these qualities. Pay attention to people serving mankind in some way or who seem blessed with an abundance of energy and wisdom. Read biographies of people with great achievements in their lives; watch the media for stories of individuals making a difference in the world.

> ### MORE-SEL
>
> *"To me, real friends are those people who will stand for you expressing yourself fully, who will go out of their way to support you to keep your word, to go the extra mile, to get out of the box, to make your dreams come true. The only people who will do that are those who are doing it themselves."*
>
> —NICHOLAS LORE

One of the most inspiring lives of MORE is chronicled in *Acres of Diamonds*, by Russell Conwell. Conwell believed that all the riches in life lie within each of us and are available if only we seek them. Through his life as a soldier, a minister, an attorney, and the founder of Temple University, he demonstrated the power of making the One Decision and of living his life in accordance with it.

Consider, too, the life of Saint Ignatius of Loyola. Ignatius was a wealthy, vain party animal who spent much of his time carousing with friends. After receiving a leg wound in a skirmish, Ignatius fretted over the look of his wounded and potentially misshapen leg in the fashionable tight stockings of the day. While recuperating, the only reading material available was *The Lives of the Saints* and the Bible. To his surprise, the people he was reading about fascinated and elevated him. They led much more exciting and inspiring lives than he. St. Ignatius followed the stirring of his soul to make what we might call his One Decision. After his recuperation, he laid down his sword in an all-night vigil to Our Lady of Montserrat and continued on the path that led him to sainthood.

Getting MORE out of life doesn't mean that you seek sainthood, but the example of people seeking a deeper life can have a positive effect on your own life. Be inspired, not daunted, by people going for making a difference in the world. Recognize that you have the same hungers. They have made their One Decision and harnessed their life energies in pursuit of their dreams, and so can you.

DRAW SUPPORT FROM SPIRIT/GOD

Praying to a higher power and deepening your relationship with spirit are tremendous sources of support for people trying to live a life of MORE. You can seek this support in any way you choose. For instance:

Have conversations with God or your definition of spirit. Ask for help in adding positives and resisting soft addiction temptations.

Feel your prayer. If you say the Lord's Prayer ("Our Father . . ."), let yourself really feel the words "lead us not into temptation."

Pray for guidance. Ask to be shown ways to develop and use your gifts.

Let spirit be your guide. Develop spiritual practices and bring God or spirit more directly into the fabric of your daily life. Make God your confidant and best friend, as close as a lover, as familial as a sister or brother, as accepting as a divine, loving parent.

Reveal your heart. Tell God about your hungers and the yearnings of your heart.

As I write, I often type a prayer and then listen to the response of spirit. It connects me with a sense of something greater. I no longer feel alone; I feel that I can draw upon vaster resources than my own. Do the same thing when you're struggling with your soft addiction routines and attempting to pursue more meaningful activities and moods. Say a prayer about your struggle and leave yourself open to a response.

(MORE TO DO)

Many studies now indicate the efficacy of prayer. Ask someone you know to pray for your success in creating MORE in your life. Watch what happens!

Look for spiritual support in the natural world. Lie on a bed of soft grass, feel the wind caress your skin, gaze on nature's rivers, lakes, and oceans. Walk in the woods, lunch in the park, work in your garden, applaud the sunset, and look for constellations in the night sky. Sense the rhythms of nature and seek the wisdom encoded in the seasons and growth cycles. The natural world inspires and enlightens us in ways that people can't. Raising our awareness of nature and attuning to its rhythms will steer you away from your old routines and toward a more fulfilling life.

PUTTING SUPPORT INTO ACTION

Now that you've learned how to garner support, it's time to revisit the Math of MORE. In the Formula for MORE, you looked at goals and action steps that added activities and behaviors aligned with your One Decision, and subtracted activities and behaviors that pushed you toward your soft addictions.

Now you'll put your newly created support system into action. Look at the Formula for MORE in the workbook section of this book. You'll notice that there is a column where you can include a reward and consequence for each goal and action step you select as well as a specific aliveline. When you complete your Formula for MORE, be sure to plan in your support. (Remember, you can visit www.judithwright.com for support, too.) Use the examples in this chapter to guide and inspire you. Commit to being supported and when you complete the form write down by whom, when, and how you'll be supported. Sharing your life with others who support you is living MORE.

GIVE YOURSELF THE GIFT OF SUPPORT

No question, asking for support can make you feel vulnerable. Whether you're offering up a prayer or requesting that a friend form a contract with you, you're revealing yourself to someone else. This can be scary. Receiving support, too, creates more intimacy in your life. While we all say we want closeness, we may be scared of people knowing us that well. We may be afraid of setting up accountability, thinking, *What if I fail? What if I don't measure up?* We may also feel like we're not worthy of receiving help from others. We're afraid of being a burden or bothering someone else. Or perhaps we feel like we should be totally independent and not need anyone.

As difficult as all these things may be, recognize that you not only need support but that you deserve it. The more we take on, the more support we need. To ask for help and sustenance is not a sign of weakness, but a sign of resolve, intent, and purpose. Think about the support Olympic athletes need. They have coaches in all aspects of their sport—chiropractors, choreographers, massage therapists, orthopedic specialists, sports psychologists, nutritionists, and business managers—to support their bodies, minds, and spirits. Going for MORE means participating in the spiritual Olympics. For athletes, support is a sign of their dedication. Let the support you generate be a sign of your resolve to have MORE in your life.

10

DETOURS ON THE ROAD TO MORE . . . AND HOW TO GET BACK ON THE PATH

*"It's not whether you get knocked down;
it's whether you get up again."*

—VINCE LOMBARDI

The road to breaking free of your soft addictions and creating the life you want is a winding road—a road that goes deeper, not just farther. Unlike predictable soft addiction routines, this road forges into new experiences and challenges. So it's easy to become sidetracked. The purpose of this chapter is to encourage success on your journey by preparing you for bumps in the road, breakdowns, getting stuck, roadblocks, backsliding, and blowouts.

Not that breakdowns are bad or blowouts necessarily to be avoided. The people I coach discover that there are opportunities and lessons in each detour. Bumps generally lead into new opportunities and territory. Wrong turns can actually enrich your journey.

Reading about a trip and going on one are two different things. Books, by their very nature, make any process appear simpler and more straightforward than it actually is. As you've read about the Soft Addiction Solution skills—from articulating a One Decision to identifying your soft addictions to developing a Vision, and so on—it might seem that if you do A, B, and C, you'll arrive quickly at the life you want and stay there.

The skills of this book aren't a simple step-by-step process that you easily complete and then you are done. They are skills to build and apply throughout your life. These aren't eight easy steps and then you are "fixed"—in any sense of the word. You are not broken, so you don't need to be fixed. These skills are guides to living that you can apply over and over again to create a richer and more meaningful life. The more you apply them, the more benefits you'll get. And achieving MORE happens only after you've tried, failed, gone down dead ends, hit reverse and then gone forward, and cleared formidable hurdles. You may even realize your Vision, live your One Decision, and still fall back into your soft addiction routines. While such stop-and-go progress can be frustrating, it can also deepen your appreciation and experience of the magnificent life you're building.

You'll need guidance to keep you on track and to keep a detour from becoming a dead end. At the end of the chapter, you will learn to use these five Rules of the Road to MORE to encourage your success by supporting you through the inevitable frustrations of your journey.

RULES OF THE ROAD TO MORE

1. Be prepared.
2. Don't panic.
3. Ask for help.
4. Keep going.
5. Learn and grow along the way.

The Rules of the Road have kept me, and hundreds of people I have worked with, on the road to MORE. Breaking free of your soft addictions means that you must deal with the challenges of going into the unknown, learn to grapple with strong emotions, and handle success and the feelings of unworthiness that often accompany that success. These challenges can derail the most dedicated road warrior without the Rules of the Road. However, forewarned is forearmed, and this chapter is written in the spirit of Rule #1: Be prepared. So, fasten your seat belt. It's a wild ride—but more than worth it, a journey to the life you want to live.

JAKE'S JOURNEY

Now let's take a look at Jake and the types of bumps you can encounter and breakdowns that can happen. By following his journey, you will learn to recognize and anticipate the most common pitfalls. You'll see Jake's triumphs and mistakes and how he benefits from both. You'll become aware of the challenges ahead and how these Rules can keep you on track despite the obstacles that arise.

Jake, a charming, successful entrepreneur, had admitted his soft addictions: overspending on clothes and gadgets, being cool, taking risks, and what he called being "on the prowl." He loved the feeling of being on the edge in his entrepreneurial wheeling and dealing and liked the high that came from taking chances in many areas of his life.

Jake began what he thought would be a journey toward MORE by deciding to tone his body and get rid of the "bumper" around his waist. He thought that this was the only barrier to true happiness for him. He lost the extra weight, but no matter how much sharper he looked, or how much stuff he bought, how many women he dated or big deals he closed, Jake couldn't shake an emptiness inside. He never felt he had enough, made enough, or was enough. Jake's daily routines were spiritually bankrupt.

Jake Uncovers His Hungers

After attending a men's weekend at the Wright Institute, Jake saw his obsessions more clearly. He began to understand how his fixation on appearance, his drive to acquire things, and his pursuit of an adrenaline rush were rooted in feeling inferior, particularly to his father and other successful men. No new Ferrari, trophy girlfriend, or million-dollar deal could ever truly assuage this feeling.

It took this realization for Jake to discover the hungers beneath his soft addictions—his need to be seen, affirmed, and loved. Once he owned up to these hungers and made his One Decision to be genuine and live a life of integrity, Jake could start taking steps toward the life he really wanted and hungered for. He reined in his recklessness in business, curbed his spending, and started spending more time with new, supportive friends who appreciated Jake for who he was, not what he had. Jake met strong men who challenged his superficiality. He shifted his focus in business from just closing deals to actually enjoying contact with his clients. As Jake's natural gregariousness and good humor emerged, clients started looking forward to his visits. Once he stopped trying to act rich and followed his Formula for MORE, Jake found true wealth in a life that was rewarding and affirming.

Jake Slips into Reverse

Yet after a while, Jake began inexplicably doing things that took him away from the MORE that he had achieved. He started isolating himself and stopped getting together with his friends. He took daredevil risks while skiing, and began overspending again. In place of the positive activities he'd developed, Jake started substituting new soft addictions, like surfing the Internet for hours at a time.

What happened? Life was giving Jake much that he'd dreamed of, but he was turning his back on all the rewards. While Jake loved the joy, bliss, and deeper connection to spirit that he felt, he hadn't prepared himself for the increased awareness and onslaught of feelings that emerged as he stopped numbing himself with soft addictions. He was becoming acutely aware of his pain, fear, and anger. And when Jake felt angry, he couldn't sustain his "good ol' boy" demeanor—nor do "good ol' boys" cry much.

Frightened by the new feelings of intimacy and closeness he was experiencing, he pulled away from his new friends and started hanging out with his daredevil, gadget-obsessed cronies again. He seemed to drop off the planet, screening his calls and never returning those from his supportive friends.

Patricia, one of Jake's most supportive and loyal friends, stopped by his house. At first Jake didn't want to see her, but she refused to leave until he let her in. As they talked, Jake claimed he didn't truly care, that this journey toward a meaningful life was stupid, and that he'd been better off before he began discovering himself. For a long time, Patricia just listened. Then she started patiently questioning Jake about his choices.

Jake Has a Breakthrough

Gradually, Jake started to see for himself where and why he'd panicked. As he admitted his fears to Patricia, he relaxed. He saw that he hadn't been bad or weak, but simply scared and ill-equipped to deal with his fears. His willingness to learn, grow, and pursue MORE reasserted itself. With Patricia's help, Jake remembered his One Decision and the things he had enjoyed about the quality life he had been creating, including his warm friendship with her. In a candid and tender moment of clarity, he admitted that while he had deeply missed her, he hadn't felt comfortable with or deserving of the warmth and caring she shared so freely with him. He didn't think he'd earned it. He saw that he'd been overwhelmed by the new richness of his life and the wealth of friendship that had come his way.

So Jake's breakdown became an opportunity for breakthrough. When he realized what was going on, he experienced an *aha* moment. Jake had used soft addictions to hide from his emotions. As he challenged those addictions and began creating a life of more meaning and connection—the life he wanted—deeply buried feelings surfaced, not all happy ones. Seeing that he was going through predictable highs and lows permitted Jake to accept himself, reorient to his One Decision, and discover additional spiritual hungers—to feel secure, to feel safe, and to trust. With these hungers firmly in mind, he began learning the skills to go about meeting them more directly. For instance, he learned to talk more about what he was feeling, which allowed others to support him and provide reassurance and comfort. He started dating women who were warmer and more available emotionally, instead of just good-looking. He shared more with everyone, and expected more in return.

Looking back, Jake was able to identify his detour as a learning experience. He saw how dealing with his "feelings overload," as he called it, had called for skills he didn't possess yet. He wouldn't have been aware of his negative beliefs or had the opportunity to shift them without the detour he

> ### MORE-SEL
>
> *"What gets in your way can take you to someplace new."*
>
> —SARAH EAST JOHNSON

took. Understanding that he could expect detours prepared him to deal with future challenges, recover more quickly when they occurred, and even learn from them as they arose.

BREAKDOWNS BECOME BREAKTHROUGHS

When you follow the Rules of the Road to MORE, you can turn each breakdown into a breakthrough. Each time you make progress and then backslide, you have opportunities to learn more about yourself and identify the new skills you need to learn. Things looked pretty bleak for Jake before he turned his situation around with Patricia's help. Jake didn't know that breakdowns are a normal part of growing and changing. So when he started feeling and behaving in unfamiliar ways, he assumed that something was wrong.

It wasn't. A child learning to walk falls many times before finding his balance and mastering this new skill. If every child waited to try walking until he could do it without stumbling, we'd crawl all our lives. In the same way, breakdowns are predictable missteps as we learn to lead bigger, more complex, less predictable lives.

From his breakdown, Jake learned to expect more ups and downs and to be compassionate with himself when they came. Breakdowns are neither failures nor excuses or reasons to give up. They teach us where we're vulnerable in our growth, so we can develop particular skills to support ourselves.

....

MORE TO THINK ABOUT

Did you ever experience a failure that magically turned into a great opportunity? Upon reflection, do you believe in the adage, As one door closes, another door opens?

....

When you discover your motivation for returning to a soft addiction routine or unearth the underlying hunger that caused you to backslide away from your Vision, you peel away the built-up layers that obscure the deeper, more essential you and your inner motivations. You'll have more data about your life, and you'll see more of what you need to learn to succeed on the journey. Remember, the win in this game is consciousness. The more aware you are, the more you will be learning and winning the game.

CHALLENGES ON THE ROAD TO MORE

There's a little (or a lot) of Jake in all of us; namely, fears of the unknown, shutting down in the face of them, backsliding, and losing our way for a while. Although challenges can come in many varieties, there are three common forms. Keep these challenges in mind as we see how Jake responded and broke the basic Rules of the Road when he needed them most.

Challenge: MORE Feelings

If we are successful in subtracting our soft addictions, we will be successful in unearthing more feelings—pleasant ones and difficult ones, but most important, *strong* ones—which are nothing like the dull, muted feelings we had when we were sleepwalking through a softly addicted life. Sometimes, on

> MORE-SEL
>
> *"Never apologize for showing feeling. When you do so, you apologize for truth."*
> —BENJAMIN DISRAELI

the way to our goal, we return to soft addiction routines to numb the freshly uncovered feelings. If you view feelings negatively, you may find yourself falling into this trap. Unlocking our negative beliefs about emotions, learning to be with our feelings, to befriend them, and express and resolve them are one of the most critical paths to living the more fulfilling life we yearn for.

Challenge: Unknown Territory

Because soft addiction routines are just that—routines—they keep us in known and predictable situations. The road to MORE is a road into the unknown, a path of change. Going into the unknown can be overwhelming and threatening, especially if we are unprepared and have not developed strong naviga-

> MORE-SEL
>
> *"I have accepted fear as a part of life— specifically the fear of change . . . I have gone ahead despite the pounding in the heart that says: turn back."*
> —ERICA JONG

tional skills. Without soft addiction routines, we experience variation and uncertainty and a very different sense of space and time. This unknown new territory can also provide many uplifting and energizing experiences. However, we need new skills to negotiate the unknown.

Challenge: Your Feelings of Self-Worth

Your beliefs about your worth can be challenged as you create a bigger life. If you don't feel deserving, it is hard to pursue MORE. Your successes, ironically, may expose mistaken, unconscious beliefs that you're unworthy, undeserving, unloved, or unlovable.

> ### MORE-SEL
>
> *"We cannot achieve more in life than what we believe in our heart of hearts we deserve to have."*
>
> —JAMES R. BALL

We yearn for success without realizing that victory can be just as destabilizing as setbacks. Tears of celebration and frustration are equally possible on this journey, and can be equally unnerving. Jake backslid because he felt uncomfortable with all the feelings that his success was bringing him. He turned back to his bad habits to help him check out emotionally.

"Compared to my wife, I grew up on the wrong side of the tracks, in a blue-collar neighborhood where status quo was the name of the game. When I started letting go of my soft addictions and creating a new life, I had great success—but then I got stuck a lot. I started my own business and was making five times more than I had ever dreamed of. I was closer to my kids and my wife than I had ever been. I realized that I wasn't very accustomed to success on that kind of scale. I kept seeing myself as a blue-collar guy from the wrong side of the tracks, but now I was on the other side of the tracks—and it was freaking me out. I had several friends who had to keep supporting me, even though I fought them tooth and nail, to tell me that I deserved everything that I was receiving. They were able to remind me what I was capable of even when I couldn't remember myself."

—Connor

BLOWOUTS ON THE ROAD TO MORE

Not all of us will have a blowout the way Jake did. We're more likely to get stuck, stall, or backslide and then rouse ourselves to get moving again. Blowouts, which happen when the implications of living differently overwhelm us, are extreme, erratic reactions caused by reliving old experiences, reawakening buried fears, or releasing old pain. They are rarely predictable and often take place following high levels of achievement. Frequently, a blowout is a reaction against a radical redefinition of the self, which can happen as we reach beyond what we've known.

MORE TO THINK ABOUT

When have you been stuck, or experienced a breakdown, backsliding, or blowout? Are there any roadblocks in your life right now? What resources could you use to help?

For Jake, changing his definition of himself was threatening. Going from a cavalier, glib, cool, successful guy with surface banter and many acquaintances to a man who was starting to invest more deeply in himself and others, tell more truth, and actually have people close to him was challenging. He saw he had the capacity to be successful as both a competitive businessman and as a friend. The support his new friends were giving him was proof he could be this different person. Combining such high expectations with Jake's relatively immature life skills and newly emerging emotions was too overwhelming. Blowouts most often occur when individuals do not have a strong relationship with their feelings. Rather than face this new force in their lives, they may instead panic and flee.

PLAYING BY THE RULES

Here's how the Rules of the Road can help you deal with these challenges. Applying these rules doesn't mean you'll never hit rough patches as you go for MORE. But they can ease a backslide, or shorten the time you spend trying to get back on the path if you lose your way.

Rule #1: Be Prepared

People who succeed at any adventure usually do a good job of preparing. And don't kid yourself, no matter how well things are going now, there will be bumps along with successes and plateaus on the journey. I have learned from backpacking and global travel that anticipating problems is key, because things often happen to me that I wasn't expecting. Yet if I've prepared well, I usually have enough tools and resources to deal with surprises.

In its early years, the Peace Corps found that nearly half of its volunteers bailed out prematurely on their two-year assignments abroad. Research revealed that the volunteers were not adequately prepared for the challenges posed by their new environments. When the Peace Corps added classes to teach volunteers how to anticipate problems and succeed in a new culture, the number of those returning home early became negligible. Later, budget cuts forced the Peace Corps to drop this training, and volunteers once again began leaving the program before completing their assignments. In other words, be prepared and beware of too much too soon. If you don't put a strong foundation under your structure, it can crash.

Jake, for instance, failed to prepare for problems. As he dropped his soft addictions and changed his life, he felt like a tourist in unfamiliar emotional territory. His usual landmarks were missing. Everything around him looked different, felt different, and seemed to operate by different rules. Because he hadn't expected daily emotional surprises, Jake hadn't come prepared with tools to help him understand or care for himself in his newly vulnerable state.

Like a tourist heading for unfamiliar parts, Jake could have prepared himself by taking classes or talking to others who'd visited this state of being. He could even have picked a buddy to check in with regularly for information and reassurance. By choosing to do it all himself, Jake increased his chances of getting homesick for his old soft addictions when he felt overwhelmed by the newness of his changed life.

Rule #2: Don't Panic

If you find yourself returning to a soft addiction routine or doing something else far removed from the Vision you've created, don't panic. Backsliding and breakdowns are part of the process. Knowing this, you'll be prepared for one of the great emotional challenges you'll face—namely, dealing with your fear.

Jake's panic showed up as a return to old patterns of addiction. Unable to admit even to himself that he was afraid and upset, Jake didn't recognize his blowout until Patricia helped him see it.

The greater our fear, the stronger and more unreasoning our attraction to old habits of being and thinking becomes. The fact that Jake didn't even want to hear from people he cared deeply about shows how powerful his fear had become. Above all, he just wanted to soothe himself, and he was willing to backslide enormously to do that.

Until we can name our panic, it runs us. Being able to accept what frightens us is like shining a light under the bed. What we think are scary monsters turn out to be little more than our own imagination. Checking out our worst fears with others can also be very reassuring, for we see we aren't alone. Everybody gets scared, and usually about the same things.

Rule #3: Ask for Help

Jake seemed to flee help rather than asking for it. We must wonder if the thought even occurred to him. Remember our earlier discussion of support? If you are nearing a hazard on the road, this is when you'll need support! Get used to asking for guidance and help early in the game, when you seem to need it less. If you use support consistently, it is already there when you most need it. Men are notorious for refusing to stop for directions when they get lost. Yet women are guilty of not reaching out sufficiently for help as well. The reason we set up MORE groups at the Institute is so that people have a built-in group of support who will hold a vision for them and keep them on track with their goals. We aren't generally trustworthy to reach out for this kind of support when we most need it.

And while we're talking about support, it's vital that you think carefully about whom you ask for help. I cannot overemphasize the importance of reaching out to people who will truly support and empower you, not those who will discourage you when you need guidance. Some people, sensing your vulnerability, might use it to drag you down. Jake's fear took him off the path until Patricia reawakened his willingness to learn, grow, and pursue MORE.

If someone asked us to lift an enormous stone or tree, we wouldn't hesitate to ask others to help. Yet we often try to shoulder enormous emotional burdens alone. If we were navigating a new country, the first thing we'd do is ask for route guidance. But we think we should be able to transform our lives and navigate new relationships without help.

It can be hard to admit "I just don't know." As adults, we think it's our job to have the answers. Jake felt increasingly vulnerable as he ventured further toward the life he wanted. He imagined that everyone understood life better than he did. The irony of asking for help is that we often find others feel just as vulnerable as we do—and out of the shared vulnerability, wonderful support can grow.

....

"I joined a MORE group as a way to ask others to help keep me on track with my Vision. It's funny because I commit to these small, doable steps each week, but many of them I end up doing right before I come into the group because I know they're going to hold me accountable. Once I had committed to exercising twice in one week. When the day of the meeting arrived, I hadn't done it yet but I wanted to make my goal. I ended up working out in the morning and then, rather than driving to the meeting, I rode my bike. It was fun and I found a new way to fit in exercise."

—*Simon*

....

MORE-SEL
....

"Even if you are on the right track, you'll get run over if you just sit there."
—WILL ROGERS

Rule #4: Keep Going

Not only did Jake fail to keep going, he had no mechanisms to help him persist and alert him of the dangers of slipping. Even when you feel yourself sliding backward, it's important to keep going. You never know what agent of Providence is

waiting to help if only you do your
part and persist.

Cling to your goals, even if you
have to start over in moving toward
them. Establish some simple action
steps in your Formula for MORE
that become regular routines and
support your new lifestyle. You may

fall off the wagon from time to time, but so what? So does everyone. Dust
yourself off and climb back on.

Jake would have helped himself if he'd set up more routines that
countered his soft addictions. For instance, working out in the evenings
with covoyagers would have cut into his time to surf the Internet. He also
made the error of losing contact with the friends who supported him.
Even if you backslide or get stuck, keep up your disciplines. Keep going
even when it seems pointless. Chances are that, with patience, your efforts will be rewarded. Eventually your clarity will return enhanced, and
with it, renewed determination.

Rule #5: Learn and Grow Along the Way

Wherever you are on your path, there is a lesson to learn or a sight to
see. This is especially true when you feel stuck, in a breakdown, or
freaked out. You can always take in new information. Learning is knowing something today that you didn't know yesterday, and growing is developing the ability to do something you couldn't have done if you hadn't
had a certain experience. Learning and growing make us much more re-
silient and better able to respond to the bumps in the road. Being able to
see the lessons that every hit, wrong turn, dead end, and backslide pres-

MORE TO DO

Keep a daily growth journal. Write down your challenges, lessons
learned, the skills you developed, or future activities needed to
develop them.

> ### MORE-SEL
>
> *"Don't go through life,
> grow through life."*
>
> —ERIC BUTTERWORTH

ents takes skill. In the workbook section of the book, you'll find exercises to help you to notice and document what you are learning and how you are growing so that it just becomes a part of your regular routine and lifestyle.

At the root of our breakdowns is our difficulty in accepting ourselves. At the deepest level, this is a question of faith rather than psychology. It is a question about our view of our place in the world. Are we embraced by a loving universe? Are some people more worthy than others? Am I worthy of a great life?

The next chapter presents the key to shifting our beliefs about our place in the world. It reveals the source of both my faith in genuine emotional expression and my belief that we are loved and worthy. Join me in the next chapter as we explore four loving and transformational truths and discover how they can inspire and support each of us on our path to MORE.

11

THE FOUR
LOVING TRUTHS

The road to MORE is a spiritual path, and all who travel it embark on a sacred journey. Following this path can lead you toward life's essential truths, as it did for me.

On a sacred journey with Bob in France, we were steeping in places where people had worshipped for millennia, communing at sites of miracles, praying in ancient cathedrals, and sharing worship with modern day monks. I was meditating on divine love, inspired by our experiences. While sitting at a Parisian sidewalk café typing into my computer, these simple yet profound truths came to me, flowing like divinely inspired guidance. I call them the Four Loving Truths, and they have helped me both when I am at loose ends and in the peak flow of joyful creativity. When I've doubted myself or lost my way, they've guided me back to the path. When I've struggled, they've brought me back to myself. When I've needed inspiration, they've made it clear why I was on my path. When I live in accordance with these Truths, I have no need for my soft addictions. Spirit sustains me instead.

As you learn to recognize and live by the Four Loving Truths, you will notice the quality of your life changing, revealing a richness and a sense of belonging. It's not necessary to believe these precepts in order to benefit from them. You just need to operate as if they are true. As you align with the Four Loving Truths and open yourself to the possibility of MORE in your life, you more easily release your soft addictions. And as you apply the eight key skills you have been learning, you will more deeply experience the power of these Truths.

As you've learned, mistaken beliefs about your feelings and your self-worth can lead to faulty thinking and send you off on detours. Orienting to the Four Loving Truths corrects these mistaken beliefs. Living in accordance with these Truths rather than with mistaken beliefs lessens the need for soft addictions.

Now let's turn to these Truths, discover the inspiration they offer, and look at how you might align your life with them.

THE FIRST LOVING TRUTH: YOU ARE LOVED

> *You are loved beyond your own imagining. You may not feel it, know it, or even believe it, but the truth remains that you are loved. You are a beloved child of a loving universe. Nothing you can do will make the love go away, for it is your birthright. Is there anything we want more than to be loved? Is there anything that we fear more than the possibility that we are not loved? Our fears are groundless. What we most wish for, we already have. Love is abundant. It is we who block the reception of love, who believe we are not loved, or lovable, or who feel as if we can never get enough.*

When you align your life with this Truth, you can experience total satisfaction. You will discover how your life transforms when you can access the infinite love of spirit each moment that you live.

We can trace much of our pain and suffering to the belief that we are not loved and that we are unlovable just as we are. We think we have to earn love and we don't feel that we are able to be good enough or perfect enough to be loved enough. Nothing is further from the truth. Love is not something that can be earned. It is an abundant resource available to all of us, all of the time.

It isn't that love isn't available; it is that we are not available to love.

Our hunger to be loved and our mistaken belief that we are not loved

lead us to seek refuge in soft addictions. We think we will be more lovable
if we have the great new car or the designer clothes. We think others will
think we are worthy if we gossip and share the secrets of others. We exercise for hours daily to be fit enough to be lovable. We feel unloved and
soothe the feeling with a soft addiction, blunting our hunger. We go to
the Internet for a false connection. We overspend, overeat, acquire,
hoard, collect, and amass substances and activities. Our mistaken beliefs
about love affect every aspect of our lives and the lives of those around us.

Many of us did not get the attention or kind of care we needed or
would have preferred when we were children. We may have decided then
that we were not loved or lovable or that there wasn't enough love to go
around. Although these conclusions, made from a younger point of
view, are understandable, they don't have to be our operating principles
today. Just because some of the people in our early life were not good at
showing us love and attention doesn't mean that we have to decide that we
aren't loved. We can make another, better choice.

The First Loving Truth corrects the mistaken belief of unworthiness
and of being unloved. When we live this truth, we don't need to participate
in costly rituals of trying to be cool enough, smart enough, handsome
enough, rich enough, or fit enough in order to be loved. Instead of turning
to numbing addictions, we can soothe ourselves and be comforted when
we feel blue or lonely by opening up to the greater truth that we are loved.

Contrary to a popular mistaken belief, being loved is not a feeling.
Being loved is a decision. Having someone love you is not a panacea for
feelings of lack, unworthiness, and pain. For example, I *know* that I am
loved, but I do not *feel* loved all of the time. My husband loves me deeply
and tells me daily. He believes in me and does whatever he can to help me
achieve my dreams. He compliments me (he calls me gorgeous every
day), lauds my successes, appreciates my way of being, gives me truthful
feedback to keep me moving toward my vision, and shows his love for me
in many ways. It saddens me that I don't always let his caring in or sometimes miss the depth of his feelings for me.

It is a form of stinking thinking to identify a feeling and ascribe
meaning to it. It is called emotional reasoning. *I don't feel loved, therefore, I am
not loved,* is a stinking thought. A corrected thought is, *I am loved. I'm simply
not feeling it right now.*

We often have unrealistic pictures of what being loved looks like. We
think things like, *If he loves me, he'll buy this for me.* Or, *If she loves me, she will read*

my mind. Or, *If I am loved, I will feel on top of the world.* We have pictures of what we think love should look like and feel like and when they don't match, we decide we aren't loved. For example, if I thought love was always gentle and kind, I would miss the love and concern that pours from my husband when he confronts me with the straight truth. Even when things don't look or feel the way you think they should, there is love.

When we decide we are loved, we begin to look for evidence of it. Because of the power of self-fulfilling prophecies, we tend to act in ways that confirm our current beliefs. If we change either our beliefs or our actions, we can shift the cycle. As you make these changes, you will feel more acceptance, more love, and more hope. Even if you can't seem to feel it in the moment, you will still see the evidence. You'll probably even attract more respect and positive attention because of the shift in your belief system, because you hold yourself as loved and deserving.

By redefining love, you will see that love isn't just romance. Love has to do with caring and holding each other close in your hearts. Evidence of being loved can range from a spouse's loving look, to a parent's stern admonition, to a chore done for you when you didn't ask, to a coworker asking you how your mother is doing after her recent fall, to a boss giving you tough, constructive feedback that will help you develop your potential.

Simple pleasures and the ability to cherish them can also be symbols of love. You can see evidence of being loved in gifts of the universe—a glorious sunset, a cleansing rain, the shimmer of the northern lights, the sunny faces of daffodils on a spring morning, or the twittering of birds at dawn. The magic that comes from human beings—an athletic triumph, an exquisitely prepared meal, a painting by Monet, the artful finishing work of a master carpenter, the perfectly executed document by your assistant—can all be seen as signs of a loving universe.

The Second Loving Truth:
Love and Peace Are the Legacy of Pain

Riding on the wave of your pain are the gift of peace and the gift of love. As you open up your heart to feel your pain, you open yourself to receive love and peace. Peace follows pain, like the sun follows the storm. The charge builds, it is released, and all is calm. Cleansing like the rain, sorrow washes your heart and peace and love remain. Bountiful love and peace flood into the tender sanctuary prepared by the vacating pain.

We have mistakenly believed that pain is the opposite of love. We haven't realized that pain and other emotions actually lead to love and can be seen as aspects of love. In addition, peace is not the absence of pain but the result of the acceptance and expression of pain. Peace awaits expression. It only arrives when we express what is in our hearts.

Inner peace does not depend on perfect circumstances or the absence of conflict. We experience peace even in the midst of chaos and upset if we are in touch with our hearts and release our pain. As we open our hearts to the feelings that reside within, we find ourselves. Knowing our inner state brings us closer to ourselves, to others, and to spirit. And when we are in contact with ourselves, we can feel the peace of truth.

Our mistaken beliefs about pain cause suffering. We resist pain, thinking that there is something wrong with it or wrong with us that we feel hurt. We may also believe that we can't handle pain. As a result, we mask our pain, we act "cool," or we numb our hurt with soft addictions. By resisting pain, we create a condition of suffering rather than a deep healing experience of our true pain. We create internal upset, anxiety, and a feeling of unease. We don't feel our pain fully and release it.

Pain differs from suffering: pain is inevitable while suffering is optional. Everyone feels pain, sadness, and hurt. Suffering, though, occurs when we have feelings about our feelings, when we revisit our pain again and again. We feel sorry for ourselves because we're hurting or we're mad because someone hurt us. We're upset about being upset. Often we fail to address the pain directly and it persists unrecognized. We are in pain underneath but are only aware of a vague feeling of upset. Suffering is a surface phenomenon. Instead of fully releasing the feeling underneath, we resist it on the surface with our soft addictions. We feel blue, cranky, or angry, or perhaps we act out inappropriately.

It's not surprising that we become attached to soft addictions that dull our pain, even though it means giving up love and peace. We make this terrible sacrifice because we resist our pain, mistakenly believing that it is ugly and renders us unlovable. The opposite is true. We will not feel seen, accepted, and loved without sharing our hearts, which means accepting our pain.

Accepting and expressing pain is crucial. It does not matter if you express it in words, tears, sobbing, or any other way; it will lead to peace.

Ideally, your expression will match the intensity of your pain. In other words, sobbing is a different expression from weeping; the latter may not release enough of the pain to create a sense of peace. Watch a baby to see how her release of feelings brings resolution and peace. When a baby feels upset, she cries fully and the feeling completes itself. In the next moment the baby smiles and coos until the next wave of feelings comes through her. This is how it can be for adults if we allow it.

Intimacy and love only come to a heart open to pain. A heart that shares pain is a heart that shares love. Love and peace are the legacy of pain. When we share our pain we open ourselves to the love of others, to the love of our self, and to the love of God and the universe.

THE THIRD LOVING TRUTH: FEELINGS ARE DIVINE AND TO BE HONORED

Encoded within you is a deep sensitivity, designed to provide you with exquisite information to guide you to right action, to protect you, to lead you to pleasure, to experience intimacy. Your feelings express the deepest truth of your soul. It is through your feelings that you experience spirit, the greater essence of life. Feelings are the universal human language, a conduit from heart to heart, transcending our outer differences and connecting us to all.

We become most human and alive when we cry our tears, laugh our amusement, yell out in anger, shake with fear, reach out with love, and bubble over with joy. Feeling these feelings, naming them, and being in relationship with them in the here and now is the way to a full, vibrant life.

Our emotions guide us to pleasure, alert us to pain, divert us from danger, and lead us to fulfillment. When we deny our emotions, we become depressed, anxious, and even physically ill. We may act out inappropriately rather than expressing our emotions responsibly. Being hurtful, mean, ill-willed, or irresponsible are all examples of our dark side's misuse of feelings. Even worse, such a feeling-avoidant attitude causes us to miss the wisdom and aliveness encoded in our emotions. We miss the flow of energy within us. We miss the connection to our heart, to the hearts of others, and to spirit. When we misuse or cut off our feelings, we miss their ability to lead us to the next level of exploration.

Expression of a feeling often leads to a new discovery of who and what we are. As we ride the wave of our feelings, we arrive at new understandings, and we express things we never knew. Sometimes we don't know what we think or can't define what's inside until we begin to express the feeling. Our expression then leads us to new territory where we become something that we weren't before. This process keeps us from being stagnant, from repeating the same thoughts and reactions. It is how we grow. It is what helps us create ourselves.

Without our emotions, we would not be human. Our emotions connect us to every other person. Through them, we understand ourselves and one another. We may not share beliefs or have the same thoughts, but our emotions are the language of all humankind; they transcend culture, beliefs, race, age, sex, or any artificial division. All of us hurt, hope, love, sorrow, and rejoice in the depths of our hearts.

Our feelings express truly the deepest parts of ourselves. They reveal and define us. They guide us to express, to heal, to connect, to worship, to love, and to become our most human and our most divine selves.

THE FOURTH LOVING TRUTH: GIFTS ARE GIVEN TO YOU TO DEVELOP AND USE IN THE DIVINE SYMPHONY OF LIFE

You have been endowed with gifts to cultivate and to offer to the world. Each of us is blessed with unique gifts, and every single one of these is valuable. As you express your gifts, you express an aspect of creation that could not and would not exist without you. Embark on the sacred quest to discover, develop, and contribute your gifts, your special contribution to the planet. It is your deepest purpose to magnify and manifest what you have been given. The world will be in harmony once we all develop and use our gifts collectively.

Accepting that we all have gifts, we can join the quest to discover them. We needn't be limited by mistaken beliefs that we are not talented, or that others are special but not us, or that it is showing off to share our gifts. Convincing ourselves that we lack any real gifts or have nothing to contribute leaves us with an aching void that we often fill with soft addictions. Our fear of failure and our perfectionist approaches bar us from fully engaging in life. We are willing to just get by in order to distract ourselves from our fear. If we believe we have nothing to contribute, we don't fully engage in life and we seek solace in soft addictions. Since we only discover our gifts by engaging in life, we may miss finding the gifts we surely possess.

Our gifts can be anything from artistic ability to mechanical aptitude. Whether it's a penchant for gardening, an empathic heart, a healing presence, an infectious sense of humor, solving computer glitches, being a supportive friend, or being a gifted hostess or ace organizer, we each have many gifts and many ways to contribute to the world.

Learn to lead your life by looking for ways to develop and offer your gifts. As you see new possibilities in your life, begin to recognize the multitudinous ways to contribute. You then offer the wisdom of your unique experiences, ways of thinking, insight, knowledge, and skills. You live passionately, all the while expanding and sharing your gifts.

The failure to realize and develop our gifts is perhaps the greatest cost of our soft addictions. When we make our One Decision, we rid our lives of soft addiction routines and we raise consciousness. Freedom unleashes our potential. When we assume that we have gifts, we start to look for them. We are more willing to try different things to discover our aptitudes and abilities. Once we see our potential, we take more pride in learning, practicing, and honing our gifts. We become more tolerant of our learning curve. As we accept this Fourth Loving Truth we begin to see how we can contribute to our community and the world. We all hunger to matter and make a difference, and developing and using our gifts gives us that chance.

Our gifts aren't limited to the traditional definition of talents—artistic talent, athletic talent, and so on. They flow from our feelings and perspectives, our very essence. It might be empathy and understanding borne out of your own difficult circumstances in life. It's possible your gift is the ability to see the best in others. Maybe you can make others laugh or can dance with innate rhythm. Perhaps you have a mystical access to spirit or a determined will. Perhaps you are driven to complete things and can be counted on. Perhaps your gifts include a talent for organizing, cleaning up, making a beautiful space, repairing appliances, quelling a disturbance, or inspiring others. Any contribution you make is a gift.

Once we see that we all have gifts, we know that we do not need to be good at everything. We can freely make use of other people's gifts. Your spouse possesses gifts you lack. You have exactly the skill your coworker needs to finish his project. He has the gift you need to interface with the other departments. Our teams and partnerships become swirling centers of creativity, with each person offering his or her unique gifts. We begin to crave diversity because it brings more to the table. Others have perspectives, backgrounds, and skills that we do not have and which complement ours. Diversity isn't then a mandated concept, but a heartfelt desire to bring the best possible gifts to bear.

By developing and offering your gifts, you grow. You become more skilled and more fulfilled. Something new is created and brought into the world. The creativity you express through your gifts empowers you to add meaning to your life and to the lives you touch.

LIVING THE FOUR LOVING TRUTHS

The Four Loving Truths reveal to us the love and wisdom of the universe. They clarify why we've been given spiritual hungers. Just as we are encoded to feel physical hunger so that we eat to sustain our physical body, we have spiritual hunger so that we seek the nourishment that causes our souls to flourish. As we follow the path to the life we hunger for, we come to know the differences between a soft addiction and spiritual nourishment.

It is my hope that the Four Loving Truths will inspire you on your journey. The Truths respond to the lament, there must be more than this. Yes, there is MORE—more love, consciousness, energy, resources, fulfillment, satisfaction, contribution, connection, feelings, life experience, adventure, and discovery. The Four Loving Truths are the essence of MORE. They informed and inspired every step of this book. May they inspire you and inform every step of your heroic journey.

Conclusion

The Heroic Quest
for MORE

"The good fight is the one we fight because our hearts ask it of us. In the heroic ages—at the time of the knights in armor—this was easy. There were lands to conquer and much to do. Today, though, the world has changed a lot, and the good fight has shifted from the battlefields to the fields within ourselves."

—PAULO COELHO

Inspired by the Four Loving Truths, armed with new skills, and aware of the possible missteps, you are now equipped to voyage into the land of MORE. Like any epic journey, it is both fraught with difficulties and imbued with tremendous rewards. It is a hero's journey and a journey that makes heroes.

In myths and fables, the hero ventures off to discover his own way. He doesn't follow the common path. He seeks something worthy of his efforts, and proves his courage in continuous tests. He doesn't always attain victory. But he continues on the quest, learning, developing, and growing along the way. This classic hero's journey is very similar to the one you'll be going on in your quest.

The path awaits everyone, not just a special few. Setting foot on it helps life become an adventure rather than a series of routines. Seeking MORE requires character and bravery, and the process itself helps bring out these positive traits. From the moment you make your One Decision, you embark on the hero's journey.

CELEBRATE THE COURAGE TO BREAK FREE

One of the hardest parts of teaching people about breaking free of their soft addictions is helping them understand how courageous it is to live consciously in a world that is primarily unconscious, to live deeply when there are so many invitations to live lightly. To resist the false promises, to choose what your heart asks of you—this is the making of heroes! It takes a hero full of courage and bravery to let go of ingrained patterns and go boldly into a new way of living. These choices help you develop strength of character. And, it takes character to make conscious choices.

In a society that promises that we will have the life we want if we buy the right stuff, or where fast results and quick fixes are touted as the cure to all our ills, we are constantly bombarded by temptation. It is not pandering to yourself to celebrate small victories in the face of these temptations. In fact, it is imperative. Don't take these victories for granted, even if they seem small. Be aware and congratulate yourself on every positive choice you make, because that choice has a far greater impact than you may realize. A choice that gets us off track puts us on a trajectory toward other poor choices, causing us to spiral downward. On the other side, a positive choice in alignment with our One Decision makes our next success more likely and keeps us spiraling upward.

Every choice that helps us spiral up is a victory, bringing us more light, awareness, and consciousness. It is a vote for life itself. So I sincerely mean it when I say that eating two doughnuts instead of three is a victory! Turning off the TV after watching one program is a huge success! Turning off your computer, cell phone, or PDA, even for a little while, is a big deal. Walking away from a bargain you almost could not resist, calling a friend instead of slumping in front of your computer, getting

> **MORE-SEL**
>
> *"Heroes take journeys, confront dragons, and discover the treasure of their true selves."*
>
> —CAROL PEARSON

out of the house to go to a lecture or an event rather than isolating—these are battle victories and need to be honored.

Make it a point to celebrate each success. There is no step too small or insignificant. Each act that adds more to your life is a significant victory. Exult in taking another route to bypass your favorite coffeehouse. Triumph in eating half a candy bar instead of the whole thing. Revel in the success of reading great literature instead of the tabloids. Celebrate limiting your Internet surfing by walking in the park before work or singing a hymn. Rejoice when you add beauty to your life, buying flowers and feasting on their beauty. Delight in listening to soul-stirring music as you get dressed in the morning.

"I turned left instead of right!" Cindy proclaimed with excitement. No one but her knows that this was a monumental achievement. This thirty-year-old mother of two and chronic shopper explained, "Every time I drove down that road, I turned right to go to the mall to shop before I went home. This time, I hesitated for a very long time at the stop sign, debating back and forth, my hands ready to turn the steering wheel . . . but then I turned left toward home instead!" Yes! A major victory! "I listened to the little angel on my shoulder rather than the little devil!" she added.

This is the stuff of heroes—resisting the forces of temptation and responding to all of MORE.

FIGHTING THE GOOD FIGHT: THE BATTLE OF LIGHT AND DARK

As you develop your Soft Addiction Solution skills, prepare to fight for a more meaningful life. While the battle is fought with the weapons of humor, compassion, understanding, love, and awareness, do not kid yourself, it is still a battle. You are engaged in a battle of light and dark, consciousness and unconsciousness, life and death. It is a constant battle, requiring vigilance and perseverance. Your soft addiction "demons" won't go gently into that good night without a fight. While you won't win every skirmish, you can win the war.

In this war, do not underestimate the power of your soft addictions or how unconsciousness renders you vulnerable to them. Be prepared.

Your journey is a noble endeavor, worthy of your preparation. And every battle that you win is a vote for consciousness, a vote for the light, a vote for life. Breaking free of your soft addictions is not just a minor exercise to do so that you can feel better, you are fighting for your life—and the quality of life in our world.

....

MORE TO THINK ABOUT

Warriors celebrate their victories. What have you achieved today? What battle, big or small, have you won today? Applaud yourself. Lift your cup of coffee (decaf, of course) in a salute. High-five yourself.

....

GUARDING YOUR GAINS

With every battle you win, you gain territory—more time, consciousness, feelings, awareness, energy, connection, inspiration, money, productivity, motivation, and clarity. Like any warrior, you must guard your gains. As a warrior of consciousness, shield your moments of hard-earned awareness from the onslaughts of unconsciousness.

Once you have created more awareness by clearing away some of your automatic behavior, become increasingly protective of your clear space. Don't give ground easily. Don't go to places, people, or activities that will challenge your success. If you have fought to feel better about yourself, don't call someone you know who will be likely to belittle your victory or dishonor your journey. If you've avoided dessert at the office party, don't go home and pig out. If you have been successful in turning off your TV, don't go celebrate at the sports bar with wide-screen TVs on every wall. Instead, use your victories as momentum to gain even more territory. Be constantly on the alert to add more spiritual nourishment to your life.

Recognize, too, that you're going to be faced with many choices along the way. It is easy to make one positive choice and then let your guard down too soon—a warrior knows that the moments after a victory are the most vulnerable and the ones to be most protected. After all, you worked hard for the territory, so don't give it up to an unworthy opponent. Align to your One Decision and it will guide you through the maze of choices.

While at times you're going to be discouraged, challenged, and doubtful as you make your choices, don't forget that all this comes with the territory. You're a hero, and by definition, heroes have to overcome setbacks and self-doubt in order to triumph. Fortunately, heroes don't have to face their challenges alone. As you'll recall, King Arthur had his Knights of the Round Table, Don Quixote had Sancho, and the Three Musketeers had one another. They shared codes of honor, behavior, and training that made success more likely. Battles are better fought with armies. Triumphs are better realized with friends. Knowing that others are on the path with you can help sustain you in your quest.

The students at the Wright Institute have access to people who can help them during every step of the process, and this helps them both through the rough spots and in celebrating their victories. If you lack this access, you should be aware that it's not all going to be smooth sailing. Join with others to create a support group and log on to our Web site (www.judithwright.com) for more support and resources to encourage and celebrate you.

THE REWARDS ARE MORE THAN WORTH IT

Even though challenges abound, the fight for MORE brings with it immense benefits. I often refer to the people who have done this training and apply these skills in their lives as Conscious Warriors because they are willing to face the challenges, fight through the brambles, and battle the dark to reap these rewards. And the rewards are more than worth it.

These Conscious Warriors discover the freedom available when they no longer feel controlled by their ruts and routines. They gain the gifts of endless time and energy because they are no longer mindlessly passing through their days. They experience more financial abundance because they are more genuine and true to themselves and the people they serve. They have more feelings and are able to see, hear, touch, and taste all the experiences that life has to offer. They laugh at themselves when they make mistakes and can see the humor in these situations. They are more aware of each moment and can derive meaning and satisfaction from all the small things that make up a day. Relationships become deeper and more intense, and a sense of spirit touches their lives.

It's tremendously gratifying when people realize that these rewards far outweigh any challenges they must face. They really do experience MORE—more time, money, energy, intimacy, satisfaction, and love. They have broken free of their soft addictions and are living the life they always wanted to live.

CREATING A WORLD OF MORE

The road to MORE is not only a path to personal fulfillment, it is a path that can revolutionize our world. Carlos Castaneda affirms the hero's path as a reformation and a revolution:

> I came from Latin America, where intellectuals were always talking about political and social revolution and where a lot of bombs were thrown. But revolution hasn't changed much. It takes little daring to bomb a building, but in order to give up ciga- rettes or to stop being anxious or to stop internal chattering, you have to remake yourself. This is where real reform begins.

You are becoming a revolutionary—one who lives in new ways. This then is a revolutionary war fought by Conscious Warriors. You are en- gaged in battles for consciousness within yourself and in the world. You are revolutionizing your internal landscape and revolutionizing the world around you.

MAKING A DIFFERENCE, CHANGING THE WORLD

Living a life of MORE benefits both you and the people around you. Many of the people I work with find MORE by contributing to others, making a difference, and having an impact. In a very direct way, their pursuit of a more fulfilling life involves helping others. In an indirect way, their quest contributes to a better world because they are becoming more empathic, spiritual individuals. Their transformation adds a little bit to the transformation of the world.

If we were all increasingly aware, our world would transform itself. We would meet our spiritual hungers directly, designing our lives to meet our deepest needs. We would know that we had the power to create our lives, instead of just reacting to situations.

MORE-SEL

....

*"Without heroes, we are all plain
people, and don't know
how far we can go."*
—BERNARD MALAMUD

Our world needs more heroes—people who are willing to do the right thing, make the hard decisions, and stand up for the highest principles and values. The more aware people are, the better their decisions will be. We need leaders who are conscious, awake, and operating from their highest values. We need people who are productive and achieving levels of excellence, while also feeling satisfied and fulfilled. We need those who model a different way of living so that others can draw inspiration from them. We need brave souls who are willing to listen to their own hearts and inspire others to do the same.

Imagine a time when everyone fights for more love, more connection, more spirit, and more fulfillment rather than for territory. This would be a world where all people would live according to the Four Loving Truths—knowing that they are loved, developing and offering their gifts to the world around them, expressing their emotions responsibly, and honoring the revelations of their hearts. This would be a place of balance and harmony, a place we all dream about.

You can help create this world. You may start on the path to MORE to feel better, but in the process you *become* better and our world becomes better. You create a living example and help to affirm others who want to live a more meaningful, significant life. You develop more awareness and generate more truth around you. You share and contribute your gifts, making the world a better place.

As you go forth, I'd like to leave you with some words to sustain you on your journey.

You are about to begin the hero's journey. Travel well on the quest. A life of MORE is your birthright. Know the vast resources that reside in you and are provided for you in the world. You have raised the battle cry and are fighting the good fight, fighting for MORE. And by doing so, you are becoming a hero of our modern age. It is in your hands that our future lies. You are a living example of the power of the human spirit, creating hope and possibility for others. Together, may we create heaven on earth.

THE
SOFT ADDICTION
SOLUTION WORKBOOK

1

GETTING MORE
OUT OF LIFE

Who doesn't want to get MORE out of life? No matter how much love, satisfaction, money energy, time, resources you have, chances are you would like to experience MORE—or you wouldn't be reading this book.

What if you could feel like the master of your life? In control, directing your life, with satisfying days, making a difference rather than feeling like your life is happening to you? Luckily, mastery in life doesn't require us to be world-class athletes or CEOs of Fortune 500 companies. We achieve mastery in life when we move beyond our soft addiction routines and create a life of MORE.

In this chapter, we'll look at the promise of MORE, the importance of wanting MORE, and the challenges in our society that make it difficult to live the life we want. The exercises in this chapter will prepare you to apply the eight key skills discussed in the sections that follow and to break free of your soft addictions.

REVIEW YOUR DAY

Before you can move forward, it's important to get a picture of where you are now. Let's explore your days to see how you create MORE or less love, meaning, intimacy, and energy in your life.

As much as we might want to live a life of meaning, we may find our lives are often full but not fulfilling. As you review your day, ask yourself these questions and circle your predominant response.

Did I move toward my goals and vision today?	Yes	No
Did I make a positive difference in other people's lives?	Yes	No
Did I take a stand for what matters most to me?	Yes	No
Was my day emotionally and spiritually nourishing?	Yes	No
Did I grow as an individual?	Yes	No
Did I experience love as a part of interactions and activities?	Yes	No

How often do you ask these kinds of questions at the end of the day? If you rarely or never do, welcome to the club. Most of us don't consciously design our daily lives to be uplifting, meditative, or deeply meaningful. We are enmeshed in routines that range from stressful to escapist, preventing us from really asking the deeper questions or living our purpose every day.

CREATE YOUR DAYS

Now go back and circle the questions that you would like to answer more affirmatively. Then, ask yourself the circled questions tonight (or tomorrow night) and think about what you could have done differently in your day to have more fulfillment. You are preparing to have MORE in your life.

WATCH "WHAT THE BLEEP . . ."

One of the most popular scenes from the movie *What the #$*! Do We Know?!* is the one called Create My Day. Rent the movie and pay special attention to that scene. You can view it with friends for some lively discussion. We are all hungry to create our days, not just let them go by.

REVIEW YOUR DAY: MORE OR LESS?

Describe your day today or at least list some activities that you did and how you spent your time. Include as much as you can.

_____
_____
_____
_____
_____
_____
_____
_____
_____
_____
_____
_____

Now, go back and circle the activities that brought you more fulfillment, meaning, recreation, or made you feel more alive. Put boxes around the activities that led to less. It is likely that soft addictions contributed to the moments of less.

EXAMINING OUR SOFTLY ADDICTED SOCIETY

Think about the technological advances that have occurred just in your lifetime—anything from cell phones, CDs, iPods, and satellite communication to TiVo and DVDs. List everything you can think of under the column marked "Item." Pick at least five of the items on the list and describe how you use them under the "uses" column. How do you use

> ### MORE-SEL
>
> *"Humanity is acquiring all the right technology for all the wrong reasons."*
>
> —R. BUCKMINSTER FULLER

them—positively or negatively? Write the description in the appropriate columns. Now, pick a few other technological items and think of both positive and negative uses for each one. Write those descriptions under the columns.

TECHNOLOGY ADVANCES AND USES

Item	Negative Use	Positive Use
EXAMPLE:		
Internet	pornography	research medical advice

Journal on Your Society and Technology

Reflect on the forces that contribute to a softly addicted lifestyle, and how pervasive they are in our culture. Think about media messages, advertising, increased technology, more disposable income, promises of quick fixes, our need-for-new society. . . . How do we live in a softly addicted society? Journal on your thoughts.

_____
_____
_____
_____
_____
_____
_____
_____
_____
_____
_____
_____
_____
_____
_____

MORE-SEL

"Think of it. We are blessed with technology that would be indescribable to our forefathers. We have the wherewithal, the know-it-all to feed everybody, clothe everybody, and give every human on Earth a chance. We know now what we could never have known before—that we now have the option for all humanity to make it successfully on this planet in this lifetime. Whether it is to be Utopia or Oblivion will be a touch-and-go relay race right up to the final moment."

—R. BUCKMINSTER FULLER

From Not Wanting Enough to Wanting MORE

One of the things we realize when seeking MORE is that we often weren't expecting or desiring enough in the first place. Often, we have limiting unconscious beliefs and feelings that keep us from desiring and pursuing MORE. Read through the list of beliefs below and circle any that you identify with. Feel free to add any other limiting beliefs that you believe are holding you back from the life you want.

I don't deserve MORE.
Only lucky people have MORE.
MORE is for special people.
I have so much already.
People will be jealous of me if I have MORE.
I won't fit in if I have MORE.
Who do you think you are, wanting MORE?
You're greedy.

Other limiting beliefs you may have:

_____

_____

_____

_____

_____

DIFFERENTIATE YOUR DEEPER MORE FROM YOUR SURFACE MORE

As you explore the promise and possibilities that life has to offer, it is important to differentiate the greater MORE from the superficial more. Use this chart to stimulate your awareness. Circle the deeper MOREs that you identify with and want more of. Underline the mistaken or superficial mores that you have been coveting.

Deeper MOREs	*Mistaken/Superficial Mores*
More love	More gossip
More life	More house
More creativity	More caffeine
More adventure	More power
More knowledge	More media
More meaning	More avoidance
More peace	More oversleeping

More abundance	More "stuff"
More feelings	More possessions
More consciousness	More diversions
More energy	More fame
More connection	More vacations
More direction	More car
More truth and genuineness	More image
More life	More status
More of a difference	More escapes
More God/spirituality	More clothing

EXPLORE: WHAT DO YOU WANT MORE OF?

Breaking free of your soft addictions creates room for the deeper MORE in your life. While there is nothing wrong with the smaller more in column 2, often we substitute the smaller more for the deeper MORE. Most people make more money, and often generate more vacations, fame, and power by living MORE. For now, let yourself want MORE. To prepare you to pursue the eight key life skills, list what you want MORE of in your life. What is the life you want?

_____

_____

_____

_____

_____

_____

_____

_____

2

SKILL #1: MAKE YOUR
ONE DECISION

You've decided to live a life of MORE and are ready to move forward on your journey. By making your One Decision, you commit to a life of MORE and to the steps that you'll take for the life you want. You have yet to formally identify your soft addictions, develop a vision of what a life of MORE looks like, and learn the skills of the process, but you stand at the edge of the possibilities that come with making the One Decision.

You have now gained an understanding of the One Decision, recognizing the difference between the One Decision and a goal or resolution. The One Decision is the difference between a "life lite" or a "life deep"—a choice between opposites. You have learned how the power of your One Decision can act as a foundation for all other decisions and a guiding philosophy when making common, everyday choices. Use the following exercises to help you make and articulate your own One Decision.

ONE DECISIONS IN HISTORY

When you make and live your One Decision, it begins to define your life. You become known for the quality of your life. Without a One Decision, you are often known by your soft addictions. A true One Decision impacts every area of your life—your lifestyle, career, relationships, well-being, service, and leadership. Think about people you know who live satisfying lives—in every area of their life. Think about people in history who have been known for the quality of their lives or for a consistency of purpose. Review the sample below and in the space below that, list some of these people and the qualities of their life that might indicate a One Decision.

Who	Qualities	Possible One Decision
EXAMPLE:		
Mother Teresa	determined, caring, compassionate, dedicated	I honor life in all its forms.

WATCH *THE MATRIX*

To broaden your understanding and awareness of the One Decision, rent the movie *The Matrix*. In a graphic illustration of a One Decision, the hero is given a choice of which pill to take—the one that shows him the full reality or the one that numbs him into a contrived, unfeeling, consensual fantasy.

As you watch, note any examples of "life lite" or "life deep" that you see in the movie. Even if you have seen this movie before, re-rent it and watch it from this new perspective.

GO TO THE MOVIES

Many of your favorite inspiring movies demonstrate the power of the One Decision. Use this chapter as an opportunity to watch some great flicks and notice when the characters make their One Decision. What qualitative changes happen after they do? How does it help them have the life they truly want?

Here are some suggestions:

Field of Dreams	*The Lord of the Rings*
Last Holiday (with Queen Latifah)	*Jerry Maguire*
Cinderella Man	*It's a Wonderful Life*
Elizabethtown	*A Christmas Carol*
My Big Fat Greek Wedding	*Pay It Forward*

What other movies can you think of that illustrate a One Decision? (If you think of any others I'd love to know about them. Please e-mail me at contact@judithwright.com.)

THE ONE DECISION: A CHOICE BETWEEN OPPOSITES

When you make your One Decision, you can use it to guide your everyday choices. It can help you start to notice the daily choices you face and the degree of satisfaction your current choices bring you. Below is a list of common choices. Circle the option out of each pair you would be most likely to choose. Remember this is simply an awareness exercise, so pick realistically, not idealistically.

A. Zoning out in a daze on the train ride to the office

B. Listening to some inspiring music on your iPod and reading the files you brought home to be prepared for your meeting today

> MORE-SEL
>
> *"I guess it comes down to a simple choice, really. Get busy living, or get busy dying."*
>
> —THE SHAWSHANK REDEMPTION

A. Plop the kids in front of the TV after school to get them to be quiet

B. Engaging with your children after school to understand their thinking, their challenges, their feelings, their accomplishments

A. Noshing on snacks and watching reruns of *Friends* after work

B. Meeting a friend for dinner to catch up and discuss your lives and your dreams

Review your common choices and note any patterns you see when you chose As and when you chose Bs. Use the next exercise to explore other common choices you make during a typical day, and what guides those choices.

REVIEW TODAY'S CHOICES

What choices were you faced with today? Think of three you made today. Under Choice A below, list what you actually chose. For Choice B, imagine an alternative choice you could have made. Next, on a scale of 1–10, rate the degree of satisfaction each choice holds.

Choices	The Degree of Satisfaction I Experienced
Example:	Least Satisfying____Most Satisfying 1 2 3 4 5 6 7 8 9 10
Choice A: Doughnut for breakfast *or*	1 2 ③ 4 5 6 7 8 9 10
Choice B: Eggs and whole-wheat toast	1 2 3 4 5 6 7 8 ⑨ 10
Now, it's your turn:	
1. Choice A: *or* Choice B:	1 2 3 4 5 6 7 8 9 10 1 2 3 4 5 6 7 8 9 10
2. Choice A: *or* Choice B:	1 2 3 4 5 6 7 8 9 10 1 2 3 4 5 6 7 8 9 10
3. Choice A: *or* Choice B:	1 2 3 4 5 6 7 8 9 10 1 2 3 4 5 6 7 8 9 10

What are you learning by looking at common life choices? What brings you the most satisfaction? When are your choices more influenced by the craving for a soft addiction and when are they influenced by a commitment or desire for something MORE? Journal your answers in the space provided below.

_____

_____

_____

_____

_____

_____

_____

_____

$$\boxed{\text{MORE TO THINK ABOUT}}$$

You are seeing how some life choices bring you MORE and some bring you less. Using your One Decision to guide more and more of your daily decisions helps you to live the life you want, rather than feeling like life is just happening to you. It helps you to choose activities and ways of being that nourish and inspire you. You are less likely to use your resources on the "empty calories" of soft addictions.

A TEST-DRIVE ONE DECISION

To experience the benefits of living a One Decision, you don't necessarily even need to make one. Test-driving a One Decision will provide you with the foundation you need to take advantage of all the skills in this book. Right now, what's more important than making your One Decision is becoming aware of the importance of *having* a life-orienting decision. What you learn as you apply the other seven skills will ultimately help you define or refine a One Decision that feels right for you.

To test-drive a One Decision, simply pick a sample as a placeholder until you are ready to make your personalized commitment. Again, what matters is *that* you commit to something, not exactly *what* you commit to.

Below are some sample One Decisions. Circle the one that most resonates with you. For now, act as if it is your One Decision and let it guide your choices until you find one to replace it. As you look at your daily choices, think to yourself, *What would I do if I were orienting to my One Decision?* You will begin to

MORE-SEL

"A promise has real power. A promise made from the stand that who you are is your word, engages you as participant. You cease to be a spectator, and your words become actions that actually impact the world. With a promise, you create a condition that supports your commitment rather than your moods."

—VERN WOOLF

discover its power to help you break free of your soft addictions and live the life you want.

I follow my deepest, most genuine desires.   *I live my life with an open heart.*
I am fully present, awake, and engaged.   *I live my life as an adventure.*
I am a vessel for spirit.   *I live as if every moment matters.*
I am a person of integrity, a stand for truth.   *I choose a life of MORE.*

MORE ALERT

Be aware of any fear or discomfort you may have about committing to MORE—perhaps it's fear of failure, or making mistakes, or outgrowing your friends. It's important to articulate your fear and discomfort to keep it from sabotaging your pursuit of MORE.

MAKE AND CLAIM YOUR ONE DECISION

Let the following exercises help you to claim your One Decision. Take some time to journal and reflect upon why you want to make your One Decision. Find a quiet, peaceful spot and ask yourself the following questions.

1. What's prompting you to make your One Decision?

Why do you want MORE in your life? Do you want to be more fulfilled? Have more meaning in your life? Are you dissatisfied or unhappy? Do you lack focus or direction? Are there times when you feel empty and disconnected? Are you unable to experience great joy, backing away from even positive, strong feelings? How would you like to feel? Do you have yearnings that you want to fulfill? What excites you about a different type of life?

_____

_____

_____

_____

_____

_____

> ### MORE TO THINK ABOUT

To learn more about making and living your One Decision, you may want to consult my book *The One Decision*, and follow the 30-day plan at the back of the book. The step-by-step exercises and assignments will lead you to the benefits of living your One Decision whether you are ready to claim one or not.

2. What do you want MORE of in your life?

Remember, MORE means MORE satisfaction, love, intimacy, time, money, energy, sense of purpose, meaning, life, contribution, self esteem, and self respect.

What other words would you use to describe MORE? Which aspects do you want MORE of in your life? What do you hunger for deep in your heart? What would make your life a well-lived one? What do you want to be able to say about your life at the end of it? Proclaim what you want MORE of in your life by writing it down.

_____

_____

_____

_____

_____

_____

_____

_____

3. What is your One Decision?

Compose a rough draft expressing your One Decision. Use your answers to the previous two questions as raw material. Be reinspired by the MORE-sel quote by Jack London. Refer to the examples below to see how others expressed their One Decision. As you write your One Decision, enjoy playing with possibilities. Write your decision in the affirmative, not as a wish or by saying "I want to." Create a living statement that

ONE DECISION TIPS

1. Write your One Decision in the present tense.
2. Word the decision positively, not reactively.
3. Remember that your One Decision is claiming a quality of being, not a goal or concrete focus. While it may help you decide, say, to go back to school, or lose weight, or get a promotion, these are not One Decisions; they are goals. Your One Decision is not choosing what to do, but rather choosing the quality of life that will pervade everything you do.

can grow with you and become clearer as your One Decision comes to greater focus throughout your life. Remember, while the decision is final, the wording and understanding may vary over time. You are deciding to live a life of MORE.

MORE-SEL

"I would rather be ashes than dust! I would rather that my spark should burn out in a brilliant flame than it should be stifled by dry rot. I would rather be a superb meteor, every atom of me in magnificent glow, than a sleepy and permanent planet. The proper function of man is to live, not to exist. I shall not waste my days in trying to prolong them. I shall use my time."

—JACK LONDON

Examples:

I live an exceptional, conscious life.

I engage fully in the adventure of life.

I am a person of integrity and genuineness.

I live from my heart.

I live deeply, feel deeply, and open myself to all life has to offer and greet it boldly. I feel my feelings and let them wash across my face.

WRITE YOUR ONE DECISION

1. Now write your own One Decision (or claim a test-drive One Decision).

Use a separate sheet of paper to capture your One Decision. Feel free to draw, add photos, color—anything to proclaim your commitment.

....

"Once I made my One Decision to value myself, my relationships sorted themselves out. I got out of a relationship that was going nowhere. I started creating the life I wanted and naturally attracted a man who would empower me and who is also committed to MORE in life—now he's my husband and we have two beautiful children."

—*Helene*

....

MORE-SEL

....

"To live content with small means; to seek elegance rather than luxury, and refinement rather than fashion; to be worthy, not respectable, and wealthy, not rich; to study hard, think quietly, talk gently, act frankly; to listen to stars and birds, babes and sages, with open heart; to bear all cheerfully, do all bravely, awaiting occasions, hurry never; in a word, to let the spiritual, unbidden and unconscious, grow up through the common. This to be my symphony."

—WILLIAM HENRY CHANNING

2. Say it out loud!

After you've written your One Decision, recite it. Feel the words you've written and express them out loud, passionately. You may also find it helps to say them to another individual who you believe will appreciate the One Decision you're making. What you're asking this other person to do is witness your One Decision. Take a moment right now and read your One Decision to someone else. What was it like to recite your One Decision to another person? How did you feel before and afterward?

3. Make a reminder for yourself.

Once you've expressed your One Decision, keep it with you at all times. Even if you've memorized it, make the actual words part of your life by carrying them with you or by placing them in a special place in your home. What will you do to remind you of your One Decision? And by when?

Examples:

I commit to create a screen saver with my One Decision on it.

By when: One week from today.

I commit to calligraphy and frame my One Decision.

By when: One week from today.

Your turn:

I commit to:

By when:

CELEBRATE YOUR ONE DECISION

Your One Decision will now guide you and provide you with a foundation to support you as you learn to live the life of MORE you have chosen. It takes courage to articulate and write your One Decision. Take time today to nourish and celebrate yourself after taking this step. Perhaps you'll take time to read from your favorite book, or take a hot bath, or put on your favorite song and then dance in your living room. Identify what feels right for you and take time to do this nourishing thing. In fact, plan to do something **right now** and something a little later.

Examples:

In the moment celebration:

1. Send yourself a congrats e-card.

2. Give yourself a standing ovation.

3. Register your One Decision on our Web site, www.judithwright.com, and we'll e-mail you a reminder if you'd like.

Nourishing celebration for
   later:
1. Hot bath with candles
2. Send a thank-you letter to
   God or the universe.

Your turn:

What will you do now?

_____

_____

_____

What will you do later?

_____

_____

_____

MORE LEARNS
AND GROWS

Now that you've made your One
Decision or at least chosen a placeholder, reflect on what you have
learned about yourself, your desire
for MORE, your feelings, and
your life through the course of
this chapter and these exercises.

> ### MORE-SEL
>
> *"Until one is committed there is
> hesitancy, the chance to draw back,
> always ineffectiveness. Concerning all
> acts of initiative (or creation) there is
> one elementary truth, the ignorance of
> which kills countless ideas and splendid
> plans: the moment that one definitely
> commits one's self then Providence
> moves, too. All sorts of things occur to
> help one that would otherwise never have
> occurred. A whole stream of events issues
> from the decision, raising in one's favor
> all manner of unforeseen incidents and
> meetings and material assistance, which
> no man or woman could have dreamt
> would have come his way. Whatever you
> can do or dream—begin it. Boldness has
> genius, power, and magic in it."*
>
> —W. H. MURRAY
> QUOTING GOETHE IN A SERMON

How have you grown or done something differently based on what you
have learned in this chapter? Learning to monitor what you have learned
and how you have grown is a powerful tool of consciousness that acceler-
ates your learning, to bring you MORE. List what you have learned and
how you have grown here.

My Learns (something I know that I did not know prior to this lesson):

_____

_____

_____

My Grows (something I've done that I would not have done prior to this lesson):

_____

_____

_____

_____

3

SKILL #2: IDENTIFY YOUR SOFT ADDICTIONS

You have laid the foundation by choosing a life of MORE. Now you are ready to learn another key life skill to lead the life you want. By deepening your awareness and understanding of your soft addictions, you can begin to break free of them. By identifying them, as well as the time and money you spend on them, you can unlock the patterns and unravel the web of soft addictions.

Keep in mind that identifying soft addictions takes a bit of practice. Once you start doing it, you become more aware of the links between various moods and behaviors and your soft addictions. The following exercises are guides for you to become more self-aware and conscious of your habits.

GO TO THE MOVIES: *ABOUT A BOY*

Rent the movie *About a Boy* for an eloquent example of a softly addicted life. The main character, played by Hugh Grant, lives a life centered on soft addiction routines until he discovers MORE through his unlikely relationship with a lovable and nerdy preteen boy. As you are watching it, be aware of your reactions.

How did Hugh Grant's character spend his time? What were his soft addictions? How did he find MORE through his relationship with his preteen "friend"? What shifted in his life? How is your life like the main character's? What similarities do you see? What differences? If you've viewed it with a friend, discuss your thoughts and feelings afterward, or journal your thoughts here:

_____

_____

_____

_____

_____

_____

LIST YOUR SOFT ADDICTION EXCUSES

As you begin to look at your soft addictions, you may find yourself making excuses and rationalizations—and believing them. While we'll address this in the next chapter, it is helpful to start becoming aware of your knee-jerk reactions at the thought of your behavior being a soft addiction. In the left-hand column list a few of your possible soft addictions. In the right-hand column, list an excuse or explanation you might use for having that soft addiction. For example:

Soft Addiction	Excuse/Rationalization
Overshopping for shoes	I've worked hard and need a reward.

SOFT ADDICTIONS CHECKLIST

At this point, your goal shouldn't be to create a definitive, exhaustive list of every activity, mood, and avoidance, which are your soft addictions. Nor should it be a time to beat yourself up or feel bad about your "weaknesses." We all have soft addictions, and being willing to look at them is courageous.

Review the list of soft addictions below and place a check mark next to the ones that might apply to you. As you scan the list, you may think of others that are pertinent to you. Feel free to jot them down to keep track of them. As you'll discover, some of the items listed may sound relatively unimportant

> **MORE-SEL**
>
> *"TV is chewing gum for the eyes."*
> —FRANK LLOYD WRIGHT

(nail biting) compared to others such as Internet surfing or television. Remember, though, that a soft addiction doesn't have to be anything monumental to constitute a spiritual roadblock. Just mark the ones that are possibly soft addictions for you. The exercises that follow will help you sort out if they are soft addictions or harmless pastimes.

"One of my favorite foods is chocolate. I'm not overweight but when I started to look at it, I realized that I would inhale my chocolate rather than enjoy it. I'd even hide in a closet and wolf it down! I realized the signs of a soft addiction. I was looking for sweetness, but the food wasn't going to give it to me. Instead, when I feel that craving, I've learned to ask my family for more affection or hugs. What a difference. I'm closer to them, and when I do eat chocolate, I actually enjoy it!"

—Kaylie

Media
- ☐ Watching television
    - *Channel surfing*
    - *Program junkie*
    - *Sports*
- ☐ Surfing the Internet
- ☐ Participating in chat rooms
- ☐ Checking investments
- ☐ Checking weather, statistics, news
- ☐ Reading magazines
- ☐ Reading only one genre of novels, such as romance or mysteries
- ☐ Listening to the radio
- ☐ Checking e-mail
- ☐ Playing computer games
- ☐ Playing video games
- ☐ Checking eBay
- ☐ Instant messaging
- ☐ Text messaging

Buying/Shopping
- ☐ Shopping
- ☐ Cruising garage sales
- ☐ Collecting
- ☐ Antiquing
- ☐ Bargain hunting
- ☐ Hanging out in the mall
- ☐ Perusing catalogs
- ☐ Clipping coupons

Maintenance
- ☐ Overeating
- ☐ Overexercising
- ☐ Glamorizing
- ☐ Hygiene
- ☐ Housekeeping
- ☐ Being a pack rat
- ☐ Caregiving
- ☐ Sleeping too much

Physical Mannerisms
- ☐ Hair twirling
- ☐ Twitching, jiggling, picking
- ☐ Gum chewing
- ☐ Nail biting

Sexual
- ☐ Flirting
- ☐ Sexual obsessions
- ☐ Phone sex
- ☐ Pornography
- ☐ Masturbating compulsively
- ☐ Being a voyeur
- ☐ Babe or dude watching
- ☐ Being promiscuous
- ☐ Leering
- ☐ Fantasizing

Work
- ☐ Overworking/keeping busy
- ☐ Overscheduling
- ☐ Overcommitting

Risk Taking
- ☐ Speeding
- ☐ Gambling
- ☐ Seeking danger
- ☐ Making deals

Social/People
- ☐ Name-dropping
- ☐ Following celebrity news
- ☐ Gossiping
- ☐ Storytelling

- ☐ Cell phone conversations
- ☐ Fantasizing/daydreaming
- ☐ Lying

Other Diversions
- ☐ Checking sports stats
- ☐ Doing crossword puzzles
- ☐ Playing card games
- ☐ Fantasy sports leagues
- ☐ Crafts
- ☐ Sports

AVOIDANCES

- ☐ Procrastinating
- ☐ Isolating
- ☐ Being late
- ☐ Playing dumb
- ☐ Living in clutter
- ☐ Acting helpless
- ☐ Playing the victim
- ☐ Hypochondria
- ☐ Phobias
- ☐ Stonewalling
- ☐ Being too busy
- ☐ Oversleeping/napping

MOODS/ WAYS OF BEING

- ☐ Being sarcastic
- ☐ Being cranky/irritable
- ☐ Indulging in self-pity
- ☐ Being "in the know"
- ☐ Being a drama king or queen
- ☐ Always being happy; always "on"
- ☐ Being a Pollyanna
- ☐ Chameleonlike behavior
- ☐ Acting like a sad sack
- ☐ Moping
- ☐ Blaming
- ☐ Looking good
- ☐ Complaining
- ☐ Constantly trying to please people
- ☐ High energy
- ☐ Jokester
- ☐ Perfectionism
- ☐ Fanaticism
- ☐ Being argumentative/conflictual
- ☐ Acting cool

THINGS—EDIBLE AND CONSUMABLE

Edible
- ☐ Sugar
- ☐ Chocolate
- ☐ Fast foods
- ☐ Carbohydrates, high-fat foods, etc.
- ☐ Coffee
- ☐ Snack foods

Consumable
- ☐ Cigarettes
- ☐ Gadgets
- ☐ Electronics
- ☐ Designer clothes
- ☐ Shoes
- ☐ Collectibles
- ☐ CDs
- ☐ DVDs
- ☐ Brand-name merchandise

REVIEW SOFT ADDICTION PATTERNS

What do you notice from your list? Were there any surprises? Do your soft addictions seem to cluster in one category? Or are they widespread? What patterns do you see from your list? Do any of them seem to "go together"? Journal on your impressions.

_____

_____

_____

_____

. . . .

MORE TO THINK ABOUT

What role does television play in your life? Take at look at these startling statistics.*

Time per day that a TV is on in an average U.S. home	7 hrs 40 min
Americans who always or often watch TV while eating dinner	40%
Chance that an American falls asleep with the TV on at least three nights in a week	1 in 4
Americans who say they watch too much TV	49%
Amount of TV the average American watches per day	over 4 hours
Amount of TV the average American one-year-old watches per week	6 hours
Hours per year the average American youth spends in school	900
Hours per year the average American youth spends watching TV	1,023

*TV-Turnoff Network, "Facts and Figures About Our TV Habit," June 3, 2004, http://www.tvturnoff.org.

KNOW THE MOTIVATION AND FUNCTION OF YOUR SOFT ADDICTIONS

How do you know if your behavior or activity is a soft addiction? Your motivation and function of the behavior determines whether it is a soft addiction or a meaningful pursuit. Do you use the behavior to create more meaning, fulfillment, spiritual nourishment, to learn and grow, to express your values, to develop your gifts? Or do you use it to escape, tune out, avoid, or zone out? In the left-hand column below, list some of your behaviors or activities. In the right-hand column, guess at your motivation or its function. Keep in mind that you may use the same behavior or activity for positive reasons and as a soft addiction. Don't worry now about making the distinction. Just list all your possible motivations and functions.

MOTIVATION AND FUNCTION AWARENESS

Activity/Behavior	Function/Motivation
Watching TV	Zone out
Late-night snacking	Numb my anxiety

MEET ELLEN

Read Ellen's story below. See if you can identify the motivation for her soft addiction.

"What do you mean soft addiction? Shoes are a necessity item. I write for a fashion magazine. I need them," replied Ellen, a young freelance writer, when challenged about her shoe habit. Well, she must have really needed them because she had managed to accumulate more than one hundred fifty pairs—ten of which were an almost indistinguishable type of black loafers. It wasn't until she did the Soft Addictions Solution training that she realized that she bought shoes whenever she was upset and wanted to feel better about herself. "After one particularly bad day at work, I left upset, feeling like a failure, like I could do nothing right. I went to the store and bought four pairs of shoes. I felt great because I thought, *I can get a lot accomplished and only in a half hour!* I felt better . . . but only for a little while. By the time I got home, I felt guilty about spending so much on the shoes. I just hid them away so I could pretend that I never bought them." Ellen could no longer deny that her shoe shopping was a soft addiction.

SEE HOW YOU FEEL WHEN DOING YOUR SOFT ADDICTIONS

How do you feel around an activity or mood? The most common soft addiction-induced feelings are the numbed, zoned-out state, or a kind of neutered emotion, such as a mildly pleasant buzz. This is a very different experience than a sense of joy or transcendence, states in which feelings are intensified rather than muted. In the chart below, list the activity or potential soft addiction in the left-hand column. In the right-hand column, jot down any feelings or states you experience at three points: before, during, and after the activity or mood. Some possible feelings related to soft addictions are listed at the top for reference.

ACTIVITY	BEFORE	DURING	AFTER
	Anxious/jittery	Zoned out	Embarrassed
	Sad	Buzzed	High
	Bored	Numb	Shameful
	Driven	Getting high	Glazed
	Excited	Glazed	Agitated
	Compulsive	Unconscious	Buzzed
	Angry	Increased	Numbness
	Self-pitying	agitation	Forgetful
	Afraid		(can't recall
			what you've
			done/seen/
			heard)

TAKE THE SOFT ADDICTION QUIZ

If you're still wondering if something is a soft addiction for you, take the quiz on page 52.

BUILD YOUR SOFT ADDICTION HIERARCHY

Remember that soft addiction success is not about going cold turkey and eliminating all of them. But it is about telling yourself the truth about what you see and what you are willing to do about it. Now that you've identified your soft addictions, you can decide what you want to do about each one. In the spaces below, build your own soft addictions hierarchy. Choose which soft addictions you'd like to release at this point and which ones you wouldn't. You can always revisit this list in the future, but an honest assessment will support you in breaking through these habits.

Soft Addictions Hierarchy

Soft addictions I know I have and will actively work on releasing:

_____

_____

_____

Soft addictions I know I have and am not willing to do anything about right now:

_____

_____

_____

Soft addictions I know I have but don't intend to do anything about:

_____

_____

_____

Things I'm not willing to admit are soft addictions:

_____

_____

_____

Soft addictions I may not even know I have:

_____

_____

_____

IDENTIFY/ANALYZE YOUR SOFT ADDICTION COSTS

While most people can admit they have soft addictions, they often deny the cost and impact soft addictions have on their lives. Analyzing the costs of your soft addictions is an eye-opening experience. How much money do you spend a year on soft addictions? How much time? What are the costs in your life from lack of awareness and consciousness? What about opportunity costs—of what could have been? These are resources you can use toward having MORE instead.

In any of the Soft Addiction Solution seminars we have done, when participants calculate the costs of their soft addictions, no one has spent less than $3,000 a year on soft addictions. In fact, the majority of people have calculated spending between $15,000 and $18,000 a year. And a large portion of participants have calculated $25,000 to $30,000 and more a year. These are just out-of-pocket costs, not considering opportunity costs or costs from not investing this money in other ways.

Use the following cost charts to evaluate your soft addictions. Consider the following different types of costs for your soft addictions. For financial and time costs, list or circle the activities that apply to your soft addictions and mark the money or time spent. For the consciousness and opportunity costs, simply record to the best of your ability the costs of your soft addictions as they apply to those categories.

> ### MORE-SEL
>
> *"The world we live in facilitates both soft addictions and spiritual enlightenment. The opportunities for fulfillment and meaning are equaled by the opportunities for creatively wasting time."*
>
> —JUDITH WRIGHT

"My soft addiction was an unusual one—parking tickets. When I was young and had my first car I lived in an area in California where it was hard to park. I got very lazy about tickets and my bad habit followed me as I moved and got older. I finally woke up to it when my husband was furious one year—I had accumulated $2,000 in tickets. But even though he was angry I don't know that I would have done anything about it if I hadn't done the full cost assessment. I tallied up my lifetime spending on parking tickets and realized I had spent over $20,000. It was very humbling, especially when I thought about all the other things I could have done with that money. The strange thing was that even though the costs were sobering, I also had more compassion for myself as I realized that it definitely was a soft addiction, and I needed some skills to break it. I've been free of tickets for years now, and my money is going to much better use."

—*Joy*

FINANCIAL COSTS

ACTIVITY	*Money Spent*		
	WEEK	MONTH	YEAR
Health club memberships			
Excessive Internet services			
Latest high-tech gadgets			
Designer clothes			
Expensive restaurants			
Telephone bills			
Gourmet coffee			
Premium or satellite TV hookups			
Attendance at sporting events			
Excessive magazine subscriptions			
Clothing for different sizes from overeating			
Total			

TIME COSTS

ACTIVITY	Time Spent (Including time planning soft addictions, doing them, and thinking about them)		
	WEEK	MONTH	YEAR
Total			

....

"As a professional woman nearing forty I had a very active life and never seemed to have enough time to spend with my husband or for doing good things for myself like yoga or working out. It wasn't until I started to look at how I actually spent my pre-cious time that I realized that my choices were part of the problem. I would come home, all revved up from a full day at work hungry for affection, and I'd sort the mail and dive into catalogs. When I started to calculate the time I spent doing mindless stuff like reading catalogs and this or that I was shocked to find that I spent five hours per week, twenty hours per month, 1,040 hours per year, which equals fifty (fifty!) whole days per year. I couldn't believe the costs or the amount of denial I had been in. Now I still might look at catalogs and freak out over bills but I realize when I am

indulging and obsessing. I am able to choose more wisely and go on dates with my husband. And I'm doing yoga!"

—Jamie

....

Consciousness Costs

In the right-hand column below, make notes of the costs to you in consciousness.

	Notes
Being distracted	
Lack of awareness of your surroundings	
Not catching cues that might have been there for you	
Being unable to respond quickly because you were in a zone	
Not being able to account for what you did during a given period of time	
Feeling like you're insulated from your thoughts and feelings	
Lack of intimacy	
Lost quality time with your family	

Opportunity Costs

If you hadn't spent the majority of your money, time, and consciousness on your soft addiction routines, what might you have done with your life? Look specifically at areas in your life and how they might be af-

fected. How might your career have
benefited from a better use of your
time? Did you lose out on jobs,
chances to develop your skills, or
sales? If you are a stay-at-home
mom or dad, are there ways you
could have empowered your partner to go further in their career or
make more money or better in-

MORE-SEL

*"My problem lies in reconciling my
gross habits with my net income."*
—ERROL FLYNN

vestments? Could you have used your money to further your education,
help those in need, take a meaningful trip; do you feel you missed out on
valuable experiences? If you had been more conscious, would you have
been in better touch with your feelings; would you have been able to take
advantage of opportunities to connect deeply with people? Use the chart
below to track all of the opportunity costs of your soft addictions.

OPPORTUNITY COSTS

Opportunities Lost	Money Spent	Other Costs
Lost job		
Lack of retirement plan		
Closer connection with friends		
Business opportunity lost		

DRAW YOUR SOFT ADDICTIONS WEB

It's rare that you have one isolated soft addiction. Instead, soft addictions generally evolve into a carefully woven web with one leading to and supporting another. Use the sample and graphic below to draw your own web.

I feel tired, so I drink a cup of coffee. THEN . . .

I feel jittery from the caffeine and bite my nails and nervously nibble pretzels. THEN . . .

I feel cranky as I come down from the caffeine, so I have some chocolate. THEN . . .

I'm hopped up on the sugar in the chocolate and so I surf the Web to relax. THEN . . .

While I'm surfing the Web, I eat more pretzels. THEN . . .

I feel burned out and sleepy from the pretzels and Web surfing, so I get some coffee to perk up. . . .

EXAMPLE:

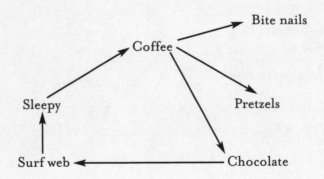

MORE Review

You've begun to see the insidious nature of soft addictions in our lives and in our society, and the costs associated with them. With this new awareness, you have been discovering what soft addictions you may have and what they have cost you in time, money, consciousness, and missed opportunities. As you use the eight key skills to begin to break free of your soft addictions, you will be able to recoup the money, time, energy, and resources that have been devoted to your routines—and use them for a life of MORE instead.

MORE Learns and Grows

Reflect on what you have learned about yourself from identifying your soft addictions, their costs, and the pervasiveness of the web of interrelated soft addictions. How have you grown, or done something differently out of doing this work? List what you have learned and how you have grown here.

My Learns (something I know that I did not know prior to this lesson):

_____

_____

_____

_____

_____

_____

_____

_____

My Grows (something I've done I would not have done prior to this lesson):

_____

_____

_____

_____

_____

_____

_____

_____

4

SKILL #3:
MINDING YOUR MIND

Break Your Denial
and Catch Your Stinking Thinking

By better understanding your mind and the variety of unruly thinking patterns—stinking thinking—and denial, you will see the patterns that keep you stuck in your soft addiction routines. Being able to think clearly is critical to leading the life you want.

Without understanding your thinking, you are likely to just replace one soft addiction with another. The point isn't just to stop a soft addiction, but to manage the thinking that leads to and perpetuates it. We all use stinking thinking and denial to justify our behavior, avoid feelings, and deceive others as well as ourselves. It is this faulty thinking that prevents us from viewing our routines objectively and honestly. Based on mistaken beliefs, our denial and stinking thinking create a false reality, keep-

> ### MORE-SEL
>
> *"The greatest revolution of our generation is the discovery that human beings, by changing the inner attitudes of their minds, can change the outer aspects of their lives."*
>
> —WILLIAM JAMES

ing us in a web of illusion, a web of soft addictions. Prepare yourself to tap into powerful yet simple ways to mind your mind, break the cycle of denial, and live a conscious life with the exercises that follow.

BREAK YOUR DENIAL: THE DENIAL QUOTIENT

The exercises from the last chapter have helped you begin to break your denial about your soft addictions and their costs to your life. Yet you can still easily slip into denial when your routines are threatened or when you start to change your behaviors. Watch for evidence of your denial as it crops up. Denial is the refusal to admit that something exists or that it has a negative impact. Use the following exercises to break your denial.

See if you can recognize the denial contained in the following responses. Check the ones that are similar to ones you have used to deny the reality of a situation:

- ❑ Who made you so high and mighty to challenge me? You should see yourself!
- ❑ It's not that bad!
- ❑ I'm just relaxing. You're the one who's so uptight. You should try to relax!
- ❑ But everybody is doing it.
- ❑ In Italy they eat all that pasta and drink red wine, and they're all thin, so I am sure this won't hurt me this time.
- ❑ I work hard, I deserve this treat.
- ❑ I'll start my diet tomorrow.
- ❑ I don't have time to manicure my nails. That's why I bite them.
- ❑ I just have to have this dress—think of what people will say when they see me in it.
- ❑ It's the latest thing; I really couldn't live without having it.

- ❐ I only did it once!
- ❐ What's your problem?
- ❐ I *need* these shoes.
- ❐ It's OK if I have that dessert, I'll just go to the gym tomorrow.
- ❐ If I weren't so tired, I would do it tonight.
- ❐ After the big project is over, I'll have time to . . .
- ❐ It's really not that expensive.
- ❐ You should see how bad Jennifer is—she spent three times what I spent!
- ❐ Joe had one and I couldn't let his sound system outdo mine.
- ❐ I am in a IT-related field—I have to have the latest technology.

Total checked =_____ = Denial quotient

Now, add up your denial quotient. The more you checked, the more you use denial, in its many forms, as a coping mechanism. The higher your score, the more vigilant you will need to be to ferret out your denial and face the reality of certain situations. If you didn't check any, you get the highest score, because you are really in denial!

THE MANY FACES OF DENIAL—FIND YOUR BRAND

Denial comes in many forms, as you will see below. Which categories have you used to justify and maintain your soft addiction routines? Circle the ones you most commonly use and then use the space below to write examples of the thoughts or statements that you have made in those categories to deny, justify, or minimize your soft addictions.

Defensiveness: reflexively defending your activities or moods, acting as if you were indicted.

_____

_____

_____

_____

_____

_____

Rationalizing: creating superficially convincing and often ingenious arguments about why soft addiction routines aren't bad or even why they are good; explaining and justifying.

_____

_____

_____

_____

_____

Minimizing: acting like a soft addiction really isn't a problem or if it is, it's not a big one; trivializing or downplaying.

_____

_____

_____

_____

Lying: an extreme form of minimizing; fibbing about the scope and depth of soft addiction routines.

_____

_____

_____

_____

Postponing: admitting soft addictions aren't good for you but put off resolving the problem; excusing current soft addictions by making a vague promise to do something about them in the future.

_____

_____

_____

_____

Comparing: a subtle form of denial; excusing your routines by comparing them more favorably to others who have even worse soft addictions.

_____

_____

_____

_____

SNIFFING OUT STINKING THINKING

Stinking thinking is related to denial but can be more subtle and sometimes more difficult to detect and neutralize. Stinking thinking seems so reasonable that we often don't realize it exists—it actually constitutes a great deal of our background thinking and our conversations. We think our stinking thoughts are facts, not arbitrary decisions based on faulty beliefs. Stinking thinking normalizes our soft addictions. Learn and beware. Use the following exercises to help you sniff out your stinking thinking.

··

(MORE TO THINK ABOUT)

Stinking thinking stems from your mistaken beliefs about yourself (_I am not worthy. I'm not lovable. I'm not OK._); about your feelings (_Only wimps cry. It's not OK to be angry._); or about the world (_The world is dangerous. Other people are out to get me. The world is an uncaring place. There is no support for me._).

··

THE MANY FORMS OF STINKING THINKING

What are your favorite categories of stinking thinking? Circle the categories that you use the most. Write in your own examples in the spaces below.

Overgeneralizing: viewing a negative event as a never-ending pattern; blowing things out of proportion; imagining things are impossible; being hopeless; and thinking in extremes—all or nothing, black and white, always or never.

_____

_____

_____

_____

Jumping to conclusions or irrational conclusions: deciding things are bad without sufficient evidence; mind reading and fortune-telling; assuming negative reactions and outcomes; projecting your feelings onto others; magical thinking—imagining connections where none exist.

_____

_____

_____

_____

Emotional reasoning: reasoning based on how you feel without comparing it to reality; thinking that because you feel a certain way, that is the way it is.

_____

_____

_____

_____

Should and shouldn't statements: criticizing yourself or others with should, shouldn't, must, ought, and have to; moralizing the behavior.

_____

_____

_____

_____

Blame/shame: combines overgeneralizing and should/shouldn't; blame yourself when you weren't entirely responsible; blame others and disregard your part.

_____

_____

_____

_____

Labeling: name-calling; attributing limited qualities to yourself and others; categorizing.

_____
_____
_____
_____

(MORE TO THINK ABOUT)

The Ultimate Test for Stinking Thoughts

Any thought that is not consonant with these beliefs is a stinking thought:

I am worthy and lovable.
My feelings are valid and worthy
The world is a caring, supportive place, which wants the best for me.

Other Categories:

Irrelevant excuses or funny logic—I can't work out, I already showered.

_____
_____
_____

Limited or scarcity thinking—I'm not smart/old/young/rich enough. It's not possible, I don't have enough time, money, energy.

_____
_____
_____
_____
_____
_____
_____
_____
_____

MORE-SEL

"You cannot always control circumstances. But you can control your own thoughts."
—CHARLES E. POPPLESTONE

JOURNAL ON YOUR STINKING THINKING

What stinking thoughts have you had while reading this section? Take a moment to journal on these thoughts. Becoming aware of your thinking is essential to creating MORE. If you are aware of the stinking thinking you are winning already.

_____

_____

_____

MORE ALERT

Stinking thinking can be costly. Perhaps you've talked yourself out of asking for a promotion, postponed career moves, assumed people would reject you and didn't make the sales you could, or blamed others for your situation rather than doing what you could to generate and receive more abundance.

STINKING THINKING SCORECARD

Make a scorecard with the major stinking thinking categories and put a hash mark or check mark on it for every stinking thought you catch. Jot down any thoughts that keep you stuck in those categories. Copy this scorecard and carry it with you. Use the situations below to help you recognize stinking thinking as it happens.

Category	Checkmark	Thought/Statement
Overgeneralizing		
Jumping to conclusions or irrational conclusions		
Emotional reasoning		

Category	Checkmark	Thought/Statement
Should and shouldn't statements		
Blame/shame		
Labeling		

Scoring at the Movies

Using the scorecard, watch a movie and pick out stinking thinking. Look for excuses, self-deprecating remarks, blame and shame, defensiveness, and evidence of the different categories. Once you start looking, you will start to see stinking thinking everywhere.

....

MORE ALERT

Mean Voices

Be on the alert for your mean voice—the one that thinks bad thoughts about you or about others. You may think it is accurate—but it is most likely based on mistaken beliefs. This kind of thinking is the most likely to derail you and send you to soft addictions to "feel better." Change your thinking instead.

....

Scoring on the Phone

Set up a tape recorder in your house near your phone. Switch it on the next time a friend calls and record your part of the conversation. Listen to your dialog and keep score of your own stinking thinking. In what ways do you limit yourself?

Scoring in Conversations

Watch for stinking thinking in everyday conversation—yours and others. You'll see that what often passes for conversation is an exchange of stinking thoughts! Listen at work, in your family, in social situations. Better yet, if you are feeling adventurous, point it out and discuss it with friends. Be prepared to deal with their initial defensiveness.

MORE TO THINK ABOUT

You know you are with someone caught in stinking thinking when their "logic" goes around and around and you can't seem to get anywhere in the conversation. It keeps looping around and they counter any new information you share. It is like talking to someone under the influence of drugs or alcohol. In contrast, when you are dealing with truth, there is resolution, awareness, understanding, and corresponding shifts in behavior. Don't confuse an intellectual rationalization with fact.

ENROLL YOUR FRIENDS AND FAMILY

Let your friends and family know what you are working on and ask them to catch you in the act of stinking thinking.

"I was so amazed by the power of shifting stinking thinking that I asked my family to get on board. Now whenever I say I can't do something, my seven-year-old daughter busts me, 'Mom, that's stinking thinking!'"

—Gabrielle

STRATEGIES TO BREAK STINKING THINKING

The point isn't to get rid of your stinking thinking; it's more about lightening up to think more clearly. With a sense of humor and compassion for our personal flaws, we find it easier to see and accept how our behavior is misaligned with our dreams. Humor gives us the distance and space necessary to admit that there's something wrong with our soft addiction routines. Below you'll find a few techniques for developing self-acceptance, compassion, and a sense of humor.

....

"I used to sit in front of the TV and just shove food in my mouth. But after I made my One Decision, I was committed to taking care of my body and my health—except my stinking thinking was always waiting to rear its ugly head: 'If I don't work out today it really won't matter—it's just one day. I can go tomorrow.' Except I didn't. I was feeling really bad and confessed to my husband one day how I had walked into the gym, touched the treadmill, and walked right back out. He just started laughing and laughing. He helped me see how my workout foibles were not as serious as I made them. Once I regained my lightness about it, so did my body. I worked out a little bit when I could and, one year later, I am forty pounds lighter. I'm still able to laugh at myself . . . except now I actually get on the treadmill!"

—Jackie

....

Keep a Humor Journal

Use your imagination to creatively and lightly examine yourself. Write something funny you said or did. Use it to gain distance on something you felt bad about. Make fun of your neurotic tendencies or your workaholism or being a couch potato. Jot down a soft addiction and then write a humorous line about it. Although your entries might seem forced at first, you'll gradually have fun with it. And it will help you to stop taking everything you do so seriously.

EXAMPLE:

Soft addiction: being overly dramatic.
I just found out I was nominated for an Academy Award for Best Supporting Drama Queen.

Write an entry for your humor journal:

_____

_____

_____

_____

_____

EXPRESS YOUR HUMOR CREATIVELY

Pick at least one of the following and use it to spur you to apply humor to your stinking thinking and soft addictions.

- Put different words to a popular song, with lyrics reflecting your soft addiction routines.
  Example (to "Respect" by Aretha Franklin):
  C-O-F-F-E-E, Find out what it means to me
  C-O-F-F-E-E, Who cares about stupid tea!
  Pour it for me, pour it for me, pour it for me, pour it for me
- Draw a cartoon that pokes fun at yourself.
- Create a satirical sketch about how you act.
- Create a pseudonym for yourself and write an anecdote that captures you at your most absurd.
- Write a ridiculous news story about your soft addiction routine.
  Example: Josie won the snooze alarm Olympics today. She faced tough competition but after twenty-nine hits delivered with perfect style, she was declared the winner. She received double technical credit for the slap-and-punch technique that sent the alarm flying across the room.

CHECK OUT BRIDGET JONES'S STINKING THINKING

Sometimes it is easier to see stinking thinking in someone other than yourself, and even easier in a movie. View the opening scene in *Bridget Jones's Diary*, the Dear Diary scene. Catch the stinking thinking and see the humor.

READ THE SHOPAHOLIC SERIES

Read the whole Shopaholic series by Sophie Kinsella for humorous views of stinking thinking. See how much you can relate to the main character's hilarious rationalizations and loopy thinking.

DEVELOP COMPASSION AND FORGIVENESS

Practice daily forgiveness. At the end of each day, grant yourself a pardon for whatever "sin" you think you committed. Review what you beat yourself up for, such as missing a workout or a deadline, having an argument with a friend, spending too much or too little, losing your keys, etc. Now choose one thing for which you feel you deserve forgiveness. Then say out loud an affirmation that communicates your forgiveness: "I forgive myself for spending so much time searching the Web for a deal on running shoes."

My so-called sin	Statement of forgiveness

THE SOFT ADDICTION TEMPLATE

Over the next several skills, you will be learning to use the Soft Addiction Template. This powerful tool can help you track your soft addictions, become aware of the stinking thinking and replace your stinking

MORE-SEL

"A man is but the product of his thoughts; what he thinks, he becomes."
—MAHATMA GANDHI

thoughts with more empowering thoughts. Students at the Wright Institute have found this to be an invaluable tool to clean up their stinking thinking and unlock their soft addiction patterns.

Any time you are having stinking thoughts, you can use the following template to "reprogram" your thinking. Below are the questions that are relevant to the skills you have learned so far. There is a full template in the Appendix that includes the questions for the eight key skills. Make copies of the template so that you can practice using it to better understand your soft addiction routines. Or use the interactive version of this template on our Web site, www.judithwright.com. It is designed with drop-down responses and suggestions to facilitate its use.

1. What event or situation triggered your stinking thinking? What soft addiction(s) did you turn to?
2. What feelings were you having?
3. What thoughts were going through your head during or after this event? How do those thoughts keep you from pursuing MORE?
4. What positive thoughts could you think instead (thoughts reflecting the reality of the situation, or thoughts that are humorous, compassionate, or forgiving)?

As you look over your responses, can you see your soft addictions with greater clarity? Can you see how stinking thinking prevents you from recognizing the routines that cause you to get less out of life?

....

"I had stinking thinking about the stinking thinking template. I was convinced that this was some stupid form of busywork and there was no way it was going to work. My thoughts are my thoughts and that's it. Well, I had to admit, every time I used it, I unlocked my stinking thinking and was able to shift my thoughts. I felt better. I felt affirmed, and like I had unlocked some tension inside myself. I realized that I was addicted to being critical—especially to myself. Now I can see what I am feeling, which triggers my cranky criticisms, and find other ways to tend to myself. (Just don't tell anyone.)"

—Kaylie

....

MORE REVIEW

You have begun to look at thinking patterns, denial, and stinking thinking—and how your thinking patterns keep you locked in your soft addictions. Recognizing your stinking thinking will help unblock you and move you in the right direction. You've identified these counterproductive patterns and are in a better position to change them so they're in alignment with your One Decision. You are taking steps toward being more conscious to recognize truth—in yourself and in others. Developing awareness, a sense of humor, and compassion toward your stinking thoughts and behavior will help you break free of your soft addictions and have the life you want.

MORE Learns and Grows

My Learns (something I know that I did not know prior to this lesson):

_____

_____

_____

_____

_____

_____

My Grows (something I've done I would not have done prior to this lesson):

_____

_____

_____

_____

_____

_____

5

Skill #4:
Discover the Why:
Cracking Your Own Code

When you explore the Why—the underlying patterns and triggers—behind your soft addictions, you will see that all soft addictions have a positive intent because they spring from a desire to take care of yourself. There is a positive intent behind each addiction, an attempt to meet the deeper hungers that lie beneath. Soft addictions are usually well intended yet misguided attempts to fill this deeper hunger.

You can gain valuable information and important clues about yourself from decoding your soft addictions—discovering your unmet needs, understanding the impact of your upbringing, and uncovering your mistaken beliefs. Discover both the historical Why—why you developed your soft addictions patterns—and the in-the-moment Why—why you have an urge to indulge right now.

MORE-SEL

"There are occasions and causes why and wherefore in all things."
—WILLIAM SHAKESPEARE

WHAT ARE YOUR HIDDEN BENEFITS?

We would not indulge in our soft addictions if we didn't feel we were getting something out of it. What benefits do you think you are deriving from your soft addictions? Choose one of your own primary soft addictions and begin to guess the Why beneath it by answering these questions.

My Soft Addiction:

What am I getting out of this? What is the secondary gain from my soft addiction? (i.e., attention; others don't expect much from me; numbs me; suppresses my feelings; gives me a break; fills some empty time; makes me feel cool)

_____

_____

_____

_____

What might be the positive intent behind this routine? What needs might I be trying to meet through this pattern? (i.e., comfort, trying to relax, protection)

_____

_____

_____

_____

DISCOVER THE ORIGIN OF SOFT ADDICTION ROUTINES: MISTAKEN BELIEFS

We all have mistaken beliefs about ourselves and our worth, our feelings, and the nature of the world. Soft addictions arise from these mistaken beliefs and our attempts to deal with the feelings and thoughts that result from these

> **MORE-SEL**
>
> *"You have to know the past to understand the present."*
>
> —CARL SAGAN

beliefs. Many of us learned as children to hold back our tears, fear, anger, and even joy and love in the face of family disapproval or discomfort. We begin to stuff these feelings and try to manage them with the beginnings of our soft addiction routines. It is likely that there is some pattern in our upbringing and childhood that served as the breeding ground for every soft addiction routine.

What mistaken beliefs can you identify from your upbringing? Can you identify experiences that might explain these? These experiences will be logical conclusions from a child's limited experience. Fill in the chart below.

My Mistaken Beliefs	Experiences Related to Belief
About myself (i.e., I'm not lovable; I'm not OK; I am not deserving.)	
About my feelings (i.e., My emotions aren't important; I should hide my feelings; Feelings are scary; Anger is bad; Crying is weak.)	
About the world (i.e., The world won't meet my needs; The world is dangerous, or uncaring; There is no support for me.)	

JOURNAL ABOUT MISTAKEN BELIEFS

How did you deal with some of these beliefs, feelings, experiences, and situations? How did you cope as a child? What did you do when you were upset, stressed, having strong emotional feelings?

_____

_____

_____

_____

FIND THE WHY AT THE MOVIES

Watch the movie *The Great Santini* and monitor the dialogue for limiting beliefs. Pay special attention to the creative adaptation of the children.

> ### MORE-SEL
>
> *"Every time I am upset, there are probably false beliefs. If I just get to spiritual truth, all is well."*
>
> —JUDITH WRIGHT

MORE TO THINK ABOUT

Think about how your upbringing and your early perspective still influence how you feel about yourself today, like this quote from Faye Dunaway reveals: "I'm still the little Southern girl from the wrong side of the tracks who really didn't feel like she belonged."

IDENTIFY THE WHY OF YOUR MOODS

You probably have been looking at your activity addictions or avoidance addictions up until this point. As you explore the Why, you may discover the roots of your moods and ways-of-being addictions—the persistent mental habits we developed to escape our emotions and avoid responsibility for our lives. The following list can help you identify your mood addictions and addictions to certain ways of being. Look at the following list of common patterns and see which ones feel familiar to you, starting from your childhood experiences. In the chart below, rate each category from 1 to 5, with 1 being "Not me at all" and 5 being "This is *so* me."

Category	Rating
Avoiding or minimizing: put your head in the sand, isolate, or pretend things aren't as important as they really are	1 2 3 4 5
Attacking and feeling superior: criticize, point out other people's inadequacies, or put others on the spot	1 2 3 4 5
Self-pity/shame/inferiority: act like a sad sack, beat yourself up, put yourself down, sink into hopelessness and despair, indulge in self-pity, whine, and feel like a hapless victim	1 2 3 4 5
Passive-aggressive: procrastinate, say yes without meaning it, or punish people indirectly by withdrawing from them	1 2 3 4 5
Manipulation: making indirect requests, thereby shifting the focus but never asking directly and forthrightly for what you need and want	1 2 3 4 5
Defensiveness/lying: outright lying, lying by omission, distorting the truth, rationalizing, justifying, or deflecting	1 2 3 4 5
Obfuscation: vague, spacey, divert attention from yourself, bring in irrelevant information, and make mountains out of molehills	1 2 3 4 5

"I was in a good-natured argument with a friend, when I saw the shocked, hurt look on her face. I suddenly realized that my last sarcastic comment had hurt her to the quick—it was much more cruel than I had realized. I knew that I had a soft addiction to sarcasm, but this woke me up to the fact that my addiction was not funny; it was a major problem. In fact, it had almost cost me a dear friend. As I searched for my Why, I realized that in my large family, sarcasm was not only a survival mechanism, but it was also a way to belong. In many ways, it truly was survival of the fittest. You had to have a quick wit and be armed with fast retorts to survive. If you weren't attacking, you were getting attacked. I didn't have my sisters' sharp wit,

so I turned to sarcasm as my verbal assault tool. Once I realized where this habit came from, I had a lot more compassion for myself. I saw that I had turned to sarcasm as a way to get through my childhood, to be part of my family, but it wasn't serving me anymore. Now when I start to turn to sarcasm, I'm able to catch myself quickly, have compassion, and make a different choice. I'm proud to say my circle of friends is now expanding, not shrinking!"

—*Brad*

JOURNAL ON MOODY CLUES

Remember, our mood addictions have the same positive intentions as our addictions to things; we developed them as coping mechanisms in response to our environment. Think about the Whys of your moods and ways-of-being. Why might you have become addicted to a certain mood or way of being? Maybe you attack because you felt attacked at home growing up. Or, you obfuscate because you felt put on the spot by a powerful teacher at school. Think about how you grew up and how you may have developed a certain mood addiction to cope with that environment and journal your thoughts here:

> ### MORE-SEL
>
> *"Use missteps as stepping-stones to deeper understanding and greater achievement."*
>
> —SUSAN TAYLOR

_____

_____

_____

_____

_____

_____

_____

_____

_____

_____

JOURNAL ON CHILDHOOD COPING

How did you cope as a child?

Review your answers to the last questions. Review the soft addiction checklist from Chapter 2. Think about how you dealt with upset, feelings, and challenges as a child. Which soft addiction patterns did you start as a child? Which categories did you indulge in the most? Overdoing activities? Avoidances? Moods and ways-of-being? Things you ate, consumed, bought, or collected? Summarize your findings to date as to why you developed the soft addictions you did. Journal on your thoughts and feelings:

> **MORE-SEL**
>
> *"All truths are easy to understand once they are discovered; the point is to discover them."*
>
> —GALILEO GALILEI

_____

_____

_____

_____

_____

_____

_____

MORE TO THINK ABOUT

As you learn about your Why, be vigilant and watch your judgments of yourself. Take time to notice your thoughts and feelings. Try to develop compassion for the creative way you developed coping mechanisms as a child. Now, as an adult, you can do better than to escape into fantasy, overeat to numb your upset, and zone out in front of the television. Instead you can deal directly with what's upsetting you.

BREAKING UP IS HARD TO DO: WRITE A DEAR JOHN LETTER TO YOUR ADDICTION

Recognizing childhood experiences and the ways in which you used your habits to get through them is a multifaceted skill that you will uncover more fully over time and with prac-
tice. One helpful way to release your soft addictions is to acknowl-edge them for how they served you in the past, but "break up" with them as an adult since they are no longer serving you. Writing a Dear John letter is a perfect method for breaking up. When our students write letters to specific addictions as if they were people, they often understand why they are drawn to them. The following exercise is a powerful tool for articulating the

> ### MORE-SEL
>
> *"I've never tried to block out the memories of the past, even though some are painful. I don't understand people who hide from their past. Everything you live through helps to make you the person you are now."*
>
> —SOPHIA LOREN

bigger Why of your soft addictions. Read the sample Dear John letters be-low and then try writing your own. Here are some guidelines that will help you in crafting it:

- Tell your soft addiction why you're breaking up with it, as if the addiction were a former boyfriend or girlfriend.
- Compliment and acknowledge the addiction for its positive intent, how it was trying—but failing—to satisfy a deeper need.
- Describe the negative effects the addiction has had on your life.
- Use humor and compassion to explain why you're breaking up.

Dear Drama Queen,

It is time for us to part ways. I know the main things you have been trying to give me are love and attention and, occasionally, pity. You are so charming. You've been in my family for a long time and I feel so close to you that I am not sure where you begin and I end. We've even had fun together in some pretty convincing performances.

As afraid as I am to admit it, it is time for us to part ways. That doesn't mean that I am not grateful for the purpose you served in the past. As a kid, drama was a way to get attention from a single mom and parent of four. You helped me as a new kid in school, and you even helped me meet people in college. But as an adult, you no longer serve me. You create negative attention and almost trick me into believing the stories you tell: that I deserve pity and that I am not worthy of God's love. You almost had me convinced that this is all that is possible and that I can't have more.

Well, you're wrong. I can have more! I am enough! I am worthy of love and until I start feeling it inside me, the hunger will never be met. So, thank you. Bless you for serving me as a kid, and good-bye.

Pauline

P.S. I am pretty mad at all the time you've wasted in my life. Don't show your ugly face back here again!

Dear Daydreaming,

I've had many good times with you. You helped me escape when I couldn't go anywhere as a kid. I could forget my troubles for a while. I could imagine I was big and strong and could beat up the bullies who chased me.

It can be fun to daydream and think of faraway lands. However, there's a time and a place for everything. Realistically speaking, I overuse you. Instead of using you to run wild with my imagination, I use you to deaden my consciousness. That may be okay when I'm relaxing. But at work, I can't function at my best when I'm not being productive and having fun. In addition, my daydreaming affects other important parts of my life.

I forget to do chores, run errands, talk to people, and pay attention to my social life. I pay a very steep price for you and I can't afford to pay the price anymore. I have to go now. Take care.

Thanks, Jack

My Dear John Letter

In the space below, write your own version of a breakup letter to your soft addiction. Use a sheet of paper if you need it.

_____

_____

_____

_____

_____

_____

PERFORM A RELEASING RITUAL

After writing your letters, you may want to conduct the following ritual. Burn the letters and release them to the ether, to spirit, to the wind, to the universe, or whatever you wish. As they burn, affirm that you are releasing your soft addiction. Acknowledge their positive intent and the job they have done. Reassure them that you will take over and find other ways to care for yourself in more fulfilling ways. And let go.

....

MORE ALERT

Just cracking the code one time is not sufficient, just as hitting the tennis ball one time does not make you a champion. Practicing new skills is necessary. Developing your internal dialogue and the habit of recognizing the Why is a matter of repeated discipline.

....

FOLLOW THE TRAIL OF SOFT ADDICTIONS: WHY NOW?

In addition to looking at your past for clues, you can spot your unmet needs and adaptive responses by noticing what you are feeling in the moment, right before you start heading into one of your soft addiction routines. By observing yourself here and now, you'll find triggers—situations, unmet needs, and other factors—that spark certain patterns. You can answer the questions, Why am I reaching for my soft addiction in this moment? What is the function of this soft addiction routine in my life?

These exercises will help you to pin down the functional or in-the-moment Why. Use them to track what you are thinking and feeling right as you start to engage in one of your soft addictions. You'll begin to understand why you choose certain soft addictions at particular times. It's like being a detective on your own trail!

"With my job I often work late into the evenings. By the time I would drive home, I was definitely tired and ready to drop into bed. But something strange would often happen. I'd go from being so exhausted I could barely hold my head up to finding myself in front of the Internet surfing for hours on end—scoping out cars, checking out new music, or reading news I didn't even care about. As I started to look deeper, I noticed a pattern. The nights I chose the Internet over rest were the nights I had some big project due the next day or something unresolved from work. I was feeling anxious, my wife was in bed, and I turned to the Internet for comfort. But it never worked. I just ended up being more drained when I went to bed and more tired the next day. Once I realized this, I decided to use my drive time home to talk and strategize with a friend at work. It was great. By the time I got home, I didn't feel so anxious and the pull of my bed won out over the pull of mindless Internet surfing."

—Jacob

REVISIT YOUR SOFT ADDICTION TEMPLATE

Imagine that you are on a treasure hunt and that knowledge about your soft addiction is the gold. To find this treasure, you'll look for the feelings you were trying to numb or the situation you were trying to avoid, as the urge to indulge in one of your soft addictions arose. The more you do this, the more you discover about your Why. You will understand yourself better and become aware of your unconscious motivations. You begin to see how your soft addiction routines may be tied to certain beliefs, feelings, or even situations. In seeing the connections, you can start to unlock your soft addictions.

In the last chapter, you were introduced to the Soft Addiction Template. Armed with your new knowledge about the Why of your soft addictions, revisit the template and add more information to what you've already written or start a new template, using the form in the Appendix, with another soft addiction and see where it leads.

The Soft Addiction Template

Scan your day today and pick a soft addiction you indulged in. Then ask yourself:

> **MORE-SEL**
>
> *"There is a great deal of unmapped country within us, which would have to be taken into account in an explanation of our gusts and storms."*
>
> —GEORGE ELIOT

1. What event, situation, or circumstance triggered my soft addiction? What was I doing or thinking about before I reached for a soft addiction?
2. What was I feeling (any upsetting feelings, uncomfortable emotions)?
3. What mistaken beliefs about the world, myself, and others do I have that may have triggered my stinking thinking and soft addictions?

You will begin to see how your soft addiction routines may be tied to certain beliefs, feelings, or even situations. In seeing the connections, you can start to unlock your soft addictions. If you want more practice, visit the soft addictions site from www.judithwright.com for a full, interactive template to lead you down the soft addiction path to the path of MORE.

CREATE YOUR OWN SOFT ADDICTION THESAURUS

As you do the previous exercise, you're going to find that your various soft addiction moods and behaviors consistently relate to underlying feelings. It's important to become aware of these feelings so you can learn to deal with them. To develop this awareness, create a thesaurus. On the left-hand side of the chart, list the soft addiction. On the right-hand side, write the corresponding feeling. Using the style of these examples, complete your thesaurus below.

Soft Addiction	Mood/Feeling
Judging others in my head	Insecurity/feel bad about self/ scared about my day
Isolating	Fear
Gossiping	Loneliness
Working out excessively	Fear
Constant complaining about work	Anger/resentment
Fantasizing about movie stars	Feeling unloved

MY THESAURUS

Soft Addiction	Mood/Feeling

LOST IN TRANSLATION: FEELINGS INTO SOFT ADDICTIONS

Carry your Soft Addiction Thesaurus with you as a reference to the underlying feelings when you catch yourself in a soft addiction. Add to it as you continue to follow your soft addiction path. When you find yourself indulging in your soft addictions, pull out your thesaurus. It will remind you of the feelings that lie beneath your soft addictions. Think about what you could do instead to tend to your feelings, comfort yourself, or better prepare for a situation. Remember, you and your emotions are valuable and deserve to be treated with care.

MORE REVIEW

To crack the code of your soft addictions, you've explored the historical and functional Why. You've learned that there are deeper hungers under your soft addictions. You can now learn to identify and fulfill them directly. Continually deepen your journey with repeated vigilance for the whys and mistaken beliefs.

What I've Learned and How I've Grown

In this chapter you analyzed the Why behind your soft addictions and began to look at the deeper hungers beneath those soft addictions. Reflect on what you have learned about your deeper hungers. Also reflect on how you have grown as you've moved through the concepts and exercises in this chapter.

MORE Learns and Grows

My Learns (something I know that I did not know prior to this lesson):

_____

_____

_____

_____

My Grows (something I've done I would not have done prior to this lesson):

_____

_____

_____

_____

6

SKILL #5: FULFILL YOUR SPIRITUAL HUNGERS

When you indulge in a superficial soft addiction, such as shopping or gossiping, you are actually expressing a much deeper spiritual hunger, such as the hunger to be known, to be special, to be accepted, to connect. These spiritual hungers are the essential desires that drive your quest for MORE. When you discover these deeper yearnings and learn to meet them directly, you begin to design a satisfying, fulfilling life. With these exercises, you will discover the language of spiritual hungers, contrast that with the language of wants and soft addictions, and even begin translating from one language to the other, recognizing what hungers lie beneath your surface wants.

> ### MORE-SEL
>
> *"When we align our lives around fulfilling our spiritual hungers, life alters in magnificent ways. It becomes MORE; we become MORE, we create MORE. It is as if we begin to live the way we were intended to live and the universe lines up with us as we align with the universe."*
>
> —JUDITH WRIGHT

IDENTIFY YOUR WANTS

It's okay to have wants. The value is in knowing them for what they are. Take a moment to follow these steps, and have fun developing your awareness of what you want.

Step 1: Set a timer for two minutes and, on a piece of paper, make a list of your wants—from the concrete to the fanciful and from the small to the big—from coffee to reading the paper to your dream car to your salary to fantasies. Keep writing until the timer goes off.

Step 2: Enjoy the act of wanting without having to act on your impulse. Picture a store filled with every kind of thing you have on your list. Imagine you are a small child running through the aisles saying, "I want!" Little children enjoy the act of wanting, without feeling they need to possess everything they admire. Mimic their ability to just want.

Step 3: Pursue some of your wants. Feel free to enjoy the act of wanting to buy the car you want if you can afford it or indulge in some chocolate or watch some regular television shows. There's nothing wrong with wants providing they don't start limiting or harming you or others. Your wants will have less power over you if you entertain them in moderation.

WHERE WANTING GETS IN OUR WAY

While there is nothing wrong with these wants or even with satisfying them, the intensity of the desire for them is the problem. We feel like our happiness depends on getting what we want, even though getting what we want doesn't fulfill us. It's not that we shouldn't have preferences for what we eat, buy, consume, play, think about, or work

> ### MORE-SEL
>
> *"A child can always teach an adult three things: to be happy for no reason, to always be busy with something, and to know how to demand with all his might that which he desires."*
>
> —PAULO COELHO

with. It's that sometimes this preference turns into an obsession that limits our freedom.

The following story shows how obsessing over a specific want can limit our opportunity for satisfaction until we admit what it was we really craved all along. Read the story below and follow the instructions at the end.

"Where are they?" Allison cried as she ripped through her closet, tossing hangers full of clothing onto the floor. "They *have* to be here. I *have* to have those slacks!" Getting ready for a casual holiday party, Allison went to put on the festive outfit she bought for the occasion but couldn't find the matching slacks. She ripped through her closet, tossing things on the floor. Frantic and cursing up a storm, Allison is beside herself. It was only when she saw wads of clothing strewn all over the room that she realized how frenzied she was—and in the grip of her soft addictions of clothing and looking good. When Allison finally calmed down, she asked herself what she'd really been concerned about. She realized that she wanted to be seen in the "perfect" outfit but what she was really hungry for was to be noticed, to feel special and part of the holiday, and to feel loved. Once she acknowledged what she really longed for, she realized it wasn't about the slacks. She chose another outfit and went on to enjoy the party. She had a great story to tell her friends—when she came down out of her frenzied panic, she remembered she had taken the slacks in to be hemmed and never picked them up.

Now, on a separate piece of paper, write your own story about obsessing over a specific want. See if you can notice what possible hunger was underneath your want.

EXPERIENCE THE LANGUAGE OF HUNGERS

Identify Your Hungers

Now that you've had a chance to exercise your wanting muscle, it's time to become more familiar with the language of spiritual hungers, the vocabulary of MORE. Hungers point to a direction or a possibility. Any movement in that direction will address the hunger. Even better, the very

acknowledgment of our hunger satisfies us, because we are no longer
running from ourselves or hiding our deeper yearnings. This is a
deeper and perhaps more difficult
assignment than the previous wanting exercise, so give yourself time
and space to reflect. Use these steps
to help you pinpoint your hungers.

> ### MORE-SEL
>
> ----------
>
> *"It's much harder to remove the hunger
> for love than the hunger for bread."*
>
> —MOTHER TERESA

Step 1: Review the list of hungers below and place a check mark next to
the ones that feel true for you. Focus on the ones that strike a chord in
your heart.

Step 2: Try claiming some of the spiritual hungers from the list by saying
them out loud. For instance, "I hunger to be known."

I hunger . . .
To exist
To feel
To be seen
To know another human being
To be heard
To be close
To be touched
To feel connected
To be loved
To be intimate
To be affirmed
To love
To express
To do what I came here on earth to do
To experience fully
To make a difference
To learn
To please God
To grow
To fulfill my purpose

To trust
To unfold my destiny
To develop
To feel connected to the greater whole
To be known
To be one with all
To matter
To know God

EXPERIENCE THE DIFFERENCE:
SPIRITUAL HUNGERS V. WANTS

Now that you've exercised your wanting muscle and experienced the language of your hungers, let's look more closely at the difference between the two. The better you understand the differences between spiritual hungers and wants, the better prepared you will be to distinguish them in the moment you are feeling them. A hunger can be defined as a deep longing or urge to be part of something bigger or a craving to make a difference with our lives. A want, on the other hand, is more visual, easier to picture, and more specific than hungers. We want very explicit things: the exact type of gadget, a certain designer's clothing, a distinct model of car, or even certain people, moods, or fantasies. A want must be met exactly as it is pictured (the precise item, a particular rendition) to fully satisfy. Hungers are cravings of the soul; wants are demands of the ego.

> ### MORE-SEL
>
> "O God, you are my God—for you I long! For you my body yearns; for you my soul thirsts, like a land parched, lifeless and without water."
>
> —PSALM 63:2

In the left-hand column of the chart below, list five or six things that you want right now. You can even refer to the wanting exercise above to list them. In the right-hand column, guess at what the deeper hunger might be beneath that want.

I Want . . .	I Hunger for . . .
EXAMPLE:	
a shiny red sports car	to be seen
cookie-dough ice cream	to be comforted

MORE TO THINK ABOUT

Compare the characteristics of Wants vs. Hungers.

Want	Hunger
Superficial	Deep
Demand of the ego	Longing of the soul
Visual, very specific and detailed, certain brand, color, size, type	Sensed or felt, general, can apply to any situation
Must be met exactly	Can be met in limitless ways
Will never be satisfied	Can be satisfied just by naming it

GO TO THE MOVIES

Rent the movie *Jerry Maguire*. As you watch the movie, keep a notepad in front of you and try to list as many wants and hungers as you see. The more you practice distinguishing between wants and hungers, the more quickly you'll be able to notice your own and to start choosing the hunger over the want.

REFINE YOUR SPIRITUAL HUNGERS

The list of spiritual hungers that you read above is a general list. You might hunger for something different.

Here are a few more examples of people's own hungers:

Juan: I hunger for respect and admiration from my family, my
   coworkers, and people in my community.
Mickey: I hunger for satisfaction, affirmation, and validation,
   both what I can bring to myself and also receive from others.
Catherine: I hunger for caring and nourishment, to see myself as a
   blessing, to respect myself. I hunger for joy, spontaneity,
   freedom of expression. I hunger to feel alive and free.

Customize the list of spiritual hungers and make it your own. Write them below.

My Spiritual Hungers

I am hungry for . . .

_____

_____

_____

(MORE TO THINK ABOUT)

Learning to identify and articulate our spiritual hungers is like learning a new language. Most of us are far more adept at speaking the language of our wants—our cravings for our soft addictions—than we are the more poignant language of our inner hungers. We more easily say, "I want ice cream" than "I hunger for connection and to make a difference in the world."

UNCOVER HUNGERS BENEATH YOUR SOFT ADDICTIONS

Think of a recent soft addiction or one that seems to plague you more consistently. Ask yourself: as I was indulging in my soft addiction, what was I truly hungry for in the moment? What might have been different if I had been in touch with my deeper hungers instead of just my surface wants? In the future, if I am tempted to indulge in this soft addiction, what spiritual hunger might I be trying to fulfill? Journal your responses.

> ### MORE-SEL
>
> *"I felt so dried out and in need of music and fellowship. I was heavy with boredom and needed emptying out. It had been a long time since I had worshipped and fellowshipped in the Spirit. It was a need, a craving. Ordinary things, and knowledge from books wasn't enough. It was spiritual hunger."*
>
> —ROBERT MORGAN

_____

_____

_____

_____

CREATE POSITIVE THOUGHTS

While leading a pilgrimage to Israel, I discovered another way to respond to spiritual hungers by creating positive thoughts to replace the stinking thoughts. A group of us had done meaningful spiritual work on the shores of the Sea of Galilee. Deeply inspired by the words of the beatitudes and with our hearts freshly opened, we began to see the positive intention and deeper hunger beneath each other's stinking thinking and soft addiction routines. We delivered a form of blessing to one another to reflect this new, loving "frame" for each person. Here are some examples:

Blessed is she who hungers to be heard, for she shall express the sounds of her heart.
Blessed is he who hungers to be known, for he shall make his mark upon the earth in the service of all.
Blessed is she who feels deeply, for she will know the richness of her heart.

1. Write a blessing for yourself to address your spiritual hunger.

_____

_____

MORE-SEL

"Let him so hunger and thirst after the truth that the dim vision of it occupies all his being, and leaves no time to think of his hunger and thirst."

—GEORGE MACDONALD

2. Once you have created a blessing for yourself, be a renegade blesser. Create a blessing for a friend, coworker, or loved one. Write it on a sticky note and put it on their computer, hide a note in their briefcase, send it in an e-mail, or even write it in frosting on a big cookie.

IDENTIFY POSITIVE ALTERNATIVES FOR MEETING HUNGERS

In the box below, you see samples of soft addictions, the hunger they mask, and alternatives for meeting those hungers. Create your own grid by filling in your soft addictions, the hunger you think it is masking, and some possible alternatives that might help you meet that hunger. (For fun, check out the game version of this exercise under the soft addiction section of my website, www.judithwright.com.)

Soft Addiction	Hunger	Alternatives
Watching TV	To feel connected	Call a friend; go to a play.
Surfing the Internet	To learn and grow	Go to a museum or a lecture on a subject that intrigues you.
Overworking	To matter	List the ways you make a difference; take pride in your contribution.
Gossiping	To connect; to belong	Talk about yourself and the person you are with, rather than others
Shopping	To feel abundant	"Shop" for friends, ideas, possibilities instead of "stuff."
Fast food	To be fulfilled	Have quick treats that aren't food.
Chat rooms	To feel connected	Call a friend and "chat live."

REVISIT THE SOFT ADDICTION TEMPLATE

You began using your Soft Addiction Template in previous chapters to identify your soft addictions, notice what triggered it, and identify your feelings and stinking thinking. Now go back to your template in the Appendix and identify what you were hungry for when you indulged in your soft addiction. Use the experience you have gained in identifying alternatives to see what you might have done instead.

Remember, it's helpful to use the Soft Addiction Template frequently—any time you find yourself indulging in your soft addictions or stinking thinking. It will help you unlock your pattern. It is a powerful tool. Make additional copies of the blank template in the Appendix. You can also use the interactive template on our Web site at the soft addictions site at www.judithwright.com.

MORE REVIEW

Knowing your spiritual hungers and differentiating them from your soft addictions is an important skill in living MORE. The benefits of focusing on hungers will show up everywhere—including your relationships. Don't wait until you already know someone well to connect through deeper hungers, rather than wants. You'll miss out on great possibilities for connection.

WHAT I'VE LEARNED AND HOW I'VE GROWN

You've learned about the difference between spiritual hungers and wants, and started to articulate what your own hungers are—for affirmation, love, to be seen. In the space below, write what you have learned about yourself as you examine your soft addictions and the hungers that lie beneath them. Reflect on how you've grown as you've moved through the concepts and exercises in this chapter. How are you applying this new knowledge in your life now?

MORE Learns and Grows

My Learns (something I know that I did not know prior to this lesson):

_____

_____

_____

_____

_____

_____

_____

My Grows (something I've done I would not have done prior to this lesson):

_____

_____

_____

_____

_____

_____

_____

_____

7

SKILL #6:
DEVELOP A VISION

Developing your Vision helps you picture your life guided by your One Decision—a life where your spiritual hungers are met. Vision is what will motivate you to rise above your soft addiction routines. If you don't see who you want to become and how you want your life to be, you lack a compelling reason to stop your soft addictions. You don't usually put aside old routines because they are bad for you. You do so because you're hungry for something better. Your Vision gives you the momentum and velocity you need to move forward on your journey. In a very real way, it gives you a reason to move through the barriers of your soft addictions and get MORE out of life.

MORE-SEL

"No man that does not see visions will ever realize any high hope or undertake any high enterprise."
—WOODROW WILSON

GO TO THE MOVIES

Watch the movie *Field of Dreams*. What was Kevin Costner's character's Vision? How did he picture it? What were the deeper hungers being met?

How were they met? How did Kevin
Costner's character allow his life to
be guided by Vision?

VISION V. GOALS

It's important to understand the
difference between Vision and
goals. Vision changes as the environment changes. It serves as a touch-
stone and guiding principle to remind you of possibilities. Your Vision
inspires and uplifts you. Vision provides a compelling idea that encompasses possibilities toward which you are moving and all your goals fit.

Goals, on the other hand, are measurable outcomes with a specific time,
space, and quantity. A goal is specific, concrete, and measurable. It can be
accomplished and completed—unlike a Vision, which is never "over."

Vision goes beyond problem solving or just quitting something
harmful to your life. You are not just motivated to solve a problem but
are driven to create a Vision that fulfills the yearnings of your heart.

To get a better picture of what this looks like, read this quote from
Andre Agassi.

*"When I think about my life and goals, I look around and see a small percentage of
people out there who I kind of envy, because they're taken up and swept away with
what they're doing. Their work takes on its own life. It has a kind of encompassing
power that envelops them. People like that wake up with passion, have vision, and
are in the grip of something beyond their control."*

—*Andre Agassi*

List as many people as you can who fit his description. What else do
they have in common? What can you learn from them? What is one thing
you will do to make your life more like theirs?

_____

_____

_____

_____

THE ONE DECISION *v.* VISION

It is helpful to define vision within the context of soft addictions, MORE, and the One Decision. Start out with this simple definition: Vision is a picture of what your life looks and feels like when you are fulfilling your spiritual hungers. With Vision, you can imagine how to live your life according to your One Decision and achieve the MORE you seek. Vision includes the senses and feelings—how you will look, feel, act, or experience your life, often with kinesthetic, auditory, or digital images. Vision, then, is the visualization of a spiritually fulfilled life, while the One Decision states the intent to live this type of life and to pursue MORE. To keep the distinction between these two concepts straight, read the following example of one person's One Decision and Vision and then try your own.

> **MORE-SEL**
>
> *"Where there is no vision, the people perish."*
>
> —PROVERBS 29:18

My One Decision: I am awake, alive, and engaged. I choose to experience my life fully and live it deeply.

My Vision: I am present and conscious. I am alive and vibrant. There is a bounce in my step and a gleam in my eye. I experience life fully. I'm attuned to my feelings and express them. There is always "somebody home" in my body. People love to be with me because I am in touch with them and myself. I spend my time in meaningful pursuits, loving and truthful relationships, living adventurously, developing myself, and contributing to the people around me.

Now it's your turn. Use the space below to write your One Decision and Vision.

My One Decision:

_____

_____

My Vision:

_____

_____

_____

....

"I have been successful in eating better, exercising, and losing weight. But it wasn't just about looking better—I had a Vision of being my best and staying conscious and caring for myself, to learn to really love myself and to be thankful for the blessings God has given."

—Cathy

....

VISION DOS AND DON'TS

You know the importance of a Vision and what it is. How do you create one that is right for you? A powerful vision is one you can taste, feel, and hear. Keep the following Do's and Don'ts in mind to help you create a strong vision.

Do	Don't
Do fulfill your spiritual hungers.	Don't just feed your surface wants.
Do have a proactive vision.	Don't settle for a reactive vision.
Do feed your soul.	Don't just cater to your ego.
Do write your vision in the present tense.	Don't write it in the future tense.
Do create a vision that deepens your life experience.	Don't fantasize an escape from life.
Do picture your One Decision in action.	Don't picture your soft addictions in action.
Do inspire yourself.	Don't numb yourself.

Do picture how you will feel, what it will be, what your life will be.	Don't settle for a vague wish.
Do be sure it is yourself you please.	Don't worry about pleasing others.
Do keep your wording positive and affirmative.	Don't use "not" in your vision.
Do envision MORE.	Don't limit your possibilities.

MORE TO THINK ABOUT

Many people make the mistake of forming a reactive Vision, or a Vision created in response to a specific situation. As a result, they are often negative. For instance: I'm not going to be fat like my mother. A proactive Vision is: I am healthy and fit. I feel vitality coursing through me.

CREATE A VISION

Think about Vision in all areas of your life. By considering what Vision is from multiple perspectives, you can create a Vision that encompasses who you are in all aspects of your being. Review the areas of life and the sample visions, and then write your own Vision for each of the areas.

MORE-SEL

"Circumstances in our daily lives are continually blocking our true vision until our feet have been firmly set upon the path."
—HEATHER HUGHES CALERO

Areas of Life

Body: how we feel about our body, how we use it, what it means to us, how it is developed and structured, how we treat it

Self: our feelings about ourselves, our self-development, self-esteem, self-respect, our emotions, personal growth work

Family: both our family of origin and our family of choice

Others: our friends, coworkers, acquaintances, neighbors

Work and play: our vocation, avocations, weaving work and play

Principles in society: our higher principles and values and how we relate to them and express them in the world around us

Spirituality: our relationship with spirit and how we express our spirituality in our lives

Lilliana's Example

Lilliana is a video producer, mother, wife, and leader in her community. This is how she worded her Visions, which serve as a powerful inspiration for her.

My Overall Vision: I am vibrantly alive! My creativity flows freely and touches all aspects of my life. I create beauty around me and share my gift and love of aesthetics with all in my life. I joyously show my love to those around me and am buoyed by their love and support.

Body: I am vital, alive, fit, and strong. I cherish my body and tend to it well and lovingly. I plan for my nourishment and keep myself well sustained. I dance, flow, and move gracefully in my body. I am proud of the shape I am in.

Self: I respect myself and trust my intuition. I treat myself with compassion. I let my inner wisdom come out continually. I assert myself and my opinions, trusting that I contribute wherever I am.

Family: My family is a source of support and nourishment where we tell the truth to each other, connect deeply, play together, support each other in our visions, and want the best for each other. We rejoice in being vulnerable and expressive in each other's company.

Others: I am developing more and more friendships and creating relationships that are challenging, fun, and stimulating. I am "dating" women friends and couples friends. My relationships are truthful and empowering.

Work/Play: Both are a joy and feel one and the same. In this way, I take my play as seriously as my work, and use play to sustain my work. I use work to connect me with others. In my work, I serve fully and create that which is beautiful for others.

Principles and Society: I contribute my creativity and my heart connection to the world around me and help others to connect and express their creativity. I contribute my creativity in pro bono projects for meaningful causes. I am "value added" in all of my interactions. I contribute to my neighborhood, school, and community. I am a resource for my community as a networker, a font of creativity, a good listener, and an encourager.

Spirituality: I honor God. I tap into my heart space often throughout the day. I allow being nourished by my relationship with God, knowing that I am loved and cherished by a loving God, even if I have forgotten.

Now it's your turn. Use the space below to write aspects of your own Vision. Creating your Vision can feel like a big task, so don't let this exercise overwhelm you. While you can spend as much time on it as you want, you can do a Vision for each area of life in a minute or two. Remember, you can change your Vision at any time, so don't feel every word has to be perfect. If it feels right to you, it probably is a great Vision for who you are now. Review the questions for each area of life in chapter 7 and then just let your responses flow. Your Vision is there within you, just waiting for permission to be expressed.

My One Decision:

_____

_____

_____

My Soft Addictions:

_____

_____

_____

My Hungers:

_____

_____

_____

My Overall Vision:

_____

_____

_____

Body:

_____

_____

_____

Self:

_____

_____

_____

Family:

_____

_____

_____

Others:

_____

_____

_____

Work/Play:

_____

_____

_____

Principles and Society:

_____

_____

_____

Spirituality:

_____

_____

_____

VISION À DEUX

A wonderful and powerful way to create your Vision is with a partner. Ask someone to read you the questions in an area of life from the Crafting Your Vision section of chapter 7. Then just let the Vision flow from you as you speak out loud for one to two minutes while your partner takes notes for you. And then switch while you read the questions and he or she responds with their Vision while you take notes. Chances are you will be surprised by the depth that you experience in this simple yet profound exercise. You will have the added benefit of getting to know each other even more deeply.

MORE-SEL

"Each of us can choose to envision a future for ourselves that is different or better than the present. Each of us can choose to engage with others who can help us become hopeful. Each of us can develop the strength to move steadily to our envisioned future doing what we can along the way to model for others the change we wish to bring about in the world."

—TOM HEUERMAN
AND DIANE OLSON

Many couples have done this together and have been amazed at the depth they experience.

....

"What a vacation—Becky and I interviewed each other about our Visions. It was like getting to know her all over again. I feel closer to her than I have in a long time. It's like I understand her better and know what matters to her. The next morning, we remembered our Visions for our bodies and it helped us get up and run along the beach together. It felt great!"

—Jerry

....

INSPIRE YOURSELF WITH YOUR VISION

- Now, do something with your Vision. Share it with a friend. Make it into a screen saver on your computer. Embroider it on a quilt. Put a note on your bathroom mirror.
- Make contact with your Vision again and again. Use it to inspire you and guide your actions. Review it so that it continues to feed you. Make a creative collage that represents the Vision. Light a candle and pray over it. Write it in your journal.
- Put a notice in your calendar to review it daily for one week, then weekly (at least) after that. E-mail it to a friend and ask her to e-mail it back to you at sporadic intervals. Ask your friend to create a Vision and share it with you.
- Enter your Vision on our Web site (www.judithwright.com), and we'll send it to you periodically to remind and inspire you. You can also read the Visions of others living MORE.
- Write a letter to yourself, stating your Vision. Give it to a friend and ask him or her to mail it to you in a year, accompanied by a note from that person asking how you are living your Vision.

MORE ALERT

Though we are all capable of creating Visions, we are also vulnerable to mistakes that can derail these visions. Be aware of the factors that can potentially distort your vision:

- Being embarrassed of your dreams
- Listening to stinking thinking that ridicules you for dreaming big
- Being overly concerned with other's reactions to your dreams
- Confusing vague wishes or fantasies with Vision

PUT YOUR VISION INTO ACTION

When you remember your Vision, it gives you a compelling reason to break free of your soft addiction routine—or to even notice that you are in one. For example, if you remember your vision of your relationship is to be honest, truthful, and intimate, then there is a reason to break your soft addiction of lying or hiding and tell your husband the truth—even to admit how much those shoes really cost!

Pick one of the Visions you just created and apply it to a situation coming up in your life. How can it help you live more powerfully? How can it help you resist your soft addictions? Record a few possibilities here.

My Vision	Application in My Life

"I had a Vision of people coming together to help each other to help others—the helpers network. And finally, it was happening. Our first event was a huge success! But then I realized that rather than living the Vision of helping helpers myself, I had been checking out every single woman in the place and turning on the charm. The whole night, I was in my soft addiction of flirting. I wasn't talking to people the way I needed to in order to grow the organization. Without my Vision, I don't think I would have even noticed what I was doing. I conducted the next meeting very differently. The ironic thing is, I actually had better conversations with women and really got to know some high-quality women—and lived my Vision."

—Jack

MORE REVIEW

Your Vision is a living part of yourself. It defines what is important to you; it grows and develops with you as you apply yourself to it. Vision is your One Decision applied to all areas of your life. While it can guide you on an ever-expanding journey to

> ### MORE-SEL
>
> *"Dreams provide nourishment for the soul, just as a meal does for the body."*
> —PAULO COELHO

meet your deeper hungers, you must be aware of reactive vision and the seduction of your wants. You will need the resolve of your One Decision and the strength of your life Vision to overcome their charm and challenges.

MORE Learns and Grows

My Learns (something I know that I did not know prior to this lesson):

_____

_____

_____

My Grows (something I've done I would not have done prior to this lesson):

_____

_____

_____

8

Skill #7:
The Math of MORE:
Add and Subtract to
Achieve Your Vision

By adding nourishment to your life and fulfilling your spiritual hungers, you will begin to naturally subtract your soft addictions. By subtracting your soft addictions, you automatically add more time, money, consciousness, satisfaction, and love which multiplies your pleasure. This is the Math of MORE—a formula that will help you implement your Vision to live the life you want: **Life + Spiritual Nourishment − Soft Addictions = MORE.**

The main assignment of this chapter and the next will be to build your Formula for MORE template. This template is a working document where you formulate your plan to break free of your soft addictions and claim a life of MORE. Then, apply the plan to your life, and let it guide your activities.

> ## MORE-SEL
>
> *"If you only keep adding little by little, it will soon become a big heap."*
>
> —HESIOD

REVIEW ADDS AND SUBTRACTS

Start by reviewing the list below of the wide range of things you can add to your life, then the things to subtract from your life. Once you add and subtract, you will build your plan to guide you to break free of your soft addictions and claim the life you want.

ADDING FOR A LIFE OF MORE

+ Add Nourishment and Self-care—for your body, mind, and spirit
+ *Nourishment and maintenance*—regular self-care and in the moment self-care, from scheduling workouts, massage, medical check-ups to treating yourself with loving care
+ *Ability to be with feelings*—develop your emotional skills to recognize, name, fully and responsibly express, and resolve your feelings

+ Add Personal Power and Self-expression
+ *Asserting your will*—discern your desires, ask for what you want, say no when you mean it, be on your own side, learn to fight responsibly
+ *Developing and sharing your gifts and talents*—recognize your gifts and share them in service
+ *Creative expression, humor, and positive ways of being*—choose positive ways of being—the opposite of mood and way of being addictions

+ Add Intimacy—get close to yourself and others

+ Add Life Purpose and Spirituality—live your One Decision and find your purpose
+ *Being awake, alive, and spiritually nourished*—the power of presence and finding the sacred in the mundane
+ *Beauty and inspiration*—surround yourself with beauty; don't wait to be inspired—keep inspiring things around you at all times
+ *Add activities specifically designed to fulfill your hunger*—review the chart of hungers and life assignments in Chapter 8.

....

"I added candlelit baths at night instead of plopping in front of the tube."
"I added fifteen minutes of reading every morning before I go to work—it's easier to get up because I have something to look forward to."

"I'm adding taking a sauna at the gym—it's like a reward for working out."
"I'm taking a walk with my husband along the lake after work instead of going online."

—Students in a MORE group who are using the Math of MORE

....

SUBTRACTING FOR A LIFE OF MORE

Subtract the amount, frequency, and duration of your soft addictions in any of these ways.

- **Subtract temptation**—identify the initial step in the cycle
- **Subtract in stages**
- **Subtract negative thoughts**
- **Subtract clutter and confusion**

MORE-SEL

God is not found in the soul by adding anything but by a process of subtraction.

—MEISTER ECKHART

ADD ASSIGNMENTS FOR MEETING YOUR HUNGERS DIRECTLY

In the left-hand column, list some of the spiritual hungers you uncovered in Chapter 6. Then in the right-hand column, list any ideas for activities or assignments that would feed these hungers for you. Review the list on page 142 in Chapter 8 that matches hungers with life assignments to meet those hungers. Which ones sound appealing or doable to you? Record them here.

My Spiritual Hunger	Assignments/Activities

NOURISH YOURSELF NOW

Now add possible assignments or activities to the list above that would directly meet your spiritual hungers. You can use the list to build your plan. Pick one now and spend some time doing it. Write down what influence it had on you. Can you see how adding will cause you to push out or replace some of your soft addictions?

> ### MORE-SEL
>
> *"In this life, if one's soul or spirit remains undernourished, underdeveloped, and unrelated, then it cannot enter into or function freely in the highest form of life that it is capable of attaining."*
>
> —JULIA PHILLIPS

_____

_____

_____

_____

_____

THINGS I'D LIKE TO ADD TO MY LIFE

Review the list of things to add from the summary above and from the things that appeal to you from chapter 8. Record them here and add any other ideas that occur to you to use as your wish list of things to add to your life. Then, when you prepare your plan, you can select some from the list and enter them into your Formula for MORE.

To add to my life:

_____

_____

_____

_____

_____

> ### MORE-SEL
>
> *"Your net worth to the world is usually determined by what remains after your bad habits are subtracted from your good ones."*
>
> —BENJAMIN FRANKLIN

THINGS I'D LIKE TO SUBTRACT FROM MY LIFE—MY SOFT ADDICTIONS

List the things that you'd like to release from your life. When you prepare your plan, you can select some from this list to enter into your Formula for MORE.

To subtract from my life:

_____

_____

_____

_____

_____

_____

"I was a major TV addict, but there was no way I was going cold turkey. After looking at my Formula for MORE, I decided simply to move my TV out of the bedroom. I kind of got used to not having it there and I liked the quiet before bedtime. So then I decided to limit my TV to two hours a day. Once I was used to that, I decided to cancel my cable service. Eventually I went down to only watching TV five days a week and also keeping my back to TVs when I'm in a restaurant. These were small steps but they've made a big difference. Of course, I still watch TV, but it's not nearly as big of a deal as it was. Plus, I was able to do it one step at a time, no big deal!"

—*Jessica*

DOS AND DON'TS FOR A FORMULA FOR MORE

In the next exercise, you will begin building your Formula for MORE. But before you embark on this journey, review the following dos and don'ts to help keep your plan on track.

Dos	Don'ts
Do relate goals and action steps to your Vision.	Don't treat action steps like a heavy to-do list.
Do things that feed your spiritual hungers.	Don't feed your surface wants.
Do have additions.	Don't just have subtractions.
Do add beauty, expression, inspiration, gift developing, compassion, humor, gratitude.	Don't add more soft addictions!
Do plan for success.	Don't plan huge steps.
Do have small steps.	Don't think that any step is too small.
Do enjoy the learning journey.	Don't go for a quick fix.
Do have goals that are measurable.	Don't have vague wishes.
Do have fun.	Don't get too heavy.
Do remember every little step counts.	Don't get overwhelmed.
Do pick just one thing to do, if you will do it.	Don't overload.
Do add support and accountability.	Don't be a lone ranger.
Do keep your Vision before you.	Don't forget you are making your dreams come true!

....

"I began losing weight during Lent and kept losing until I dropped thirty pounds. When people ask me how I did it, I say, Math of MORE! It wasn't so much about subtracting as it was about adding. I added reading inspirational passages every day,

a date with my partner every week, running along the lake in the morning, playing the piano after work . . . and food wasn't the only way I nourished myself. It was pretty easy to lose that extra weight. I felt like I 'cheated' over Lent—I didn't feel deprived!"

—Joe

CREATE YOUR FORMULA FOR MORE

You can make your dreams come true by living according to the Math of MORE. You're now prepared to create a plan to achieve your Vision. This plan will help you determine the specific additions and subtractions that make sense given your Vision and will establish goals and action steps to turn your Vision into reality. Articulating your Vision, identifying your hungers, and being aware of your specific soft addiction routines all have moved you closer to your Vision. Now it is time to develop goals, longer-term results, action steps, and concrete tactics to live your Vision.

> ### MORE-SEL
>
> *"God's arithmetic: happiness adds and multiplies as you divide it with others."*
>
> —UNKNOWN

GUIDE TO YOUR FORMULA FOR MORE

Overall Vision and Visions for Areas of Your Life

You developed an overall Vision and also a Vision for each area of your life in the previous chapter. Now you can create goals and action plans for each area. You may also want to choose one area that feels the most pressing or significant or the one in which you are most motivated to make a change right now. There is no wrong way to do this. The important part is to choose a place to start and do it.

Hungers (What I Am Hungry For?)

These are the hungers that you named in Chapter 6. Or you can choose from the list of spiritual hungers that we all have.

Blocks to My Vision—My Soft Addiction Routines

In Chapter 3, you identified your soft addiction routines. Write them again in the form that follows. Add any others that you have become aware of in reading the book. You don't need to work on all of these at the same time. Working on any one of them will influence the rest of them.

Goals and Action Steps

Additions and subtractions translate into goals. As you work on your plan, describe your goals in measurable results rather than wishes or vague desires. Choose action steps that are concrete and achievable, and which you are fairly certain that you can accomplish. Simplify at first to build in certain successes, keeping in mind that any step toward your Vision helps create MORE.

Pick a time period for your goals—you can try starting with a year and breaking it down into thirds or quarters. Then choose powerful action steps that cover no more than three to four weeks. You can choose action steps that only take a day or week to accomplish and then recommit or add.

Now, create your own Formula for MORE with your Math of MORE template below. You can create a template for each area of your life, and create new templates as your Vision for yourself develops by copying the blank form in the appendix. You can use the sample of Tyler's plan at the end of Chapter 8 as a guide. Also check out our Web site (www .judithwright.com) for other tools that will support you in building your Formula.

Taste of MORE

To get you started, here are some action steps to take to get a Taste of MORE. Try them out and then add them to your plan if you like, or let them inspire other action steps.

MY ONE DECISION

_____

_____

_____

MY VISION

_____

_____

_____

MY SOFT ADDICTIONS

_____

_____

_____

MY HUNGERS

Primary spiritual hungers I wish to address

_____

_____

_____

MY ADDITIONS

My Goals: what do I want to add in my life

to feed my spiritual hungers?

_____

_____

_____

My Action Steps: what steps will I take toward my goals?

_____

_____

_____

MY SUBTRACTIONS

My Goals: what will I reduce or subtract

to curb my soft additions?

_____

_____

_____

My Action Steps: what will I limit or omit?

_____

_____

_____

ADD CREATIVITY THROUGH A MEAL

The next time you cook a meal, no matter how simple, enjoy the creativity in the act of preparing the food. Appreciate how this creative activity can be spiritually and physically nourishing for you. Then have fun serving it—dress up in the nationality of the food, play native music, decorate the table or serve it on the floor picnic style or . . . a meal has transformed into an event!

ADD BEAUTY AND SUBTRACT CLUTTER

Identify one way to add beauty into your life and do it now or before the end of the day. At the same time, identify one way to clear some of the clutter that may be in the way of your adding beauty and do it. And do it today. You might find opportunities to do both at your desk, work space, next to your bed, or at a spot in your house that you pass frequently.

ADD SPIRIT THROUGH AN INSPIRATION KIT

Create your own God bag, spirit bag, or life bag full of nourishing, inspiring items that lift your spirit so that you always have instant inspiration (i.e., journal, spiritual reading, great music, joke book). Pack an inspiration bag for when you travel. What have you included? What can you always have with you to inspire you and lift your spirits?

ADD FEELINGS THROUGH COACHING AND TRAINING

To add more feelings to your life, consider seeing a life coach or therapist or attending a personal growth training that will support your emotional development and expression. You may want to try rebirthing, dynamic breath work, bioenergetics, or other techniques that help you access your emotions. Contact the Wright Institute about our Feelings Curriculum for a step-by-step program. Pick one way to add more feelings to your life.

MORE REVIEW

In this chapter, you learned the Math of More: adding things that en-hance your vision and subtracting things that take away from it. You've also developed your Formula for MORE with Vision, goals, and action steps to take. Adding real nourishment to your life naturally subtracts your soft addictions, literally pushing them out of the way. And when you subtract your soft addictions, you automatically add more time, re-sources, and consciousness.

MORE Learns and Grows

My Learns (something I know that I did not know prior to this lesson):

_____

_____

_____

_____

_____

_____

_____

My Grows (something I've done I would not have done prior to this lesson):

_____

_____

_____

_____

_____

_____

_____

9

SKILL #8: GET SUPPORT
AND BE ACCOUNTABLE:
A LITTLE HELP FROM YOUR
FRIENDS AND YOURSELF

Your Formula for MORE is a blueprint to make your dreams come true. Guided by your One Decision and your Vision, you are developing goals and action steps to add MORE to your life and to subtract your soft addictions. To ensure the successful implementation of your plan, you will need accountability and support.

These exercises will help you develop strategies to build accountability into your life, solicit support, and create a strong network of support to enhance the quality of your life. It may make you feel vulnerable to reach out for support, but your plan is vulnerable without it. Support and accountability make the difference between a good plan on paper—the blueprint—and a plan in action. You will complete your For-

mula for MORE by adding deadlines (alive-lines), rewards and consequences, and specific forms of support.

ASSESS YOUR RELATIONSHIP WITH ACCOUNTABILITY

Accountability simply means to take account and assess where you are in
relationship to your goals. Does the word bring up positive or negative
feelings for you? What experiences can you remember in regards to accountability that may bias your feelings? Can you imagine positive supportive ways to experience accountability? Journal your thoughts and
reactions about accountability.

_____

_____

_____

_____

_____

_____

_____

_____

_____

_____

TAKE ACCOUNT

There are several ways to hold yourself accountable to your goals and
Vision:

- Tell-a-Vision
- Set time frames for goals and action steps
- Assess progress with another person
- Reward rewards
- Establish truth or consequences

Pick from the following ideas to add accountability and timelines to your
Formula for MORE.

MORE-SEL

....

*"We are ill equipped for
self-assessment in activities that do not
have discreet ends—we see everything as
a TV show or athletic competition."*

—UNKNOWN

Tell-a-Vision

Tell someone about your Vision
and your new goals and action steps.
Ask a friend to check up on your
progress, but tell them to hold back
on pushing you or making judgments. Who will you tell? Call or
e-mail someone now.

Set Time Frames for Goals and Action Steps

All of your goals and action steps should be assigned a time frame. Your
goals should cover longer periods of time—monthly, quarterly, by season
or within a year. Your action steps can be planned for anywhere from a
few days, a week, or a month at a time. Consider these as alive-lines
(rather than deadlines) for all of your goals and action steps.

Be realistic and don't make too big of a leap from where you are now.
Don't worry about making too small of a step—you can always add more
to your plan.

Use the "By When" column in your Formula for MORE for each of
your goals and action steps and put the steps in your date book or calendar. Assign a frequency, duration, and start and due date for each step as
appropriate. You can write your steps below, but then transfer to your
Formula for MORE template found in the Appendix:

Use Jerry's Formula for MORE as a guide.

_____

_____

_____

_____

_____

_____

_____

_____

_____

_____

Goals	Action Steps	By When (Alive-line)

My Vision: to be a playful, alive guy who engages with others, feels like I belong and have fun!

Goals	Action Steps	By When (Alive-line)
+ Add "playing" with others—average once a week	+ Add playing basketball with my friends	by Sunday night
— Subtract playing computer games	+ Go bowling, biking, and play board games with the kids	Do one of these a week
	— Erase computer games from my hard drive	by Sunday night

Assess Progress with Another Person

Think about someone you can ask to review and renew your plan with you on a regular basis—your spouse, a friend, a coworker, your MORE group, or even do it together as a family every week. Who will it be?

Now add this person in the support column of your Formula for MORE template from the last chapter and assign a timeline under "By When."

> ### MORE-SEL
>
> *"It is easy to dodge our responsibilities, but we cannot dodge the consequences of dodging our responsibilities."*
>
> —E. C. MCKENZIE

Reward Yourself

Accountability is not just assessing your goals; you also need to reward yourself when you meet them. Treat yourself to the play you've wanted to see when you successfully curtail your television watching for a

> ### MORE-SEL
>
> *"Responsibility is the pitchfork that cleans out the mess in our lives."*
>
> —BOB WRIGHT

MORE-SEL

*"You get what you reward.
Be clear about what you want to get
and systematically reward it."*

—BOB NELSON

month. Relax in the sauna after your workout. Read the great book you've had your eye on or take a great bubble bath to relax after completing the task that you had previously avoided through your procrastination. Plan conscious breaks for yourself and use them to celebrate the completion of your action steps. Besides reinforcing your behavior, rewards have the added benefit of creating MORE in your life.

Brainstorm possible rewards for meeting your goals or doing your action steps.

_____

_____

_____

_____

Now, select a reward and enter it into the Rewards/Consequences column in your Formula for MORE.

Establish Truth or Consequences

While rewards are powerful incentives, it can help to have a consequence when you don't meet your goal or timeline. A consequence can be supportive, helping you strategize how to achieve your goal: journal on your feelings and resistance, or call a friend for support, or write a check to your favorite charity. Set educational, logical consequences that don't feel punishing, but that help you to be successful in the future.

Brainstorm possible consequences here and then pick one to add to your Formula for MORE.

_____

_____

_____

DETERMINE YOUR CURRENT STATE OF SUPPORT

By enlisting support, you increase the likelihood of implementing your Formula for MORE. You'll find people who validate your One Decision, celebrate your victories, and keep you from losing faith when the going gets rough. Without support, your plan has little chance of being put into action. With it, you can make your Vision a reality.

Start by taking account of support in your life right now. Where are you well supported? Where could you use more support? Do you give support more than you receive it? What judgments and reactions, or resistance, do you have about getting support from people (even though you know it may be "good" for you)? Journal your responses here.

_____

_____

_____

_____

_____

....

"Now I recognize when I am going into a tailspin and I reach out for support. When I feel hurt, I want to get away from myself—and everybody else. I isolate and start stuffing my face, trying to stuff my feelings. Finally, I'm seeing that overeating doesn't feed my true hungers, and I have started to make better choices, like talking with a friend. Not only am I eating less and losing weight but I also feel so much closer to my friends! I am even being more effective in my day and have a greater sense of purpose in my life. I am beginning to know that I am capable of creating what I want in life."

—Joanie

....

CREATE SUPPORT

Review the following ways to create support and then select the action steps you will take to begin to build and strengthen your support system.

Prepare to Create Support

- Clear barriers to support.
- Discover supporters through new activities.
- Solicit support from family and friends.
- Come to terms with your decision to change.

Create Fresh Sources of Support

- Talk to people—just about everyone can support you in some way.
- Give support to others.
- Participate in a MORE group.
- Contract with others to support you.

Develop Your Support Network

- Ask others to remind you of your Vision, and be a Vision-keeper for others.
- Create a life team.
- Seek role models and inspiration.
- Draw support from spirit, God, and nature.

CHOOSE ACTIONS TO TAKE

Review the list above and choose some of the actions you will take to add support to your life. What steps will you take to be more supported in your life?

List them here and then enter into your Formula for MORE.

_____

_____

_____

_____

_____

_____

TRY IT OUT

Use these as possible actions to get you started.

Ask Friends or Family for Support

Pick a friend or family member and share from your heart about your One Decision, your Vision, and how you want to share your path with them. Let them know they matter to you and you want their

> ### MORE-SEL
>
> *"Nowadays women can do anything they set their hearts to do. They pretty much have access to all the centers of learning and to almost any job that men can do. But this is meaningless as long as they don't have a support system, a support base."*
>
> —FLORINDA DONNER

support. You may find that others may not agree with you but may be willing to support you because they know it is important to you. If they don't support you, remember that you can find others that will. To empower yourself around your commitment, it is critical that you allow yourself to feel hurt, angry, or afraid when others don't want to change with you. And, be pleased when they do. Journal on any feelings that come up as you share your Vision with others and your feelings about their reactions.

Join or Start a MORE Group

Don't underestimate the power of a group of people all going for MORE. Encourage the people around you to join you in a MORE group. Or join an ongoing group. There are groups that meet regularly by telephone that you can participate in from wherever you live. Log on to www.judithwright.com for information on joining or starting a group. Post a note in your neighborhood grocery store, coffeehouse, library, or café. Write the step here you will take toward creating or joining a MORE group—with an alive-line by when you will do it—and then add it to your Formula for MORE.

_____

_____

_____

_____

"I've cut down on TV watching, am no longer known as the 'gadget king,' and am spending better time with my daughters and my wife. I'm coaching the girls' soccer team and going on weekly dates with my wife. I don't know that I'd be doing all this without my MORE group. There is something about meeting regularly with them that takes away some of my shame and allows me some compassion—and I'm more likely to laugh at myself and my wild rationalizations! I'm prone to hide and lie about my soft addictions and being part of the group helps me to tell the truth. I don't feel so strange or alone. And, they give me great ideas for next steps to take—and make sure I take them."

—Dick

MORE-SEL

"I don't know if people are alike or not, and I don't know if people ever really understand each other. But I still think we're all akin inside, at the place where we feel things and know things. And I think we have to help each other out; otherwise there's no hope at all."

—ROBERT MORGAN

Register Your Vision

Enlist a Vision-keeper for yourself. Ask a friend, coworker, family member, or even your boss who is supportive of what you are trying to change in your life to be your Vision-keeper. Give him or her your written Vision and ask her to read it to you on a regular or as-needed basis. Ask them to remind you of it when you are faltering. Call them when you are having doubts.

E-mail someone your Vision right now. Register it on our Web site at www.judithwright.com and we'll randomly send it back to you to inspire you. Do it now.

MORE ALERT

Most of us don't consciously decide who might best help us achieve our Vision. As a result, we surround ourselves with people who like to do the same things we like—this often means we hang out with soft addiction buddies.

CREATE A LIFE TEAM

Achieving MORE is an ongoing process, and while it's important to have people supporting you as you move toward your goals, it's just as important to have people helping you after you've achieved them. A network of support may be different than the circle of people who you currently consider your friends. Your life team needs to be made of people who are going for MORE in their own lives. Use the Support Pipeline to assess who might be good for your life support team. You might want to use our online version of the Support Pipeline as well and it will tabulate your results.

Develop Your Support Pipeline

- Make a list of possible life team members.
- Create a set of five to ten values/criteria for rating these relationships. Your criteria might include truthfulness, playfulness, gives good coaching, or any other quality you value.
- Rate each person on each of your criteria, using a scale of 1 to 5, and then total each person's score.

Use Sara's pipeline as a guide:

Name	Qualities	Truthful	Responsible	Trustworthy	Supportive	Going for it	Score
Joanne		4	3	4	2	3	16
Phil		5	4	4	4	4	21

My Support Pipeline

Write your values in the columns, and then rate people you are considering.

Name	Qualities						Score
1.							
2.							
3.							
4.							
5.							
6.							
7.							

Look to those people whose scores are the highest to depend upon for support and to offer your support to them. Surround yourself with people who reflect the values that help you to have MORE. You may be surprised to find that your highest-quality support comes from unlikely people in your life.

WHO WILL
YOU SUPPORT?

List the people from this list and
others whom you choose to support to live the life they truly want
to live.

_____

_____

_____

_____

_____

_____

_____

_____

_____

PUT SUPPORT
INTO ACTION

Put your newly created support system into action. Revisit each goal
and action step you selected in your
Formula for MORE and complete
the support column in your plan.
Put what steps you will take to create
support, or name the people who
will be supporting you in the support column.

MORE Review

By definition, a Vision is a big thing, and it's difficult for one person to realize this Vision without help. The support of other people gives you resources you can use to bring this Vision to life, while accountability makes sure you take account of your progress and receive feedback to tell you how you're doing in your quest.

MORE Learns and Grows

My Learns (something I know that I did not know prior to this lesson):

_____

_____

_____

_____

_____

_____

My Grows (something I've done I would not have done prior to this lesson):

_____

_____

_____

_____

_____

_____

DETOURS ON THE ROAD TO MORE . . . AND HOW TO GET BACK ON THE PATH

You've been learning the eight key skills to break free of your soft addictions and live the life you want. Applying any one skill will help you to shift your patterns, and applying all of them will transform your life. This is a lifetime journey—and a journey of a lifetime.

On this journey, you are changing your habits to become more conscious, aware, and alive. But, remember, you have been dulling your consciousness and feelings for a number of years with your soft addictions. These new ways of being will likely stir up feelings, and challenge your belief systems, friendships, and familiar habits. You are likely to run up against roadblocks on the road to MORE and will need the Rules of the Road to navigate back onto your path.

Use these exercises to be aware of the inevitable challenges and detours so that you can navigate back onto the road to the life you want.

> ### MORE-SEL
>
> *"Mountains cannot be surmounted except by winding paths."*
> —JOHANN WOLFGANG VON GOETHE

THE CHALLENGE OF MORE FEELINGS ON THE ROAD TO MORE

There are three major challenges on the road to MORE: more feelings, going into unknown territory, and challenging your beliefs about your self-worth. Each of these three challenges stirs up feelings. Develop the ability to deal with your feelings, and you will be more prepared to deal with these challenges. Breaking free of your soft addictions means that you stop numbing your emotions. If you are not prepared to deal with your feelings, you are likely to have some sort of breakdown and return to soft addictions to numb the feelings you have unearthed. To prepare you to overcome the emotional roadblocks on the way to the life you want, take this Feelings Survey.

Complete Your Feelings Survey

Complete the following Feeling Assessment. Rate yourself on the question from 0 to 5, and write the number of your rating in the blank provided.

0 = never
1 = rarely and under no pressure
3 = occasionally under moderate pressure and
5 = impeccably under high pressure

Or simply rate each question from 1 to 5 for how often and how well you think you do what it asks.

___ Do you know when you are having a feeling?
___ Can you identify how emotions feel in your body?
___ Can you identify your feelings and express them fully?
___ Are you at ease with your emotions?
___ Do you welcome your feelings as an important part of your experience?
___ Do you feel comfortable with a full range of feelings?
___ Can you express all feelings in a way that completes the emotion; that leads you to more truth and understanding?
___ Do you look for cues in the information your feelings offer?

___ Do you learn about yourself and understand yourself from being with your feelings?

___ Do you use your emotions to help you find ways to handle situations effectively?

___ Do you use your emotions as a source of joy rather than to fend off pain?

___ Do you have a full range of emotional expression (or do you overexpress one type of feeling over another, say, anger instead of hurt or perhaps pain instead of anger)?

___ Does expression of anger bring you more clarity, understanding, and resolve?

___ Does expressing your pain result in feelings of peace and relief?

___ Do you have frequent moments of unmitigated joy? Frequent feelings of overall well-being?

___ Do you express your love fully?

___ Can you receive expressions of love and take them in?

Use your responses to these questions to help you see where you can grow in relationship to your emotions. Most people don't answer a 4 or 5 to every question. Even for the questions where you have answered affirmatively, you may still want to deepen your relationship with your emotions in that area. The more you can accept and express your feelings responsibly, the less likely you are to have a breakdown or turn back to soft addictions to numb them. There is no end to learning about yourself and your feelings; it is an ever-deepening journey.

Now, go back and circle the top five questions that you would like to respond to with a resounding 5. Use these questions as an invitation for yourself to develop your relationship with your feelings more deeply.

> MORE-SEL
>
> *"God gave us tears so we could water our feelings and grow as people."*
> —NOAH BEN SHEA

Unearth Your Mistaken Beliefs About Feelings

Think about the messages you received about emotions from your family and community. What negative and mistaken beliefs have you formed about your emotions? Write down your negative beliefs in the form of thoughts, such as:

> My feelings are bad.
> I shouldn't feel.
> I must hide my feelings.
> Being emotional is wrong.
> I can't handle my feelings.
> Only wimps have feelings.
> People who emote openly are weak or weird.
> Buck up. Suck it up.
> If I started letting my feelings come up, I wouldn't be able to function.

_____
_____
_____
_____
_____
_____
_____
_____
_____
_____
_____
_____
_____
_____
_____
_____
_____

How Do You Want It to Be?

Now, write a statement of how you would like to be with your feelings. Your One Decision and your Vision may remind you of the importance of feeling and expressing yourself. Carry this statement with you or post it in a prominent place. Put it on your screen saver. Share it with a friend. Illustrate it, frame it, or add photos that inspire you.

> ### MORE-SEL
>
> *"To give vent now and then to his feelings, whether of pleasure or discontent, is a great ease to a man's heart."*
> —FRANCESCO GUICCIARDINI

_____

_____

_____

_____

_____

Improve Your Relationship with Your Feelings

Take some steps to improve your relationship with your emotions. Start by learning more about your feelings and how you can employ them, and allow yourself permission to feel. Here are some possibilities. Circle the ones you are willing to do, and then do them.

Investigate ways to increase your emotional repertoire and express your feelings responsibly, including personal growth opportunities, individual coaching, psychodrama, breath work, or biodynamics or investigate our feelings curriculum. Take acting classes that allow a full range of expression.

Go to a day-care center and watch the range of emotions expressed by little children. See how most of the children move through feelings easily, releasing them and moving on. Let them inspire you to allow feelings to move through you.

Make a collage of pictures of people expressing different emotions. Use it to inspire you to be fully alive and expressive.

Over time, make a composite, replacing the pictures you have pulled out of magazines or of friends or off the Internet with actual photos of yourself reflecting the full range of feelings. Celebrate your ability to express the full range of emotions.

Practice the Rules of the Road to MORE

The Rules of the Road can help you deal with these challenges. Applying these rules doesn't mean you'll never hit rough patches as you pursue the life you want. But they can ease a backslide, or shorten the time you spend returning to the path if you lose your way.

Rule #1: Be Prepared

> You'll be less likely to indulge in your soft addictions if you prepare by anticipating vulnerable areas in your life. Look at your day tomorrow. Are there any especially challenging situations where you might be tempted to indulge in soft addictions? What would help prepare you? Pack your lunch, arrange to speak to a friend during the day, schedule your workout right now . . . pick a situation and an action to take.

Challenging situation	*Action to take*
Job review	Rehearse responses with Larry

Rule #2: Don't Panic—remember, blowouts and breakdowns occur. Use the other rules to get back on the path.

Rule #3: Ask for Help—practice asking for help before you need it. What is one thing that you would like help with? Make it a point to ask for help today.

Write it here and then ask for the help today.

_____

_____

_____

_____

_____

Rule # 4: Keep Going—don't stop.

Rule # 5: Learn and Grow

Keep a daily growth journal. Write down your challenges, lessons learned, the skills you developed, or actions you need to take to develop them. You can do it just as you have seen at the end of each chapter's exercises. Use this as a sample for today.

> MORE-SEL
>
> _"If you're going through hell, keep going."_
> —WINSTON CHURCHILL

What have I learned today?

_____

_____

_____

How have I grown today?

_____

_____

_____

MORE REVIEW

As you've seen, the road to MORE includes detours and breakdowns that can become breakthroughs on your path. Mistaken beliefs about emotions and the inability to deal with feelings create roadblocks as you learn to live the life you want. But forewarned is forearmed. With the Rules of the Road, you can return to the path.

MORE Learns and Grows

My Learns (something I know that I did not know prior to this lesson):

_____

_____

_____

_____

_____

_____

My Grows (something I've done I would not have done prior to this lesson):

_____

_____

_____

_____

_____

II

THE FOUR LOVING TRUTHS

By understanding and living the Four Loving Truths, you will truly live a life of MORE. These essential truths correct the mistaken beliefs that keep us from living the lives we want. They help us see that our spiritual hungers are beautiful and deserve to be met. These truths can guide you in times of upset, realign your mistaken thoughts and beliefs, bring you hope, and reinforce you in your times of glory.

To deepen your awareness of the Four Loving Truths, choose one of the following statements as a meditation every day. Read one every day for thirty days, or meditate on one truth each week. Read the meditation through and ponder its significance and application in your life. Imagine living the way of the Four Loving Truths. Let their power work through you.

YOU ARE LOVED

You are loved beyond your own imagining. You may not feel it, know it, or even believe it, but the truth remains that you are loved. You are a beloved child of a loving universe. Nothing you can do will make the love go away; nor do you need to earn it, for it is your birthright. You are the only you that has ever been, the only you that ever will be—a unique aspect of creation. You are special, precious, whole, and complete. You are loved.

May you live in alignment with this loving truth and know yourself as one who is loved, one who is worthy of love, one who is beloved in the eyes of God.

LOVE AND PEACE ARE THE LEGACY OF PAIN

Riding on the wave of your pain are the gifts of peace and love. As you open up your heart to feel your pain, you open yourself to receive love and peace. Peace follows pain, like the sun follows the storm. The charge builds, it is released, and all is calm. Cleansing like the rain, sorrow washes your heart and peace and love remain. Bountiful love and peace flood into the tender sanctuary prepared by the vacating pain.

May you know the comfort and peace that follows the expression of your pain and may you know the love that flows into an open heart.

FEELINGS ARE DIVINE AND TO BE HONORED

Encoded within you is a deep sensitivity, designed to provide you with exquisite information that allows the expression of the deepest truth of your soul. It is through your feelings that you experience spirit and the greater essence of life. Feelings are the universal human language, a conduit from heart to heart, transcending our outer differences and connecting us to all.

May you know your feelings are divine, to be honored, and expressed. May you feel the cleansing of your tears, the bubbling of joy, the life force of anger, the warning of fear, the wisdom of your emotions. May you know that the cares on your heart are precious offerings of what matters most to you. Offer your feelings up to the most loving spirit, where your feelings are received like a symphony sung from your heart. There is no care too big or too small to be worthy of honor.

GIFTS ARE GIVEN TO YOU TO DEVELOP
AND USE IN THE DIVINE SYMPHONY OF LIFE

You have been endowed with gifts to cultivate and to offer to the world. You are blessed with unique gifts, and every one is valuable. As you express your gifts, you express an aspect of creation that could not and would not exist without you. Embark on the sacred quest to discover, develop, and contribute your gifts, your special contribution to the planet. It is your deepest purpose to magnify and manifest what you have been given. The world will be in harmony once we all develop and use our gifts collectively.

May you discover your talents, honor your gifts, develop your attributes and share them with the world. Remember, everything that is uniquely you—your expression, your perspective, your gifts, what you love, what comes easily to you, what is helpful or inspiring to others, is a gift. As you are a gift to the world.

Conclusion

THE HEROIC QUEST
FOR MORE

MORE-SEL

"Who is a hero?
He who conquers his urges."

—THE TALMUD

You are now ready to take the Vision you've created and launch your hero's journey into the land of MORE. You are truly on a heroic quest to live the life you desire. Declare your One Decision as your battle cry and fight the good fight that it takes to live it. Claim the rewards of a life well lived.

VICTORY!

It is courageous to live consciously in our world. Every choice you make in accordance with your One Decision is a victory. Every step you take toward the life you want is a success.

Claim your victories! Use this space to list temptations resisted, the additions you've made to the quality of your life, steps you've taken. Keep adding to the list and celebrate your battles fought and won:

I claim these victories!

_____

_____

_____

_____

_____

_____

To the Victor Goes the Spoils

Record the benefits of breaking free of soft addictions that you experience and begin an inventory of the rewards of living a life of MORE. List the rewards of your journey—both great and small, whether it is the money you have saved, the experience of clarity, the added sustenance in your life, feeling being more in control of your life, the time you have freed, the energy that is coursing through you. . . . Add to this list often:

MORE-SEL

"The characteristic of a genuine heroism is its persistency. All men have wandering impulses, fits and starts of generosity. But when you have resolved to be great, abide by yourself, and do not weakly try to reconcile yourself with the world. The heroic cannot be common, nor the common heroic."
—RALPH WALDO EMERSON

My rewards for fighting the good fight

_____

_____

_____

_____

_____

SHARE THE WEALTH

Know that others can benefit from your journey. Share your victories, successes and campaign strategies with friends and other Warriors. Learn from one another, take heart from one another's victories and defeats, and share your tactics. Log on to www.judithwright.com to share your journey—we'd love to hear from you to cheer you on and celebrate your victories.

> ### MORE-SEL
>
> *"The world you desired can be won, it exists, it is real, it is possible, it's yours."*
>
> —AYN RAND

Go forth, as the hero of this modern age. One who is willing to resist temptation, to forsake surface cravings and to pursue the feeding of your soul instead. One who is willing to make the difficult but right choices. One who is willing to fight for consciousness, true pleasure, clarity, and to reclaim the riches for which you were intended. One who is willing to claim the life you desire!

You are a revolutionary warrior of the modern age, fighting on the battlefield of consciousness. May you revolutionize your life, may you be a revolutionary agent of change in our world. May you be a harbinger of new ways of living to our world. May you experience the treasures of the life you want, the life you were destined for, a life of MORE.

ACKNOWLEDGMENTS

The writing of this book has brought me MORE! I have been blessed with the love, caring, dedication, encouragement, support, and hard work of many tremendous people. It is my hope that each of them receives in even greater measure the love and caring they have so generously poured into this book and me.

My particular thanks to the Conscious Warriors—those dedicated students of the Wright Institute who live MORE and have inspired this book through their examples. No longer compulsively watching television, overshopping, mindlessly surfing the Net, or hooked on other soft addictions, they are creative forces in the world and influential leaders in their families, businesses, and communities. It is my wish that everyone reaps the reward they have—more time, money, energy, satisfaction, intimacy, and meaning—and can also experience the outrageous laughter, fun, compassion, encouragement, and inspiration we have shared in our Soft Addiction Solution trainings and MORE groups.

Deepest appreciation is due to all the students at the Wright Institute; working with them is an honor and a delight. Not only do they continually create MORE for themselves but also in their worlds. I love what we are creating together and feel blessed to be on this journey with them. To the staff and faculty of the Wright Institute, past and present, I am deeply grateful, particularly to Barb Burgess, Angie Calkins, Kathy Schroeder, Gertrude Lyons, Beryl Stromsta, Jennifer Roberts, Sandy Mauck, Jillian Eichel, and Jennifer Panning, for their dedication, hard work, care, and especially for their belief in MORE and in me. If everyone could be surrounded by people who live the tenets of MORE and apply the skills in their daily work life what a world we would have!

To Christina and Collin Canright, Patricia Crisafuli, Bruce Wexler, Ela Booty, Marilyn Pearson, Jennifer Stephen, Michele and James Gustin, and fig media, I bestow my gratitude for their talents in editing, proofreading, design, production, and material and media development to bring this work into being.

Love and honor to the women of SOFIA, the Society of Femininity in Action, for their ever-present love and support and their deep care of and adherence to the tenets of this book. They have held this book in their hearts and helped birth it into being. And to the Women's Leadership Training Group, my deepest thanks for selfless service, late-night laughfests, and around-the-clock heartfelt support and hard work. What a joy it is to lead such magnificent women and to be inspired by their dedication.

Blessings to Gertrude and Rich Lyons, Stanislav Smith, Don and Denise Delves, and Tom and Karen Terry, who believe in MORE and share their resources to ensure that others experience MORE. May their generosity and dedication be rewarded a thousandfold.

For those students of the Summer Spiritual Training, I share my ardent appreciation for their immense creativity, hard work, good fun, and their amazing example of creativity and productivity—what is possible when people come together for a higher purpose! Their vast love and care are imbued in this book.

Thanks to my agent, Stephanie Kip Rostan of Levine Greenberg Literary Agency, for believing in this book and escorting it into being. I appreciate her care and dedication, and our talks about the bigger things of life!

Thanks to Joel Fotinos, my publisher and visionary at Tarcher/ Penguin, for his inspiration, vision, creativity, cheering, and making the impossible possible. To Sara Carder, my editor, whose care, shepherding, and skilled editing helped make this book a gift to its readers. I thank

Ken Siman, Terri Hennessey, Kat Kimball, Lily Chin, and the entire sales force, marketing, and publicity crew at Tarcher/Penguin for their enthusiasm, creativity, and support.

Thanks to my British nanny, Andrew Harvey, who used the considerable force of his personality and intellect to convince me of the importance of getting my work in print. Blessings and sincere gratitude to Virginia Rogers, Freya Secrest, Victoria Schuver-Song, and Jim Morningstar for being Vision-keepers.

To all of our friends in the media—from radio to TV, magazines to newspapers—as well as all of the book readers, talk attendees, and participants of our Soft Addiction Solution trainings for discovering and spreading the word of what is possible in a world without soft addictions.

Loving thanks to Marge Wright and to the memory of Mort Wright for their loving example of MORE and teaching Bob about love and possibilities so that he could share it with me and thousands of others.

In memory of my parents, Dick and Gene Sewell, who showed me the opportunity of service, excellence, and breaking barriers so I could live a life of MORE. May your legacy of service continue.

To all those who have touched me and blessed this book, named and unnamed, I send heartfelt thanks.

Most especially, thank you to my beloved husband and partner, Bob, without whom this book would not exist. Empowering me to write this book, he supported me every step of the way. His devotion, commitment, creativity, love, and Vision inspire me every day of my life. For his inspiring example of living MORE and his dedication to creating MORE for everyone around him, I am immensely grateful and honored to share my life with him.

With deepest gratitude to the divine spirit that sources all.

ABOUT THE AUTHOR

Judith Wright (www.judithwright.com) is hailed as a peerless educator, world-class coach, lifestyles expert, inspirational speaker, best-selling author, and corporate consultant. Judith's life has been dedicated to exploring optimum ways of living and being. A trailblazer in human development, she has been revolutionizing the personal growth industry. Judith cofounded the Wright Institute in Chicago—a cutting-edge coaching and training institute. She and her husband, Bob, train individuals, couples, families, and corporations in how to get more out of everything they do. Her students learn to live with more meaning, fulfillment, and success in relationships, career, parenting, finance, and all the areas of their lives. Judith founded SOFIA (Society of Femininity in Action), a cutting-edge women's organization, and began developing and teaching the Soft Addictions workshop at the Wright Institute more than fifteen years ago.

Called "one of the most sought-after self-help gurus in the country" by the *San Francisco Chronicle,* Judith demystifies what it takes to lead a great life as she teaches proven, time-tested perspectives on how to have it all through her writing, teaching, coaching, and public speaking. A media favorite, Judith has appeared on more than 350 radio stations and over fifty television programs, including *Oprah, Good Morning America,* the *Today* show, and *Fox & Friends.* A powerful speaker and coach, Judith inspires women's groups, couples, community leaders, and corporations alike. Her talks on lifestyles, feminine power, productivity, communications, and relationships educate, inspire, and entertain corporations such as AC Nielsen and Chase, associations like the International Association of Junior Leagues and the Society of Women Engineers, and events like the Miss USA Women's Power Summit, Mega Success seminars, and many more.

To book Judith as a speaker for your company or organization, to learn more about her trainings and seminars, or for more information on a personalized coaching curriculum with Judith, visit her Web site at www.judithwright.com. Or contact her by phone at 1-866-MORE-YOU, 312-645-8300, or by e-mail at contact@judithwright.com.

ABOUT THE WRIGHT INSTITUTE

The Wright Institute—a cutting-edge coaching and training institute—empowers people to discover and live successful lives of purpose, meaning, and fulfillment. You can recognize Wright Institute students and consulting clients by their results: They have potent and powerful relationships that last, familes that work, and businesses that contribute to staff, industry, and their communities. The stories shared in this book are only a small selection from the thousands of people who have transformed their lives through Wright Institute programs.

Anyone can have MORE in life, but few have learned the skills to lead these lives of greater meaning, satisfaction, and purpose. It takes commitment, training, and support to live a life of MORE. So over the years, the Wright Institute has developed and offered students and clients the practical and life-transforming skills they need for success in every life area, from self-esteem and relationships to career-building. Our educational methodology features our unique accelerated learning model that integrates three core developmental elements: coaching, laboratory learning, and classroom training. In our trainings, students develop vision, learn philosophy, use concepts, and engage in powerful experiential exercises. In the learning labs, they learn, apply, and practice actual life skills with group support, and in coaching they develop their personal strategies and individual skills.

Through thousands of examples and success stories, we know that there is no one perfect formula. And a perfect formula isn't the point. Our passion and mission are to support people through any means and resources available to live full, exciting, engaging, successful, satisfying lives.

Special Offer

Just by purchasing this book, you receive a special offer from Judith Wright and the Wright Institute that includes complimentary training and coaching. To take advantage of this special offer, go to www.judith wright.com, click on "Soft Addictions Book Offer," and enter the code 4M6R3. This offer is redeemable for up to one year following initial publication of this book. For questions and more information, contact the Wright Institute by phone at 1-866-MOREYOU or 312-645-8300, or e-mail us at contact@wrightlearning.com.

There is nothing I love more than helping others reach their highest potential. Let me hear from you. Tell me how you are creating MORE in your life, about your struggles and your victories along the way. If you would like to contact me for public speaking, training, coaching, or other personal development activities, you can e-mail me at contact@ judithwright.com or call 1-866-MOREYOU or 312-645-8300.

THE SOFT ADDICTIONS TEMPLATE

1. What was happening right before you indulged in your soft addiction? What circumstances triggered your soft addiction?

2. Check each primary feeling you had prior to engaging in your soft addiction:

__Anger   __Hurt __Sadness __Fear __Joy __Love __Other

What negative thoughts (stinking thinking) were going through your head during or after these circumstances?

Examples of Negative Thoughts:

Overgeneralization	This always happens to me!
Jumping to conclusions	This isn't going to work out. I should just quit.
Emotional reasoning	I feel bad, I must be bad.
Blame and shame	It's her fault we were late for the party.

4. Identify mistaken beliefs that may have triggered your stinking thinking and soft addictions.

Examples of Beliefs

I am not beloved or worthy.	My emotions are not important.
	The world is an uncaring place.

5. What positive thoughts could you think instead? Positive thoughts reflect the reality of the situation, are humorous or compassionate.

Examples of Positive Thoughts

Sometimes things go wrong, but I can handle it.	I need to apply myself to make sure this works out.
This is tough, but it's not insurmountable.	I feel upset, but that doesn't make me a bad person.
	I can learn from this mistake.

6. What spiritual hungers or deeper yearnings might underlie your soft addictions? (Circle ones that apply.)

To exist	To learn	To be intimate
To be heard	To grow	To love
To be touched	To trust	To make a difference
To be loved	To be known	To fulfill my purpose
To be affirmed	To matter	To be one with all
To express	To feel connected	To know God
To experience fully	To belong	

7. Identify positive alternatives to your soft addictions, which meet your deeper hungers.

Examples of Alternatives to Soft Addictions

Soft Addiction	Hunger	Alternative
Watching television	To feel connected	Call a friend and go to a play.
Surfing the Internet	To learn and grow	Go to museum or lecture.
Overworking	To matter	List ways you make a difference.
Gossiping	To connect and to belong	Talk about yourself, and the person you are with, rather than others.
Name-dropping	To be important	Talk about *matters* instead of *who* matters
Shopping	To feel abundant	"Shop" for friends, ideas, possibilities, instead of stuff.
Fast food	To be fulfilled	Have quick treats that aren't food.
Chat rooms	To feel connected	Call a friend and "chat live."
Isolation	To feel secure	Hang out with people you feel safe with.

Congratulations! You are on your way to creating greater awareness of yourself and beginning to live a life of MORE.

MATH OF MORE TEMPLATE

My One Decision:

My Vision:

Hungers	Soft Addictions/ Blocks	+/–	Goals	+/–	Action Steps	Support/ Accountability	By When (Alive–line)	Rewards/ Consequences